# EF BENSON

*For Cynthia and Tony Reavell*

# EF BENSON

## AS HE WAS

*Geoffrey Palmer*

## GEOFFREY PALMER
## AND NOEL LLOYD

*Noel Lloyd*

*Lennard Publishing*
*1988*

LENNARD PUBLISHING
a division of Lennard Books Ltd
Lennard House, 92 Hastings St
Luton, Beds. LU1 5BH


A CIP catalogue record for this book
is available from the British Library

ISBN 1 85291 060 7

First published 1988
Copyright © Geoffrey Palmer and Noel Lloyd 1988

The authors are grateful to Cynthia and Tony Reavell
for their considerable assistance with illustrative material.


Cover Design by Pocknell and Co

Text designed and typeset by
Nuprint Ltd, Harpenden, Herts AL5 4SE

Printed and bound in Great Britain by
Butler & Tanner, Frome, Somerset.

# CONTENTS

ACKNOWLEDGEMENTS .......................................... 6
PREFACE .................................................... 7
CHAPTER ONE ............................................... 9
CHAPTER TWO .............................................. 15
CHAPTER THREE ............................................ 18
CHAPTER FOUR ............................................. 25
CHAPTER FIVE ............................................. 31
CHAPTER SIX .............................................. 42
CHAPTER SEVEN ............................................ 53
CHAPTER EIGHT ............................................ 58
CHAPTER NINE ............................................. 69
CHAPTER TEN .............................................. 74
CHAPTER ELEVEN ........................................... 78
CHAPTER TWELVE ........................................... 87
CHAPTER THIRTEEN ......................................... 92
CHAPTER FOURTEEN ......................................... 98
CHAPTER FIFTEEN ......................................... 104
CHAPTER SIXTEEN ......................................... 110
CHAPTER SEVENTEEN ....................................... 117
CHAPTER EIGHTEEN ........................................ 128
CHAPTER NINETEEN ........................................ 135
CHAPTER TWENTY .......................................... 141
CHAPTER TWENTY-ONE ...................................... 154
CHAPTER TWENTY-TWO ...................................... 162

APPENDIX: ANNOTATED LIST OF BENSON'S WORKS ............. 164
INDEX ................................................... 205

# ACKNOWLEDGEMENTS

We would like to thank, most sincerely:

*Austin Seckersen,* for so generously making his collection of Benson material available to us

*Dr Michael Halls,* Modern Archivist of King's College Library, Cambridge, for his interest and for giving us the benefit of his specialist knowledge so willingly

*Richard Dalby,* Benson collector and enthusiast, for his help in solving some knotty problems

*Allan Downend,* Secretary of the E. F. Benson Society, for his lively interest

*Cynthia and Tony Reavell,* of Martello Bookshop, Rye, for their unstinting advice, criticism and encouragement, and for use of material from the Tilling Society Newsletters and their book *E. F. Benson and the World of Tilling*

*Roderick Brown,* for his guidance, and *Mark Booth* who started the whole thing.

# PREFACE

irst of all I have to own that I am not at all convinced as to the propriety of agreeing to write a preface to a book which is dedicated to me. But I am certain enough of Geoffrey Palmer's and Noel Lloyd's thoughtfulness and perception in matters concerning E. F. Benson and his highly complicated family to be very pleased to be asked to introduce their biography, and at the same time far too honoured to reject their friendly dedication!

In the early 1980's, just before the current explosion of enthusiasm for E. F. Benson, his admirers were numerous but isolated: each one thought he or she was the only devotee, the only one to have discovered the incomparably funny Mapp and Lucia. In those days no writer seriously considered devoting a biography to Benson, and no publisher was interested in bringing one out; of the two books on the Benson family, the better was out of print, and the other about to be remaindered. We approached one or two biographers who had written sensitively about contemporaries of Benson's, but they always had something more pressing in hand.

But then everything changed. This was largely, although not solely, the result of the television dramatisation of *Mapp and Lucia*. Even before these two series, Aubrey Woods' radio readings had attracted a faithful band of enthusiasts, and paperback publishers had begun producing the first in a steady stream of attractive reprints of the best E. F. Benson fiction and memoirs. Two appreciation societies were formed in England, then another in New York, and at the same time there was a noticeable increase in the number of Luciaphiles making the pilgrimage to Rye, the picturesque little town which is so unmistakably Tilling down to the last detail, and its creator's home for his last twenty years. Once television had brought its own interpretation of the stories into millions of homes in Britain and America, a whole new world of converts was gained, and E. F. Benson was, after half a century, one of the cult nostalgia figures of the mid-eighties – in fact, once again he was all the rage.

Suddenly it seemed that scarcely a day passed without us hearing that someone new was writing, was about to write, or was thinking of writing, a Benson biography. Had they all steamed ahead there would have been an entire shelf full of volumes on Edward Frederic Benson, from the lightweight and superficial to the In-Depth Literary Biography, all coming out about now. It seems unlikely that the majority of them will ever see the light of day. Happily this book, probably the first one we heard about – if only at that stage an idea and an intention – is one which *has* made it. The pleasing thing about it is that there is no doubt about the genuine and long-standing interest and affection that the writers have for E. F. Benson: no question of jumping on the bandwagon, no case of authors in search of a fashionable subject.

The starting-point for most people's interest in Benson is usually their delighted enthusiasm for his humorous Mapp and Lucia novels, set initially in 'Riseholme' (Broadway in the Cotswolds) and soon progressing to 'Tilling' (Rye in East Sussex). However, he also wrote seventy more works of fiction, and after his Tilling novels he is perhaps best-known as a writer of first-class ghost stories. Many older readers remember him too as the author of *David Blaize* and *David of King's*, often their first youthful introduction to his novels. And the man behind these extremely varied bestsellers? Was he the eternal schoolboy? Or the urbane socialite? A soft-hearted philanthropist and a pillar of the community? Or a lonely and aloof old man? A man of action or a thinker? A glittering success or a self-confessed failure? A writer of popular slush or of minor but enduring classics? He was certainly a little of all those things, and of course a great deal more besides: above all he never lost his wickedly irreverent sense of humour and his unerring ability to detect falseness and hypocrisy.

In addition, anyone who has grappled with Benson's out-of-print secondhand books is going to be grateful for the helpful guidance given in the section at the end: now at a glance we will recognise what we have already read, know what is worth looking out for, and see what themes and characters the various novels have in common.

And now, firmly convinced that there is nothing more tedious than a lengthy preface when one is wanting to get on with the book itself, I will leave you to do just that.

*Cynthia Reavell*

# CHAPTER ONE

dward Frederic Benson, known as Fred to his family and friends, was born on July 24 1867 at Wellington College in Berkshire, where Edward White Benson, his father, was the first Headmaster. Edward White Benson's influence on his children was to last long after his death, and his presence haunted their dreams.

The Benson family was of Yorkshire stock, solid and worthy middle class, though with a certain amount of inbreeding and a tendency to schizophrenia. Edward White Benson was born and educated in Birmingham, where his father, a somewhat eccentric inventor, had started a factory making white lead. In 1843, when the young Edward was 13, his father died in poor circumstances after the factory had failed, and his mother had to bring up eight children on a small annuity. She had wanted to restart the business but Edward, always a dominant personality, protested that the marriage prospects of his sisters would be ruined if the family was 'in trade', and that his own career in the Church (for he had already made up his mind to become a clergyman, and had even established an oratory in an office of the disused factory) would be more difficult to achieve. The responsibility thrust on his young shoulders made him determined to have his own way. As an adolescent he was over-serious and lordly. Poverty and loss had not made him at all humble, as specified by Victorian values, but instead forceful and intransigent.

Edward went from King Edward's School in Birmingham to Trinity College, Cambridge. His mother underwent great privations to provide him with even the bare necessities of life, and Edward, in his determination to do well, reduced sleep and exercise to a minimum, reading mathematics and classics far into the night. While he was at Cambridge his mother and eldest sister died. The family's financial affairs were predictably chaotic, but relatives came to his aid and his brothers and sisters were taken in by various aunts and uncles.

Edward did not achieve the brilliant scholastic triumphs that were expected of him. He never won a University scholarship nor a

Brown Medal, though he took the Senior Chancellor's Medal which made up for some other disappointments. What turned out to be of greater value, though, was that the gruff-voiced but tender-hearted Francis Martin (the Bursar of Trinity) took a great fancy to the gifted but flawed young man. Edward was good looking in a theatrical way, with long fair hair, a slightly aquiline nose, full, curving lips and large blue eyes. He had an eager manner and an abundant flow of talk. Francis Martin was so captivated by the personable young man that he paid his college fees and supported him through the rest of his time at Cambridge, even to the extent of furnishing his rooms, taking him abroad on reading trips, contributing to the education of his brothers and providing dowries of £500 for each of his three sisters.

Edward obtained his degree in 1852 and was elected a Fellow at Trinity the following year. He then took up a post of assistant master to teach Classics at Rugby, where he was ordained deacon and priest. He lodged with his cousins, the Sidgwicks, whose boys Henry and Arthur were being educated at the school, and it was there he met his cousin Mary, who had been known as 'Minnie' almost from birth. She was the youngest of the five Sidgwick children, twelve years old, pretty, plump, docile and with winning ways. Edward quickly became attracted to her, and confided to his diary that he hoped she would one day be his wife.

He wrote to her frequently from his trips abroad, letters full of vivid descriptions of things seen and heard, but designed to educate rather than to amuse. He spoke to the twelve-year-old girl of marriage, and Minnie, flattered but artless, intimated in her kittenish way that she would wait until she was grown up and then give him her hand. From that moment her suitor and her mother both took it for granted that the agreement was a solemn and binding promise, and the next six years were a long preparation for marriage to the young schoolmaster who was kind but severe, always patronising and often disapproving. Knowing that her future had been settled, Minnie felt obliged to fit herself for a destiny for which she did not feel worthy. She knew that she must grow to love her husband and she did her best. Only to her cherished diary, to be seen by no eyes but her own, did she hint obliquely that the real Minnie was not the one Edward believed he knew.

Edward and Minnie were married in 1860; he was thirty and she eighteen. The marriage got off to a bad start with a disastrous honeymoon spent in Paris, and it is to Minnie's eternal credit that never once did she let the mask of cheerful complaisance slip. She was scared. 'An utter child,' she wrote in her diary, 'with *no* stay on God. Twelve years older, much stronger, much more passionate! and whom I didn't really love. How evidently disappointed he was – trying to be rapturous –

feeling so inexpressibly lonely and young, but *how* hard for him!' And she cried every time she was alone.

At the time of the marriage Edward had been Headmaster of Wellington College for six months. The post had come to him as the gift of the Prince Consort, and the school was opened by the Queen as a memorial to the Duke of Wellington. It was set on a bleak part of Bagshot Heath, four miles from Wokingham in Berkshire and a mile from Broadmoor, the criminal lunatic asylum then being built. Being new, the school had no traditions and presented an almost insuperable challenge to a man so new to his profession. Minnie was younger than the oldest boys in the college. She and Edward lived in the Master's Lodge, and there Fred was born. He was the fifth of the six Benson children, and the third son. Martin, the eldest, was born in 1860, Arthur Christopher in 1862, Mary Eleanor (Nellie) in 1863 and Margaret (Maggie) in 1865. After Fred in 1867 came Robert Hugh, in 1871.

Minnie had a major nervous breakdown after giving her husband his sixth child, and that forced Edward to conclude that there must be no more babies if Minnie were to recover from her faints, depressions and tears. She spent a year convalescing, first in Scotland, then in Lincoln with their friends the Wordsworths, and finally in Wiesbaden with her brother-in-law Christopher Benson and his wife. During her long absence Edward grew increasingly unsympathetic, and complained that she was neglecting her duty to him and the school. Once or twice Minnie dragged herself back to Wellington for an official function, but had the courage to decide that her health was more important than standing beside her husband on Speech Day.

During the Wellington years Edward's relations with his governors and masters were constantly strained. He was autocratic, unwavering in his principles and unable to tolerate contradiction or criticism. He was a harsh disciplinarian and his temper was volcanic. At Rugby there had been an occasion when he thrashed a number of boys so savagely there was almost a rebellion; at Wellington the beatings continued. General Sir Ian Hamilton remembered that he had been caned every day for weeks for the crime of being late in school. His friends had gasped at the colours of the bruises and stripes on his body – blue, green, yellow and dark purple.

Strangely, Edward was not conscious of the terror he could inspire. To him punishment was a Christian duty; it promoted goodness and was not to be challenged. During periods of depression he thought that everything was going wrong. Then his rebukes were terrifying; masters as well as boys were on the receiving end of his wrath. However, if they burst into tears he was mollified and asked to be forgiven.

Edward's virtues must not be forgotten; his enthusiasm,

phenomenal energy and capacity for hard work. He could be generous, patient and courteous. But he was not popular. Boys were irritated that he knew so much about them, and accused him of prying; and they were bored by his insistence on keeping silly and unnecessary rules. They felt that he was often insincere and exaggerated the sinfulness of petty wrongdoings; and they were frightened by his lack of control when he was angry.

Fred and his brothers and sisters were not much concerned with what went on in the school, but life in the Master's Lodge was in many ways as uncomfortable as it was for the pupils. The children felt that they were continually poised on a knife-edge. Though their father loved them dearly, and sought to join their interests and activities as though he were one of them, he also tried to mould each member into his own conception of what an upright and incorruptible Christian should be. He could never resist the temptation to turn a moment of fun into a sermon on good conduct, as though enjoyment itself tended to rot moral fibre. A badly rolled umbrella, a crust left on a breakfast plate or slouching in a chair were signs that salvation was going to be difficult to attain.

The children were not punished physically, but their father's hurt expression and sad words were a form of emotional bullying that they felt more deeply than a straightforward beating. 'That is not the right way to behave on a Sunday, is it, old boy?' or 'Hadn't you better read a book?' were the kind of comments that paralysed the children's efforts to amuse themselves in harmless ways.

Arthur once wrote 'I hate Papa' on a piece of paper and buried it in the garden: though this incident does not appear in his memoirs, a little boy called Arthur in his partly autobiographical novel *Memoirs of Arthur Hamilton* gives expression to his feelings in this way. 'Hate' was perhaps too strong a word to describe what the young Bensons felt for their father. It was more like fear mixed with resentment at not being allowed to act like other children.

It was to their nurse, Elizabeth Cooper, known affectionately as Beth, rather than to their mother, that the children turned for comfort. Beth was born in Yorkshire in 1818. Slight and spare and with a strong constitution, as a teenage girl she went to the Sidgwicks as nurserymaid. Minnie's father, Headmaster of Skipton Grammar School, had died young. His widow, left with six children, of whom two died in infancy, eventually settled in Rugby. Beth brought them all up: William Sidgwick, who became tutor of Merton, Henry Sidgwick, professor at Cambridge, Arthur Sidgwick, master at Rugby and tutor of Corpus Christi College, Oxford, and Minnie. Beth became Minnie's nurse in 1841 and when Minnie married Edward Benson it was taken for granted that she would become part of the new household at Wellington. She nursed all the children in turn, and during Minnie's absence abroad after Hugh's birth she was, in all but name, mother to the temporary orphans. Edward Benson was far too preoccupied to give them any extra attention. Photographs show Beth as angular and severe-looking, a complete contrast to the soft and rolypoly Minnie, yet she gave to the children something that neither father nor mother could: a strong, controlled devotion, a protecting presence and a feeling of utter security. She claimed nothing and gave everything. Her heart was big enough to contain love for all the children, but Hugh, probably because he was last and had taken most rearing, had the securest place; he was her 'darlingest child'.

All Fred's memories of his very early years were bound up with Beth: exciting walks to pick blackberries, her concern when he broke two front teeth on a piece of toffee, and her ability to repair the broken legs of a dog belonging to the children's Noah's Ark. Beth was also there when Fred suffered the first tragedy of his life. One Christmas Eve, returning from a moonlit walk through the woods with Beth, he lost the brown dog with the mended legs. It slipped from his warm hand and disappeared into the undergrowth. Black misery descended on him. They looked for the toy in vain and older brother Martin continued the search when Beth decreed that it was time to go home. Fred was impressed by Martin's bravery in facing the terrors of the wood alone, but could not remember afterwards whether or not the toy was found. Probably it was not, for the next morning Fred's father gave him a cup of milk to drink in the dining-room after breakfast, and warned him to drink slowly. As the milk disappeared Fred heard a clink and found a shilling at the bottom of the cup. This is one of the rare occasions when Edward shows himself in a more sympathetic light.

Minnie Benson's relationship with her children was in some ways no less difficult than her husband's. Her love for them was eager but indiscriminate, and the children often felt suffocated. They needed Beth's steady affection more than maternal over-solicitude. Minnie Benson's emotions centred round other women. During the first years of her married life she recorded in her diary the names of various young women to whom she was attracted, sighing wistfully over the delicious times she had with Emily, Anne, Katie, and a Miss Hall in Wiesbaden. Her lasting relationship was to be with Lucy Tait, a daughter of the previous Archbishop of Canterbury, who moved in and became an intimate and indispensable member of the family after Edward's death.

Most of the Benson children were only able to respond fully to their own sex. None of them married. Martin died too young for his sexuality to be assessed. Both Nellie and Maggie had intense friendships with other women, Nellie with Ethel Smyth, the composer, and Maggie with Nettie Gourlay – though she did at one time glance wistfully in the direction of one of her father's curates.

Arthur and Hugh, particularly the latter, seemed to have a dislike of women, even though they both relied heavily on them as readers and admirers. The more worldly Fred chose friends from both sexes, though he too felt a deeper attachment to the men. The Bensons lived very sheltered lives as children, and even in adult life their father's influence was a considerable restraint; so it was almost inevitable that they should seek a substitute for real life and normal relationships. The three brothers chose literature, which became a drug that helped to sustain them against the harshness of reality. Arthur was the most affected. He led an enclosed life at Cambridge, writing and forming platonic friendships with handsome young men. Hugh chose religion. As a Catholic priest he was forced to forgo female companionship on a sexual basis. Only Fred became aware that there was a life outside the study and the cloisters. He embraced it eagerly.

# CHAPTER TWO

n 1873, when Fred was six years old, the family moved to Lincoln, to the Chancery in the Close. Edward Benson had been appointed Chancellor and Canon of Lincoln by Bishop Wordsworth, with the idea that he should start a theological college. His salary would be half of the £2000 a year he was earning at Wellington, but he was getting tired of schoolmastering and the indifference to religion which so many of the boys showed. He looked forward to moulding the minds and hearts of rather maturer young men.

The Chancery, which faced the east front of the Cathedral, was built in the fourteenth century. The front was Tudor brick, gabled, with oriel windows, and there was a double door of oak in which Commonwealth bullets were embedded. Inside there were vaulted cellars, a panelled dining-room, a wall of ancient masonry pierced by fourteenth-century arches, servants' quarters, sitting rooms, an oratory, study, nurseries, schoolroom, bedrooms, winding stairs and many passages. With its dark corners and huge empty cupboards the house was a marvellous place for hide-and-seek, and a floor of attics full of gurgling water cisterns became the haunt of goblins and ghosts, which Fred was to describe graphically in *David Blaize* more than forty years later.

The garden, which lay at the back of the stables, was bounded by a high wall fringed with wild golden wallflowers against which grew apricot and peach trees; and a pear tree might have been designed specially as a climbing frame for small children. In the north-west and north-east corners were two ivy-covered towers belonging to the old medieval city wall. One of the towers was dangerously decayed, but the other was solid and an ideal place for war games. A grassy space was given over to lawn tennis, inexpertly played by Edward and the two older boys. In the garden there was a large stone Roman sarcophagus which had been unearthed during the digging of a gravel pit nearby, and which the Chancellor had bought for a few shillings. To the ghoulish delight of the young Bensons it had contained the bones of two children.

Edward started his new job under severe nervous strain. Years later he confessed to Arthur that he had been suffering reaction to the move from Wellington, aggravated by Minnie's absence at Wiesbaden, the challenge of his new duties and the strangeness of the new environment. It was, he said, the most acute attack of depression he had ever had.

Hard work helped his recovery. In addition to the formation of the theological college he started Bible classes for mechanics from nearby engineering works and night schools in the city. All were very successful. Edward was at his best with working-class men and women. He didn't patronise them, and they enjoyed his brilliant talk. The Bishop's Palace was at Riseholme, about two and a half miles north of Lincoln. The Bensons and the Wordsworths had been friends for many years; they took holidays together at Whitby and Ambleside, and maintained close ties based on intellectual compatibility and deep affection.

The eldest Wordsworth daughter, Elizabeth, later became head of Lady Margaret Hall, Oxford. She was a year older than Minnie and much more assertive. Minnie was at first attracted by her and wished that her friend showed more positive signs of reciprocating her feelings, but later decided that Elizabeth's mind was occupied by nobler thoughts. It seems, though, that the thoughts were not particularly high-minded, being cast rather in the direction of Minnie's husband. Certainly at one period Edward confided in Elizabeth Wordsworth more than he did in his wife.

Arthur, who wrote the official biography of his father in 1889, was very reticent about the state of the Benson marriage at this time. There can be no doubt that all was not well. Edward had always taken Minnie too much for granted, and had failed to appreciate the toll that frequent child-bearing had taken of her. He had been, like most husbands of his class and period, kind but domineering, well-meaning but selfish. Minnie, still feeling guilty because she failed in her own eyes to love her husband enough, and confused by her inexplicable tendency to feel romantic yearnings for women, felt unable to cope with her own emotions and her husband's demands and criticisms. On her return from Wiesbaden she was improving physically. But mentally she was still in turmoil. Occasionally she showed flashes of independence that worried Edward, sometimes refusing to support him at school functions. 'We have been through a bad time,' he wrote to a friend in 1874, and to another friend, 'My dear wife mends so slowly.'

At first Minnie was not pleased with Lincoln. Cathedral society was not stimulating and Elizabeth Wordsworth was too much in evidence. Then her heart once again melted into love. Caroline Charlotte Mylne, whom Minnie called 'Tan', was the wife of a theological student who had decided to take orders after some years in business. She was a middle-aged woman of charm and self-possession, with strong evangelical leanings. Minnie was convinced that God had sent Tan to her, and for the first time God became real to her; not a mysterious, unknowable Being hidden behind rites and rules, but a personal Father in whom she could confide. Tan converted her to a simple but fierce Christianity that Edward didn't understand. She swept away all obstacles to become born again, her crisis resolved in a mystical awareness of the essence of religion, leaving Edward struggling with dogma, ritual, the Trinity and Jesuitism. From that time she was always the stronger character. She discovered that she had a first-class mind, untrained though it might be. She now had experience of life beyond keeping house and bearing children; she had a new certainty and a new purpose in living. For the rest of the time they lived at Lincoln she remained deeply attached to Mrs Mylne, and when they were parted by circumstances the friendship endured. Edward was puzzled and disturbed but never conceived anything but a spiritual bond between the two women. From then on there was a more equable relationship between man and wife, and for the next twenty years their married life was outwardly successful.

It is not surprising that in this highly charged atmosphere Fred also fell in love – with one of the Cathedral choristers. Cathedral services had been an interminable purgatory, but now Sunday was a day of joy – for as long as Fred's passion lasted. The chorister's solos awakened in him the first stirrings of a delight in music, bringing with it intimations of a kind of religious ecstasy, hardly understood by such a young boy, but compounded of a pure treble voice, stained glass windows and the organ's roll.

During the Lincoln years the young Bensons were encouraged to take up numerous hobbies, all of which stimulated their interest in the world around them, and which they pursued with vigour and enthusiasm. They drew, wrote poems and stories, collected wild flowers, shells and birds' eggs, and set up a museum in a room given by their father.

Maggie, being nearest in age to Fred, was his chief ally in their games and hobbies, and they began to feel a special closeness. Martin was away at school, Nelly and Arthur were generally involved in their private doings, and Hugh was too babyish. Altogether, the three and a half Lincoln years were full and rich. Fred was storing up a crop of experiences to draw on in later life, and there seemed then, with love and friendship providing such happiness, no reason why it should not go on for ever. He was the most imaginative of the children, the most extrovert, without the seriousness of the older ones and the stubborn petulance of Hugh; his vivid personality endeared him to everybody.

# CHAPTER THREE

ne winter morning in 1876 Edward Benson received a letter from Benjamin Disraeli, the Prime Minister, offering him the newly constituted See of Truro, in Cornwall, which was to be detached from the unwieldy diocese of Exeter. Disraeli knew of Edward's essentially Tory principles, his fierce capacity for hard work and his devotion to the Church.

Edward had already refused the See of Calcutta because of the children and Minnie's health, but he never had any doubt about accepting Truro. He was genuinely sorry to leave Lincoln, where he had started so many successful projects, and he feared that a salary of only £3000 a year might bring hardship to his family. He would have to provide a house out of it, and a carriage and horse to travel through Cornwall, as well as paying for entertainments and visits to London. But he was excited by another new challenge – the chance to inaugurate, administer, order. Instead of being a subordinate in a great tradition he would be pre-eminent and supreme, as he had been at Wellington, but not accountable to a Board of Governors.

Edward was consecrated to the Bishopric of Truro on April 25 1877 in St Paul's Cathedral. After living for a time in temporary accommodation he found a large Queen Anne house a mile out of Truro on a hill overlooking the town and the tidal estuary. It had been a vicarage, with an extensive glebe and a large garden. With the aid of a fund raised to provide a suitable residence for the Bishop the house was enlarged: stables were converted into kitchens, two new wings and a library were added; a kitchen became a chapel; new stables and a drive were built, and the house was renamed Lis Escop (Bishop's Court in Cornish). It was set in fifteen acres of copses, valleys and streams, and near the house were beehives, haystacks and a summerhouse. The mild climate encouraged fuchsias, magnolias, camellias and hydrangeas to grow in profusion all the year round. Fred and Maggie became even more passionately interested in natural history. In a letter to Arthur, Fred wrote: 'Maggie's and my collection of moths are getting on beautifully. Maggie found a Golden Y smashed one day. It was stiff but I managed to

get its body from under its wings and the wings from under each other.'
He went on to tell his brother that his new butterfly book had arrived and
was splendid. He and Maggie had been riding the red pony in the field,
and two black woolly bear caterpillars had made cocoons.

And in his tenth year Fred fell in love again, this time with
Mrs Carter, the organist of Kenwyn Church and his sister's music
teacher. She must have been about thirty. Fred had admired her playing
before he actually saw her face, but when he did he became so shy that he
ran away. After that the curate, the Rev. J. A. Reeve, later Rector of
Lambeth, was the transient object of his adoration, although in fact in
this case it was the curate who started adoring first. Every Sunday, after
tea, Fred went with him into a spare bedroom where, with his arm round
Fred's neck, he would read the sermon he was about to preach.

The children had not been long at Lis Escop before the
game of Pirates evolved, and was taken up enthusiastically by all the
family, all of whom had a hand in forming its complicated rules; and they
all enjoyed its tension, cunning and heart-stopping excitement. Two
pirates, chosen in rotation, were given five minutes in which to hide in a
maze of trees, hedges, paths, garden doors, beehives, kitchen gardens
and orchard. The rest, usually three, occasionally four when Minnie
played and, (once only) five when the incongruous figure of Edward
joined the line up, were non-pirates. They chose a captain who had to
decide what trophy each of them should take back to the home base (or
Plymouth Sound, which was the summerhouse) without being caught by
a pirate. The trophy might be a croquet hoop, an apple, ivy leaf or other
ordinary object. The main rule was that no one should be caught unless
he or she was carrying their trophy, and the cunning lay in the psychological trap that the pirates could fall into, by supposing that what the
player was carrying was the actual trophy when the real one could be a
leaf behind a lapel or an apple hidden in a pocket. Then it was a case of
bluff and double bluff, misunderstandings, abortive chases and desperate
sprints to reach the summerhouse. It was a very strenuous game.

More than fifty years later Fred wrote a very poignant story
called *Pirates* set in a Lis Escop which had fallen into ruin. It is visited by
a middle-aged business man who has to take life easy because of a heart
condition. He had lived there with his brothers and sisters when he was a
small boy. He has visions of the games they played, including Pirates,
and other incidents in his early life which seem to be repeating themselves. He buys the house and has it and the garden restored to their
former state. Gradually he slips into a time warp and re-enters the world
of his youth. One morning he wakes up, slips out of the house and runs to
the summerhouse to join the rest of the pirates. Next morning the
gardener finds him dead, a middle-aged man who has had a heart attack.

The story is a distillation of the happiness that Fred had felt at Lis Escop, described lovingly and with nostalgia beautifully understated.

The first great family tragedy happened when Fred's eldest brother Martin died suddenly of meningitis just before his eighteenth birthday. Martin was at Winchester; he was a brilliant scholar and was nearer his father's heart than any of the other children. When he died life seemed to have no further meaning for Edward; Martin had been everything he had prayed for. Though he accepted the boy's death as God's will he could not understand the mystery of the Divine purpose and was overwhelmed by grief.

Martin was buried in the Winchester cloisters. Fred attended the funeral and though he himself was too young to understand the depth of his father's feelings, he never forgot his pale and agonised face when he met the family at Winchester station.

Later that year Fred reached the age of eleven, a good-looking, stocky little boy with fair hair and blue eyes, and it was time for him to be packed off to school. Apart from what his mother and a couple of temporary governesses had tried to teach him, his only schooling so far had been at a day school in Lincoln, kept by a widow just outside the Close. Later all that Fred could remember about her was that she had a Roman nose and her house smelt of mackintosh.

The new school was Temple Grove, one of the oldest and best known preparatory schools in the country. It occupied a large eighteenth-century house in a part of East Sheen, near Richmond in Surrey, and accommodated some 130 boys. Both Martin and Arthur had been at the school before him, and another former pupil was M. R. James. The first house on the site had been owned by Sir William Temple, Jonathan Swift's employer. Wings of bare brick which had been added housed a dining-room, a large schoolroom and cubicled dormitories.

The Headmaster was Ottiwell Charles Waterfield, an old friend of Edward's. He was Olympian, both in appearance and manner; he was tall and square-bearded, and walked with a curious rocking movement. Fred depicted him accurately as the Headmaster in *David Blaize*. Waterfield was an excellent teacher but stern in demeanour and over-ready to chastise. Like other benevolent tyrants he could cry copiously after birching his victim, and once collapsed in floods of tears after he had broken a boy's finger with a ruler. Strangely, the boys forgave him for, unlike Fred's father, he inspired hero-worship as much as terror. The moral tone of the school was high but not priggish; the boys were allowed a great deal of scope for their individual interests, and Fred settled in quickly and happily.

Some members of the staff were Dickensian in their odd

habits. One read *The Sporting Times* openly in class, his feet on the desk; another spent most of his time cultivating a moustache; a third ended up as a bookmaker; and Geoghehan, a sentimental sadist lacking his right arm, allowed his favourite pupil to sit on his knee, pull his beard and alter his marks in the register. His favourite joke was to spear the back of a boy's hand with a pen, the nib of which had been dipped in purple ink. Mr Prior, the writing master, was hopeless at keeping order and was more terrified of Waterfield than any of the boys. Games were compulsory but nobody taught the boys how to play them. M. R. James had always assumed that they played Association football at Temple Grove. Thirty years after leaving he was told that it had been rugby. Similar misapprehensions were common among the non-sporting types.

Fred enjoyed himself immensely during his first year. Without any effort he found himself at the top of his class and was the recipient of many prizes. Thus he was able to devote most of his time to cricket, stag-beetles and friendship. One of Waterfield's most civilised customs was to allow the boys to go into Richmond unsupervised on half holidays, and Fred regularly enjoyed visiting the pastrycook's shop.

An incident occurred during his first year that shocked and frightened him. Two boys were publicly expelled, one high in the school, the other much younger. They had done something so filthy that they had brought utter ruin and disgrace upon themselves, would never be received at any public school and had, into the bargain, broken their parents' hearts. It was difficult for the young Fred to imagine what crime could have merited such devastating condemnation. The boys listened, white-faced and shaking, to the Headmaster's emotion-choked diatribe with its dark hints of unmentionable evils, and left the big schoolroom in stunned silence. Fred was immediately summoned to the Headmaster's study. A weeping Waterfield asked him if he knew why the boys had been sent away. When he answered, 'No, sir', he was allowed to go with a fervent 'Thank God for that!'

Fred was more mystified than ever but began to rummage in his mind for clues. He remembered that the elder of the two expelled boys had spoken friendly words to him, and had given him a piece of Turkish delight. Later he had taken Fred for a stroll through the woods and asked him some odd questions, which Fred could not understand and so could not answer. Their talk had been interrupted by the appearance of the Headmaster who glanced at them keenly, said nothing but took them into a nearby greenhouse and fed them on grapes. Then he had walked back with them to the school.

After the disgraced boys had been taken away the secrecy and prohibition laid on the affair by the staff meant that the school seethed with hints, rumours and suppositions. Gradually the pieces of the jigsaw were fitted together, and the boys, some with relish, some more reluctantly, began to learn certain of the facts of life.

After Fred's initial academic promise the next two years at Temple Grove were disappointing. He had reached the top form easily with little effort and continued to drift happily, but now his laziness brought him to the bottom of the form, and there he stayed. The Headmaster sent agitated letters to Fred's father and received agitated letters in return. Neither could understand why a boy, obviously not stupid, should stagnate in this way. But, though Greek and Latin, Divinity and Mathematics, the chief subjects on the timetable, failed to inspire him, he was enthralled by the beauties of the English language, which Waterfield's reading of poetry had revealed to him. Also, the glories of Bach, which Mrs Russell, his music teacher, allowed him to make a rapturous hash of, rekindled a love of music that glowed quietly in his mind all through his adolescence. Beethoven, too, had his place, so had Mozart, but Bach was the gold standard in Fred's musical coinage at that time.

Fred tried for an Eton scholarship and failed. He had written to his mother just before the exam saying that he would either cut his throat or go mad if he didn't get a scholarship. Minnie wrote back immediately to say she didn't approve of either course, although she understood the reason he was so vehement about it. 'You *will* get one,' she wrote, 'if any effort on your part can do so. I believe it can. You see your great fault is want of accuracy – I believe you have plenty of ability but great mistakes ruin an examination paper, and accuracy *is* in your power if you give your mind to it.' Accuracy, she insisted, would help character as well as work. She wanted it to be part of his very being for the rest of his life.

Three months later his mother was writing again. 'I saw your last letter to Papa and very sorry I was, dear boy, to see that you had not been quite careful in your conduct out of school.' Apparently Fred had spoken to another boy at a time when speaking was not allowed. 'Don't you see, Fred dear, you ought to be becoming *manly* and setting an example to all the smaller boys? I want you to be manly and all that we have ever talked of tends to this... accuracy and sincerity and foresight making the kind of character worthy of your great hopes and present life, in God. Stir yourself up then, my boy, and be a man.'

Thus was Fred constantly exhorted by both parents not to stray from the paths of righteousness. Letters were sermons. They could have had a disastrous effect on a twelve-year-old boy, but Fred took them all in his stride.

When Ottiwell Waterfield retired to become a director of the Ottoman Bank, Fred was tutored for other scholarships under a new

Headmaster. This was Mr Edgar, formerly the second master, an amiable eccentric with two daughters with whom it was the fashion for the boys to fall in love. Something Fred liked to remember about Mr Edgar was his hat. It was made of hard black felt, like a bowler but quite round, with a broad black brim turned upwards all the way round, and wider even than that of a floppy straw hat. It made the new Headmaster look extremely comical, and went well with his easy-going nature and lax discipline.

During his last year Fred became involved in a complicated row. Instead of yielding up to the matron a present of five shillings he had received, so that it could be doled out shilling by shilling at suitable times, he bribed a friend with one of the shillings to break bounds and go into Richmond and spend the other four on Turkish delight. Then he organised a midnight feast in the dormitory with three of his friends and they sat on his bed stuffing themselves. Not only did the sheets get covered with a sticky residue, but it was not long before the stomach of one of the boys revolted, and he had to rush off to matron to be sick. The whole story was eventually unravelled and Fred stood revealed as the ringleader. The reaction of the Headmaster was very different from what his predecessor's would have been; Mr Edgar frowned heavily, told the boys they had been very naughty, and hoped that they would never do such a thing again.

Fred's only remaining anxiety was that his father might hear of the escapade, and he went home for the Christmas holidays in a very apprehensive frame of mind. His term report arrived just before Christmas and with it a full account of the crime. Already in a fit of black depression, the Bishop was so angry that Fred stood before him numb with fear. He was told that he was a disgrace, that he was not fit to mix with the other children, and that he was to have his meals alone and stay away from civilised society. Fred had no words to challenge what seemed to him an unfair judgment.

The next day was Christmas Eve. Fred was recalled from his lonely bedroom to stand again before his father, wondering what new crime he had committed, what new shame he had brought on his father's white hairs – but to his surprise the Bishop sat him in an armchair near the fire, put a rug round his knees and shared his own tea with him. Such a change of mood was not uncommon. For no good reason, and to the confusion of the children, severity changed into love, and love into severity.

Fred's remaining two terms at Temple Grove were pleasant but uneventful. He remained placidly at the bottom of the form, but secretly his intense interest in poetry, reading and composing music was developing. Many of his poems were addressed to the friend who was the current object of his adoration, and he received flowing stanzas in return.

To balance the romantic side of his nature he conceived a passion for steam-engines, and he and his fellow engineer, only one place above him in form position, would race their model locomotives through the cloisters.

Fred's teachers and parents were very disappointed with what they considered his lack of ambition. In fact, Fred had plenty of ambition. He wanted to be the best poet, engineer and cricketer in the world. He failed another scholarship examination, this time at Marlborough, and competed again at Eton; still without success. It was finally decided that he would go to Marlborough as a fee-paying pupil. Fred accepted the idea readily because a friend who had left Temple Grove a year before had gone to Marlborough and was now tall, handsome and magnificent. Fred, always ready to adore, looked forward to seeing him again. On his last day at Temple Grove he lost a school cricket match by dropping an easy catch having already been bowled for a duck. Many boys would have felt suicidal, but it was not in Fred's nature to be cast down for long.

When Fred left Temple Grove Arthur was nineteen and had got an Eton scholarship at King's College, Cambridge. He could do everything with ease, which stimulated Fred's admiration, and he talked with his father on equal terms, a facility which Fred was a long way from acquiring. Nellie for her part had distinguished herself at Truro High School. Not only had she taken many prizes, she was a devastating underarm bowler and had a good contralto voice. Maggie, at the same school, took the prizes that Nellie didn't. She was no athlete but a painter in watercolours and oils. Hugh, at nine, now his father's favourite, was opinionated and argumentative. At that time during the holidays, but only for a short time, he and Fred formed an alliance to which not even Maggie was admitted. It was distinguished by violent quarrels and swift reconciliations. It was all too exhausting for Fred and he went back to Maggie with relief. This was to be the only time when the two brothers were close. Their normal relationship was one of little understanding or communication. They could not have been less alike.

# CHAPTER FOUR

red was at Marlborough for six years, from September 1881 to July 1887. The school had been founded in 1843 for sons of the middle classes, and had developed on Arnoldian lines, with a prefectorial system and a strong bias towards organised games. Fred was put into B House, a square brick building of three storeys which could have provided a model for an old-fashioned prison. There were stone passages, iron bars, gas jets, and inadequate washing facilities. Ten to fifteen boys slept in a dormitory in Spartan conditions. But perhaps because it was a welcome escape from his problem parents, Fred took to his new school with enthusiasm, finding everything bright and alluring.

He took in his stride the differences between Temple Grove and Marlborough. The day was longer and more strenuous. If he leapt up when the bell clanged at 6.30am he might have time for a cup of cocoa and a bath before rushing to chapel at 7, and the first lesson, which started at 7.15am and lasted an hour. A miserable breakfast followed, consisting of tea, bread and butter, and sometimes porridge: anything extra had to be bought at the school tuckshop. Before dinner at 1.30pm there were two hours of lessons, an hour of preparation and an hour and a half for leisure. Dinner consisted of meat and a pudding, adequate but unexciting. At teatime the boys brewed tea in the classrooms, and it was one of the times when special friends could be together. After evening chapel there was a supper of biscuits and cheese, and a glass of beer. There was another hour of preparation before bedtime. Fred spent all his pocket money at the tuckshop. In bed in the dormitory the head of the house might give a favoured few pieces of hot buttered toast. It was the tradition for a boy with a gift for story-telling to send the others off to sleep.

At the end of Fred's first term he took a foundation scholarship examination which was open only to the sons of clergymen, and passed, to his own relief and his father's delight. He was able to enjoy the Christmas holidays and play Pirates with a clear conscience, happily contributing reams of poetry to the childrens' *Saturday Magazine*.

This then was a happy time for Fred. Even his normally difficult home life was brightened by his enjoyment of school. He became inordinately fond of cricket; rugby and athletics ranked only slightly lower in his estimation, and racquets was a growing obsession. He made the Football Fifteen a year before he left. Away from the sports field he spent happy hours collecting butterflies and moths in the nearby Savernake Forest, and his collection won him the Stanton Prize for Natural History in 1882.

What gilded these delights was his friendships with boys, especially those who were strong and masculine, who had musical inclinations or who sang in the choir. His affections were violent but volatile and his ardent affections lasted at most a term or two. Then another blue-eyed athlete would take his fancy, and a dip at the bathing-place or a game of squash would herald the beginning of another new friendship. One of his most intense attachments was to John Shuckburgh Risley, who was about six months his junior. His diary for 1886 is full of rapturous references to Risley − falling out, making up, taking communion with him, feeling alternately hopeless and ecstatic. 'I am feeling hopeless about Risley. What on earth am I to do?' he wrote. Eventually the enthusiasm petered out and Alfred Edward Glennie, nearly three years younger than Fred, took Risley's place, the diary recording equally fervent declarations of lasting affection. 'I have felt towards him as I have never felt towards anyone else.'

Fred was quite open about the passionate nature of his friendships in his autobiographical writings, but insisted that they had a healthy open-air quality about them; that in spite of physical attraction there was no element of 'dingy sensualism', as he called it.

After Fred's first year at Marlborough he started to climb the scholastic ladder when an interest in Greek and Latin was at last awakened by A. H. Beesly, a master who became another focal point for Fred's hero-worship, and who returned the feeling with his own strong affection. Out of the schoolroom Beesly was a lonely bachelor who had never been known to speak to a woman. In it he was a brilliant teacher. He had written and published his own translation of the story of Hecuba under the title *The Trojan Queen's Revenge*, and he would read it aloud to the boys. They would listen spellbound, none more so than Fred, who now felt the first stirrings of a love for all things Hellenic. Beesly invited him to Sunday morning breakfasts, and coached him in racquets.

When Fred was in his second year his father was appointed Archbishop of Canterbury, and the family had to uproot themselves from Truro and resettle in Lambeth Palace. Their lifestyle was further changed by the state dinner parties and the summer garden parties the Archbishop was required to give. The Archbishop's time was filled with

interviews, meetings, attendance at the House of Lords and preparing
sermons and speeches. His only recreation was riding, so Fred, Arthur
and Maggie often rode with him on Rotten Row or in Battersea Gardens.
What with parties and receptions at various noble houses the family was
launched, half scared, half eager, into London society. Fred felt at home
in it straight away.

The children were delighted with their father's promotion
and for once he met with nothing but admiration from them. His
eminence in Fred's eyes was sealed by a visit to Marlborough he made
with Minnie and Maggie to confirm a number of the boys, including
Fred. It was a moving moment for the new Archbishop; he was impressed
by the behaviour of the boys and the religious atmosphere in the chapel.
Fred was more excited by the fact that the school was given a day's
holiday in honour of the visit; he basked in reflected glory quite shamelessly, especially when his friends urged him to be confirmed again.

Retreating from the grandeur and rigours of the palace the
Bensons spent the holidays at Addington Park, a country mansion that
went with the living, and which is now swallowed up by Croydon. It then
lay in the corner of a park of some 600 acres, containing a great variety of
scenery: a steep heathery valley, great tracts of woodland with glades and
open spaces, a home farm and large gardens. The house was a grey stone
building, put up in 1770, ugly in front but stately at the rear. There the
younger Bensons were able to indulge themselves in almost every outdoor
activity, shooting, riding, golf, croquet, and tobogganing and skating in
winter. The evenings were taken up with painting, writing for the
*Saturday Magazine*, playing the organ, producing plays, and there was
ceaseless discussion and argument. Addington holidays were to Fred like
the magic of a spring that lasted all the year round. He was to say that
they gave him one of his greatest gifts, the habit of enjoyment. He found
pleasure and interest in everything around him, everything he did and
everybody he met. Writing became an enthralling occupation for them
all. Nellie had published an article in *Temple Bar*, Arthur wrote his first
book, and Fred and Maggie were engaged on a joint venture which in
some ways looked forward to Fred's first bestseller, *Dodo*.

Only Sundays lacked the delightful activities that made up
the rest of the week. They were days of unutterable boredom, made
worse by the never-changing routine: early communion in the chapel,
morning service in the nearby parish church, a family walk after lunch
and a Bible reading before tea. After tea there was the evening service,
and after supper the Archbishop read improving books aloud until it was
time for compline in chapel. Secular topics of conversation were frowned
upon at meals, no games were allowed and no frivolous books could be
read. It did not occur to the Archbishop that his enjoyment of Sundays

was not shared by the rest of the family.

In the summer of 1884, when Fred was seventeen, he was promoted to the Sixth, had a study of his own, and a fag to clean his boots and to make his tea. He could now wear his cap at the back of his head. The next year he became head of his house, enjoyed more privileges, co-edited the school magazine, *The Marlburian*, with great success, and played football and racquets. A genial and energetic pagan, he continued to fill his life with friendship, games and work, in that order. The result was that he failed a series of scholarship examinations. He managed to persuade his housemaster and Headmaster to write to his anxious father, urging him to allow Fred to stay on another year before going up to Cambridge, and the appeal was successful. The Archbishop never found out Fred's real reason for wanting to stay at school. It was to help his house win the racquet house cup, the fives cup, the gymnasium cup, the football cup and the singing cup; but most of all he wanted Eustace Miles to catch up with him so that they could go to Cambridge together.

Eustace Hamilton Miles was the head boy that year and one of Fred's greatest friends, both at school and university. He was fourteen months younger than Fred and had entered Marlborough a year later. He was more academically minded than Fred but his sporting achievements were as considerable. Miles knew already that he was going up for a classical scholarship at King's College, and Fred, with his usual unbridled enthusiasm, decided that he would do the same. They were given permission to give up French, Mathematics and History and devote themselves entirely to Latin and Greek, working on their own in their studies.

Fred began then to be aware of the flexibility of language and to delight in the cadence of words. What Beesly had done to awaken for him the Greeks' genius for beauty was now complemented by his discovery that how they wrote was as thrilling as what they did. He also started to read voraciously in English literature, particularly Addison, Browning, Dickens and Tennyson. He wrote much of *The Marlburian*, with Eustace Miles as co-editor, and turned it from a dry-as-dust school magazine into a mixture of scurrility and humour. The son of a publisher, Miles was knowledgeable about printing, pulls and proofs, and the enterprise must have been blessed with journalistic flair for it not only covered its costs, at threepence a copy, but made a profit for its editors. It was then that Fred realised that writing could pay.

Eustace Miles's later career diverged sharply from the classical one that might have been foreseen for him. After a period as assistant master at Rugby he turned from Greek and Latin to athletics, self-health and vegetarianism. He became Amateur Champion of the World at racquets and at tennis, holding the Gold Prize from 1897 to 1901. He won the Amateur Tennis Championship at Queen's Club for eight years in three periods during the years 1899 and 1910. His fanatical devotion to health through natural foods led him to open the Eustace Miles Restaurant and health food shop in Chandos Street, London, and he published a number of popular cookery books as well as inventing several kitchen appliances. An offshoot of these activities was his involvement in the Pelman Institute for Memory Training. Twelve booklets were issued to the students, one every month, and each one had a supplement of physical exercises devised by Miles. He also edited the monthly magazine *Healthward Ho!*

In 1906 he married a long-forgotten writer called Hallie Killick, and in later years they occasionally visited Fred at Lamb House in Rye and were entertained to vegetarian meals, which the meat-eating, spirit-drinking and tobacco-addicted Fred shared. Miles died in 1948, having outlived Fred by eight years. Almost as prolific as Fred, he had written more than forty books, earnest and dogmatic, on a variety of subjects: physical culture, lawn tennis, racquets and squash, reincarnation, philology, and control and self-expression for boys. He also wrote 150 booklets on various aspects of health and efficiency. It is mainly by his long friendship with Fred that his name is remembered today. It is hard to see in the fun-loving Marlborough schoolboy the stern bigot that Miles became, but the seeds must have been there, in the capacity for hard work, the self-discipline, the strength of his opinions, and his restraining influence on some of Fred's wilder flights of fancy.

For the last two years at Marlborough, Miles and Fred worked and played together and lived their lives to the exclusion of all others. The attractions of Risley, Glennie and their successors had faded. Miles had entirely captured Fred's heart. Their exclusive alliance aroused no comment or disapproval; such situations were common in public schools and were regarded as quite natural.

And so Fred's last term at Marlborough was one of the happiest times of his life, and when it was over so too was the wonder of boyhood – though Fred never stopped trying to find it again. Apart from brief holidays at Addington and in the Lake District Fred's whole life had, for six years, been bounded by chapel, sportsfields, schoolrooms and studies. Now he could see that all he had loved about Marlborough would become obscured by the mist of the years ahead. But one thing that would never be lost was the quality of his friendship with Eustace Miles, many years later lovingly portrayed in *David Blaize*.

Beesly was on Marlborough Station platform when Fred left for the last time. He was pretending to look at the magazines on the bookstall but just as the train was about to leave he hurried to the carriage door and looked up at Fred's mournful face. 'Just come to see you off,' he said. 'Don't forget us all.'

That summer the Benson family went to Easedale in the Lake District. The Archbishop had taken the Rectory, and eight people were forced to shelter from the incessant rain in cramped and uncomfortable conditions. Nellie fell ill, then Fred contracted jaundice. He was relieved when it was time to go to Cambridge.

# Chapter Five

n October 4 1887 Fred became an undergraduate of King's College, Cambridge. Miles followed him four days later. He spent his first year in lodgings. His father was there to see him into his rooms and remembered that it was thirty-nine years, almost to the day, since he had begun his own university life. Edward could not help remarking that he disapproved of the way gowns had been shortened into jackets and that undergraduates had lost the old grave look which symbolised dignity and self-respect. He was particularly incensed that Colleges had become secularised.

It was not until the Michaelmas Term of 1888 that Fred moved to Gibbs's Building, into rooms known as E1 on the ground floor, on a rent of £18 a year. There he lived for two years, sharing the rooms with Charles Stevenson, an old Harrovian, the son of an M.P.

Dr Waldstein lived above Fred, and above him Professor Middleton, both of whom he found inspiring teachers. Oscar Browning lived in Wilkins's Buildings, as did H. M. Mozley, a wildly eccentric Fellow. If Mozley was seen coming out into the court at King's for a walk and some unkind person whistled from a window, no matter what the tune was, the old man, probably thinking that the sound was inside his own head, would turn round and scurry back to his rooms. It would be ten minutes before he ventured out again.

In 1890 Fred moved to F rooms, also on the ground floor of Gibbs's Building, and these he shared with Vincent Wodehouse Yorke. Fred had met Yorke two years earlier and had immediately fallen in love with him. 'I feel perfectly mad about him just now,' he wrote in his diary. 'Ah, if he only knew...' Fred felt that this attachment would yield happier results than others in the past and regretted nothing that he had said or done; he was sure that Yorke knew of the situation and he believed that everything would be all right.

But whatever responses Yorke made at the time the friendship was not to last beyond Cambridge. Yorke was an old Etonian, two years younger than Fred, and got his degree in 1891, after a First Class Classical Tripos the same year. He was an excellent tennis player and took part in the Inter-University Tennis Doubles. He became a Fellow in 1895, did some research in Greece and Asia Minor, then gave up University life for a business career in London. In 1899 he married and so passed out of Fred's life to Fred's great sorrow and lasting regret. In 1905 the Yorkes had a son, later to become 'Henry Green', the novelist. Yorke had been Mozley's chief tormentor. He would send the poor fellow back time and time again, until he relented and let him off the hook so that he could at last take his walk.

In the beginning Fred's proclivity for romantic friendships may have been little more than the relic of the kind of semi-religious eroticism that public schools foster, but the fact that, starting with his childish crush on a choirboy, they continued into adult life indicates that his sexuality had been fixed early on. After Cambridge he drifted into the Oscar Wilde/Alfred Douglas set; he also got to know Robert Hichens and Reggie Turner (whom Wilde called 'the boy-snatcher of Clement's Inn').

It is likely that Fred and Oscar Wilde were introduced to each other by Robert Ross, Wilde's devoted friend who spent a year, or part of a year, at King's College from October 1888. He and Fred moved in the same circle of undergraduates and dons. Fred was charmed by Wilde; they often met and talked about their writing projects. Wilde told him once that he was busy with a small volume of ethical essays designed to be given as tokens of ill-will at Christmas, and that the Bishop of London had agreed to write a preface hoping that the brief sermons would carry their message of sorrow into many otherwise happy homes. As Wilde described the so-called book it soon turned out that it was a figment of his outlandish imagination, a flurry of brilliant words that had no substance. On another occasion he said to Fred, 'Pray come to this symposium. Everything nowadays is settled by symposiums, and this one is to deal finally with the subject of bimetallism – of bimetallism between men and women.' Lord Alfred Douglas says in his autobiography that he was on terms of great friendship with Fred Benson. Fred attended the first night of *Lady Windermere's Fan* with Max Beerbohm and Reggie Turner, each wearing a green carnation.

Some of the characters that Fred met at Cambridge provided him with subject matter for comedy in more than one of his future books. One of them was the wildly sociable J. E. Nixon, Dean of the College and one of the Life Fellows. His activities were prodigious and his energy phenomenal. He was only just over five feet tall, had only one eye and an artificial right hand, but these disabilities didn't prevent him from taking part in games. Even when playing lawn tennis he wore a black tail coat and long boots with turned-up toes. He rode a tricycle around Cambridge at top speed. At his weekly glee-singing meetings he dispensed Tintara wine, hot tea-cakes and Borneo cigars, and sang in a cracked tenor voice, beating time faster and faster with a paper-knife until it flew out of his hand.

Nixon had more new ideas in a day than most people have in a lifetime, and all of them useless. He thought up ways of turning envelopes inside out so that they could be used again, sharpening pencils without getting the forefinger blackened and using different coloured inks for correcting essays. He was argumentative about the most trivial things, and whatever the issue, deliberately perverse. His conversation consisted of a stream of observations, not one of them connected with any of the others.

The most notable of the Life Fellows, however, was Oscar Browning, whose large and pungent personality pervaded the whole of Cambridge. O. B., as he was called, had been a notable Eton master and house tutor, a compound of Arnoldian earnestness, ludicrous tuft-hunting, acuteness and buffoonery. In 1875 he was suddenly dismissed from Eton in circumstances which are unclear but seem to have revolved round some questionable behaviour towards one of the boys. He had a habit of making pets of those who were handsome and attractive. As he was already a Fellow of King's, he retired to Cambridge and took an active part in the teaching of History and in the social life of the College.

Short, bald and stout, his garish behaviour and adolescent cavortings made him both a laughing-stock and an object of disapproval. He was an enormous snob. He bought a hockey stick when he was forty-five and took up the game so that he could be hit on the shins by the Duke of Clarence, then an undergraduate of Trinity. He also claimed friendship with the Empress of Austria, Lady Salisbury, Lord Acton, and many others. Nobody attended his lectures in English History, but everybody went to his 'At Homes' on Sundays, when he would play on one of his four harmoniums, then lead a quartet which massacred Beethoven, Brahms or Mozart. He took a great interest in young men, including Fred. As O. B. grew older he quarelled with every board or committee member he was associated with, left Cambridge for Bexhill, became a Christian Scientist, and finally settled in Rome to write a history of the world (never published).

Fred found himself part of a small group of like-minded young men. Most of them had been at Eton, their leader being Montague Rhodes James, known as Monty. He had been at Temple Grove, though five years before Fred, and then at Eton and Cambridge. Monty James was on terms of great intimacy with the Bensons, often visiting them at Addington, and was entrusted by the Archbishop with a kind of watching brief over Fred, whose character his father held to be too frivolous, wishing he were as grave as Arthur. Fred was still 'a dear boy', however, in his diary.

Other members of the James group were Walter Headlam, a very fine Greek scholar, and Lionel Ford, who later became Headmaster of Harrow. Fred also had a tremendous admiration for James Kenneth Stephen, editor and parodist, who became a Fellow in 1885. He was a barrister and later Clerk of Assize for the South Wales Circuit between 1888 and 1890, but died insane in 1892. For a time he was suspected of having committed the Jack the Ripper murders of 1888.

J. K. Stephen had been tutor to (and reputed lover of) Prince Albert Victor, Duke of Clarence and grandson of Queen Victoria. He was a member of the Apostles, a semi-secret society of intellectuals with a strong homosexual flavour. Another member was Henry Cust, who was at Trinity, a young man of great promise who later ruined his career in politics by excessive indulgence in various vices. Arthur Benson failed to gain entry to the Apostles, but his intense friendship with Cust (which had begun at Eton) meant that he knew Stephen and the Apostles well. His friendship with Cust collapsed in 1883, and Arthur was left deeply wounded.

Another friend of Cust was Henry Wilson, one of Stephen's protégés, and it is supposed that Wilson, Cust and others of the Apostles had all known Montague John Druitt, failed barrister and teacher and suspected murderer of five prostitutes in London's Whitechapel area. When Druitt was being investigated the spotlight moved from Stephen. It was proved that the Prince could not have been present at the scenes of the crimes so he was cleared too. The police were on much firmer ground in suspecting that Druitt was Jack the Ripper, and it has been suggested that some of the Apostles murdered Druitt, whose body was found in the Thames (after which there were no more murders) because they had inside knowledge that he had committed the ghastly deeds.

The evidence that Druitt was the murderer is no more than circumstantial, and the link between Fred and the suspected participants in the alleged plot to kill the Ripper is tenuous to the point of non-existence; though it is interesting to note that, at that time, the University had its share of equivocal characters and that strange things stirred beneath the placid exteriors of the venerable buildings and their inhabitants. Fred was only on the outermost fringe of these goings-on, but he could not have been ignorant of the muddy waters in which some of his contemporaries dabbled.

Fred joined the Pitt Club, whose members had their letters stamped without having to pay postage, and a literary society called the Chitchat which met on Saturday evenings, when each member in turn gave an original paper on a subject of his choice. They drank coffee and claret-cup, ate anchovy toast and took snuff in such quantities that the proceedings were often interrupted by embarrassing sneezes. The most important meeting that Fred attended was when Monty James read his first two ghost stories. They were received with unanimous appreciation, but Fred was the only member of the ten present who was inspired to follow Monty's example.

An offshoot of the Chitchat was the TAF (Twice a Fortnight), a weekly gathering which J. K. Stephen started. It was composed of his friends from King's and Trinity, old Etonians and Harrovians who met on Sunday evenings instead of going into Hall. Monty James was the central figure, though he later resigned, saying that it was too exclusive. The 'Love-Feast of the Clan', as it was nicknamed, was renowned for its conversation, readings from Dickens, rags and horseplay.

Fred also joined the Decemviri Debating Society, and distinguished himself by saying absolutely nothing whenever he attended a meeting. His only speech was to protest against an effort to expel him. The motion was carried and he never went to another meeting. He felt he had accomplished something, though he was not quite sure what.

At the end of his first term Fred won an exhibition at King's, but for the next year he slacked alarmingly, for there was no incentive to attend lectures. Their standard was so low that he temporarily deserted the Classics for more attractive occupations, one of which was to launch the *Cambridge Fortnightly*, with the help of Roger Fry.

It is not surprising that the venture didn't last more than five issues – between January 24 and March 13, 1888. Published by Octavus Tomson from 16, King's Parade, it cost sixpence and was a flimsy affair of twenty pages. Its opening declaration of policy was unpromising.

> The *Cambridge Fortnightly* will not sully the purity of its pages with the contaminating commonplaces of ordinary politics. The only policy of the paper will be one of freedom of discussion in matters of University or general interest. Any of our readers who may have a grievance to ventilate, a theory to propound, a moral or intellectual problem to solve, or a joke to cut, will find in the pages of the *Cambridge Fortnightly* an open field for protest and discussion.
> The subsequent issues of the *Cambridge Fortnightly* will be adorned with a lithographed title-page of high allegorical beauty. We regret that our artist has been summoned to Windsor to paint a portrait of Her Majesty, and has therefore been unable to complete his design in time for this number.

The artist in question turned out to be Roger Fry: the high allegorical beauty was a scratchy view of Cambridge buildings.

In the second number it was evident that the rot had already set in. The editorial declared:

We are becoming sceptical about the Cambridge Undergraduate. He is not as adventurous as we thought. Last fortnight there was put before him an intellectual feast of no ordinary description. It was not large it is true; but is not 'enough is good!'? And this seems to have been positively too much to judge from the numbers still left at the publishers. We envy the sale of our Oxford twin, *The Undergraduate*, who has sold eleven hundred copies of the first number. We understand that the way to success is by interviewing actresses and defaming Dons. Are we to be forced to tread in their steps? It lies with the Undergraduate.

But the Undergraduate yawned and left the magazine to limp along without his participation in freedom of discussion of moral and intellectual problems; and issue No 5, without any warning, saw the end of the venture.

In its short life the *Cambridge Fortnightly* published articles about ways to increase the University's income by raising the Capitation Fee, about the place of women in University life (it was pro-women), Cambridge rowing, Lacrosse, accounts of Union debates, a long story by Christopher Carr (Arthur Benson), an obituary of Sir Henry Maine, Master of Trinity Hall, by Oscar Browning, a letter from Davos by Arthur Sidgwick (Fred's uncle) in Greek, and various unsigned humorous poems of little merit. The only exception was Barry Pain's brilliant parody called 'The Tea Party' – its first appearance in print. There was also a prose parody called 'The Anglo-Saxons', by H-nry J-m-s. Most contributions were unsigned; apart from the editorials it is likely that the James parody was written by Fred; it is definitely in his style.

One of the interesting things about this forlorn little undertaking is that it probably provides a clue to where Fred lived during his first year at Cambridge. Roger Fry, two years before, had had rooms at 16, King's Parade, and that was the address from which the *Cambridge Fortnightly* was published. As Fred and Fry were the main begetters of the periodical it is possible that Fred took over Fry's rooms before he moved into Gibbs's Building, and Fry would have visited his old rooms to help get each issue together. They may have called themselves 'Octavus Tomson' as a bit of undergraduate humour. No.16 is now a men's outfitters.

When the *Cambridge Fortnightly* expired Fred was five pounds poorer, but true to his nature, he did not grieve for long. Soon, working on his own, he was writing *Sketches from Marlborough*, which he had started while he was still at school, and some of which had appeared in *The Marlburian*. It was privately published in 1888 and printed by the Marlborough firm who, to their surprise, had benefitted financially from printing the school magazine.

Fred admitted later that the ominous part about this first book was the extreme facility with which it was written. Knowing what his father's response would be to the use of time that could have been spent in study, he didn't tell him about the venture. When the Archbishop found out he wrote Fred a letter of remonstrance couched in such loving terms that Fred's guilt was doubly severe.

*Sketches from Marlborough* is Fred's rarest book and copies seldom surface. It is not known how many copies were printed, but five hundred is a generous estimate. It contains 105 pages and was sold at one shilling and sixpence, printed and published by Chas. Perkins, the 'Times' Office, Marlborough. The title-page bears a sentimental verse from *Ionica*:

> *I may have failed – my School may fail;*
> *I tremble, but this much I dare;*
> *I love her; let the critics rail,*
> *My brethren and my heart are there.*

The book deals lightly and humorously with the final weeks of the narrator's schooldays. In the preface Fred claims that the 'I' – the narrator of the story – is not strictly 'I', and that is easy to accept. He comes across as a charmingly deprecating fellow, not very good at anything, grossly but endearingly incompetent as a sportsman, as his observations on cricket show: 'There must be a fatality about first balls this evening...I was got out by one too. However, first balls usually are rather fatal to me; I don't suppose second balls would be, but I haven't often tried them.' Nor is his bowling any better than his batting, but he takes solace in a friend's reflection that 'if you don't ever hit anything and if nothing ever hits your wicket you can't possibly get out.'

Are there, in this youthful work, intimations of things to come? It would be overstating matters to see too much, but one can catch glimpses of the kind of humour that came to such fruition in the Lucia books and, indeed, some of the bizarre situations. Sporting interests are described with an enthusiasm that is followed through in many of the later books. Fred himself appears, though still as 'I', as having a passionate interest in natural history, chasing butterflies in Savernake Forest.

There is nothing cloying in the book, no mooning over the unattainable ideal friend, no nostalgic references to past loves. The characters are a bunch of fun-loving, games-mad, workshy boys who are, in spite of outdated slang, thoroughly credible.

Once Fred returned to Marlborough, breaking a journey to Truro to attend the opening of Truro Cathedral, and spent half a day at his old school. As he had expected, things had changed, (or rather he had) though quite how and why he could not explain. He had once looked upon Marlborough as a planet, fixed and shining: now he realised that other bright planets had swung into his life, and Marlborough had dimmed by comparison. But Beesly had not changed, so for a few hours he shed his Cambridge sophistication and was a schoolboy again, friend-ship glowing as richly as it had ever done.

He spent most of his vacations at Lambeth and Addington, although he remained at Cambridge for part of the long vacations spending them with Vincent Yorke. One summer the family went to Switzerland where the Archbishop told Fred that he would pay for the guides and porters for any two first-class peaks that he wanted to climb. Fred had no hesitation in choosing the Matterhorn first. Starting off at midnight, the party stumbled upwards by lantern light until dawn broke and the surrounding peaks and valleys were gradually revealed as the rising sun flooded them with dazzling brilliance. It was almost a mystical experience for him. Soon, however, dark clouds began to form and mists wreathed round them. They reached the peak as quickly as possible, opened a bottle of champagne and began the descent without delay. Now the sun disappeared, snow fell heavily and visibility dropped to nil. There was thunder, and the air was electric. It took forty minutes to crawl down through the storm, and the adventure left Fred shaken, glad that he had had such an experience, but determined never to undergo it again.

His second selection was the Zienal Rothorn, and this time Nellie went along with him. They climbed through the night and nothing untoward marred the ascent. They were able to sit at the summit for an hour in brilliant sunshine, sheltered from the wind by a cowl of snow, marvelling at the sights and colours spread out for them. On the ground the Archbishop looked at them through his telescope and saw them waving to him and shaking hands with their guides.

The pleasure that writing *Sketches from Marlborough* had given him, the ease with which his pen had raced over the pages, and the modest acclaim that the book had brought him made Fred decide that eventually he was going to devote most of his time to writing. With that decision firmly established he was willing to work hard at his classical studies during his third year. With Eustace Miles as his mentor he settled down to serious work – intensely boring work as he soon discovered. There was no artistic appreciation of the sort that Beesly had inspired,

only learning by rote words and phrases that might be useful in trans-
lations. He would have drifted away to more enjoyable activities had it
not been for Miles, who kept him anchored to the rock of industry. After
two terms he grew tired and stale, and Monty James came to the rescue
by taking him on a walking tour of Normandy and Brittany. They
travelled by train more than they did on foot, but Fred returned refreshed.
The last paper in the Tripos was in Classical History, of which he knew
nothing, and he had to sit up most of the night before cramming his brain
with a vast number of unrelated facts.

Before the results came out Fred went home to Lambeth
Palace for a couple of nights. He wrote to Minnie who was holidaying at
Rhyl. He couldn't tell her how he had done in the Tripos because the
results would not be out for a week, but he felt no bitterness towards the
examiners, which he thought was a favourable sign. Miles had stayed for
a night at the Palace and they had been seeing pictures and gone riding
before breakfast. He signed himself, 'Best of love, Your lovingest son.'

To Fred's great astonishment he took a first, as did Miles.
Fred was further dumbstruck when the examiner congratulated him on
his grasp of the subject and suggested that he take up History for a second
Tripos. Fred remained silent about the method he had employed and
politely declined.

Delighted at Fred's success, the Archbishop was anxious
that he should stay up at Cambridge for a further year to take another,
preferably a theological Tripos with a view to ordination. His over-
whelming desire had been that all his sons would enter the priesthood.
Arthur, now a master at Eton, showed no signs of wanting to be a
clergyman, so his father's hopes now rested on Fred all the more heavily.
But Fred had no vocation. He decided on Archaeology for a second
Tripos, and the Archbishop sighed but said nothing. It was Hugh, due to
enter Trinity after failing an Indian Civil Service examination, who
eventually gladdened his father's heart by entering the Church.

During the next long vacation Fred began to write the first
draft of *Dodo*, at first for his private amusement, but as he became more
and more involved with his fascinating but heartless heroine he began to
hope for publication. His ambition was not to be printed by a little
provincial firm, but in brave hard covers with his name on the front, and
on sale in bookshops all over the country.

He wrote enthusiastically and speedily, but without self-
criticism. There was no plot, the minor characters circled round the
central figure and occasionally clashed with her, without interplay of
character, development or depth of feeling. What made the story different
from other novels of its time, and was the reason for its ultimate success,
was the original idea of making Dodo reveal herself by what she said;

what she did therefore required no comment. Dodo was rich, attractive and adored. She flirted and smoked and outraged conventional society; and she talked and talked. But on the last page she was the same Dodo as she had been on the first. After a few weeks scribbling Fred found that he had lost direction. He became conscious of some of the story's inadequacies and felt disinclined to spend any more of his precious time on it. He decided instead to concentrate on his archaeological studies.

At the beginning of October, 1890, Fred was briefly at Addington before returning to Cambridge for his final year. Arthur was already back at Eton and Hugh had gone to Cambridge for the assembly of freshmen. His parents and Maggie were away on a visit so that, apart from Beth, he was alone with Nellie. For a few days he and his sister reverted to childhood games and pursuits, riding, playing lawn tennis, enjoying their freedom from parental restraints. Neither of them realised that this was the last time youthful and carefree exuberance would be theirs. For soon after Fred had returned to Cambridge Nellie died of diphtheria. She was only twenty-seven.

Nellie had resembled her mother both physically and in character, being short and plump, ready to please and of a naturally happy nature, in spite of an occasional bout of the family curse of neurasthenia. 'Gay, adventurous, brave', Arthur called her. Emotionally too, she resembled Minnie with her preference for her own sex. At Lady Margaret Hall, Oxford, she experienced a number of sentimental relationships, and wrote and received reams of schoolgirl love letters. But her deepest feelings were reserved for Ethel Smyth, a woman of formidable passions, a committed militant in the cause of women's rights, and a composer whose talent was yet to be recognised. She came into the Benson's lives in 1886 at a dinner party given by the Dean of Windsor, and was immediately smitten by Minnie's intelligence and the sympathy that was, she said later, like a visible aura. Ethel Smyth, whose emotions always seemed to be in a state of turmoil, was convinced that Minnie could solve her problems, and she resolutely attached herself to the older woman. Their friendship blossomed into an intimacy that alarmed the Archbishop and he took a great dislike to Ethel. Maggie, too, had little time for Ethel who, despite rebuffs, had made several bids for her friendship. When Ethel met Nellie during the summer of 1889, she was more successful. Their friendship sprang up on the cricket field. She, her sisters and Nellie were all members of the White Heather Club, the premier women's cricket club of the time. Minnie was disturbed by the new relationship, but was compelled to accept the situation and regretfully relinquished Ethel. After that there was a coolness between them. It was Nellie's first grown up relationship, and although it lasted less than a year, it was intense. When Ethel left London for Munich they wrote to each other every day, letters in which expressions of love were mixed with accusations of misunderstandings and lectures on behaviour.

Two years after Nellie's death Minnie was still feeling a sense of outrage. She wrote to Maggie, first about Fred, saying that he was a perfect dear, but London didn't suit him; he felt demoralised and couldn't take enough exercise, 'bless the darling'. She went on to say that when Ethel had arrived the day before they had talked a little, and then she had told her plainly that she had disgusted her. Ethel was very serious too. She had found Fred in the smoking-room, had stayed with him for two hours and told him the whole story, but in such an unfair way that he couldn't help but agree with her. Fred then went straight to Minnie and heard her version of the story. 'I'm sure she doesn't intend to lie but it comes to very much the same thing in the end. Oh, she *is* a beast!' Minnie finished vehemently.

Meanwhile the Archbishop maintained his uncompromising disapproval of Ethel Smyth, and it was not until after the publication of *Dodo* that she was welcome at Lambeth. His opinion of her had not changed but, believing that Fred had lampooned her in *Dodo* as the composer, Edith Staines, he sought to make amends for his son's offence. To Ethel's mingled terror and gratification the Archibishop almost embraced her, and all through the evening he was over-solicitous. When she was leaving she asked Minnie why the Archbishop had been so amiable. Minnie explained that he thought she might have been hurt about Edith Staines. In fact, Ethel had been pleased to be included among the social celebrities that Fred had parodied; in any case she considered that Edith Staines was the one decent character in the book.

When Nellie died the gap in the family circle, first opened by Martin's death twelve years earlier, grew wider, heralding the disintegration of the Bensons' corporate life. The paths of Arthur, Fred, Maggie and Hugh were diverging. Their old intimacy was losing its glow. Although they regarded each other with unsentimental affection they were sometimes violently critical of each other, and future events pulled them further apart.

# CHAPTER SIX

red was now twenty-three years old but still boyish-looking, in spite of a new moustache, with an athletic figure, and an attractive face. He had a sensitive mouth, and intensely blue eyes that were perhaps his most remarkable feature. He was bursting with health; his prowess as a sportsman and his sunny nature ensured his popularity at King's and elsewhere. His mind, which had been darting from one passion to another, at last settled firmly on one subject – the Greeks, and as an ardent Hellenist he reacted vigorously against Roman art and architecture.

His enthusiasm was fired by two teachers, Dr Waldstein in the Museum of Casts, and Professor Middleton, who made all things Greek as real as the living world. Three mornings a week Fred would go to the professor's room with his books, but would neglect them in favour of listening to the professor and examining the Greek artefacts that he produced from pockets and drawers, all of which revealed aspects of Greek life and art that he found fascinating. Fred's appreciation of the language which he had learned from Beesly at Marlborough now burst into fervent love for the people and their way of life. He believed that the Greeks were the supreme race; he cast a romantic and uncritical eye on all their achievements and was captivated by their artistry. He longed to know all about the god-like people to whom he had given his heart.

His studies were rewarded: he gained his Tripos in Archaeology and was given an open scholarship at King's. Immediately he applied for a grant to excavate the town walls of Chester in a search for tombstones of the Roman legionaries who had been stationed there. Fred had little time for the Romans because they weren't Greeks, but the grant was available and he thought the task would fill up the autumn nicely and might yield material for a fellowship-dissertation. His application was successful.

Before he began work at Chester he went to Pontresina for a fortnight with his family, and had a most frightening experience on the Piz Palu, one of the peaks of the Bernina, in Switzerland. He and Hugh, with two guides, planned to ascend the peak on one side, pass over the top and descend on the other side. The first two parts were accomplished without incident but on the way down they encountered so fierce a wind that loose snow from the rocks was hurled against them. Hugh suddenly became sleepy, stumbled and collapsed. He seemed to be barely conscious but opened his eyes and begged to be allowed to go to sleep. They poured brandy down his throat but this only revived him momentarily, and the guides had to carry him along the rest of the ridge, trying to find shelter from the wind. They took off the rope which bound them all together, the guides carried Hugh and Fred followed on his own, lagging behind when descent without a rope became awkward.

The journey back took an hour. Occasionally Fred would see the guides and their burden, then the rocks would hide them again and he would have no idea whether Hugh was alive or dead. He caught up with the others when they had at last escaped from the wind into sunshine – and found the guides roaring with laughter and Hugh quite drunk, trying to sit on the point of his ice-axe. In thick and stumbling speech he told them that he had only felt very sleepy and not on the point of death. The half pint of brandy had had a delayed effect on the nineteen-year-old youth not used to strong drink. So there was no need for Fred to send the telegram that he had been composing in his mind to inform his father that his youngest son was dead.

Fred's work at Chester took six weeks and was very successful. The City Council had given their approval to the scheme and the city surveyor helped with technical problems. Important tombstones were found which showed that a legion *Legio Decima Valeria Victrix* had been stationed at Chester; their presence in England had hitherto been unknown. He was congratulated by Professor Mommsen, a prominent historian, and was invited by the Prime Minister, Mr Gladstone, to visit Hawarden and tell him about his finds. The Gladstones and the Bensons were on very friendly terms, in spite of the Archbishop's unswerving Toryism.

Fred's exploration funds were now exhausted and he returned to Cambridge to write up the results of his work. On an idle impulse one day he took out the incomplete manuscript of *Dodo* and read it again. His interest was rekindled, but before he did any more work on it he decided to get an expert opinion. He sent the story to his mother and asked her to pass it on to Lucas Malet, a family friend and best-selling novelist, the daughter of Charles Kingsley. He was astonished and rather scared to hear later that his mother had instead sent it to Henry James.

'Very dear Mrs Benson,' Henry James wrote in October 1891, 'It is charming to hear you on so interesting a topic. It'll give me great pleasure to look at your son's story – though I suspect that if he knew into what deplorable fastidious habits I have let myself lapse (in such matters) I mean how seriously I take the whole business – I can take it in only one way; he would perhaps withdraw some of the friendly confidence with which he honours me – little cause as he may have to fear the critical spirit . . .'

The manuscript was roughly written, full of erasures and illegible interpolations, and when Henry James delivered his judgment he prefaced it by remarking that he had over-estimated the attention he would be able to give to a manuscript of such substantial length, adding that he had taken for granted that the work would be type-copied and not hand-written. James confessed to being rather a cold-blooded judge, likely to be offensive to a young story-teller on the question of quality. Fred's story fell short of his ideal of literary ferocity. 'Make yourself a style,' he wrote. 'It is by style that we are saved.'

Fred was not too discouraged by the tortuously worded condemnation, but further work on the book was interrupted by a journey to Algiers at the end of December 1891, undertaken by him, his parents, Maggie, and Lucy Tait, sister-in-law of the Dean of Windsor who, after Nellie's death, had made her home permanently with the Bensons.

At Marseilles the Archbishop was in one of his depressed moods which Fred tried to alleviate by reading aloud the family's favourite pieces of *In Memoriam*. From Algiers the family wended their way eastwards, visiting Constantine, Tebessa, Timehad, Fort National and Biskra. Next they went to Carthage, and the Archbishop found it a most moving experience. He had been writing a book about Cyprian, Bishop of Carthage, for thirty years, and at last he had reached the site where the bishop had worked. He had no idea that his pilgrimage had a less than enthusiastic response from the rest of the family, who could only see a bare and bleak hillside. Fred left the others at Tunis and arrived at Athens by way of Malta and Brindisi. Once there his love of all things Greek leapt into urgent life, and his account of his first sight of the Parthenon on a January afternoon shows that it was as intense as a religious experience. It was the moment in his life when everything that had previously moved him – friendships, games, music, mountains, forests, poetry – seemed to be distilled into this ultimate happiness. What he saw was the epitome of Greek nobility, and nothing ever again caused such a mixture of emotions.

Athens was not a totally solemn experience, however; in fact, he found it a somewhat comic city. In Constitution Square he saw a Regiment of Guards suddenly dispersed by an irritated cab horse, causing the soldiers to break rank in a very unmilitary way and seek refuge among the orange trees. He had an audience with King George, which gave him further amusement because the King always stood when giving an interview and kept rising on tiptoe, then dropping his heels, and doing this in rapid succession. It was impossible for someone with as keen a sense of the ridiculous as Fred not to mimic him unconsciously, so as they talked it was like two seesaws going up and down. He learned that the King and the Crown Prince, both very bald, wrote testimonials in praise of a hair restorer. He also met the beautiful Queen Olga, daughter of the Grand Duke Constantine of Russia, and other members of the royal family. He always retained a snobbish regard for the mystique of royalty, though writing amusingly about their odd mannerisms.

Fred was by now used to mixing with the upper echelons of society into which, as the son of an Archbishop, he had entry. He was certainly not over-awed by the company he kept. He kept a quizzical eye on everything he saw and heard, and stored in his mind the amusing or outrageous antics, and the stuffiness and snobbery of court circles, all of which were to be recalled and presented to the public in the books that were to come.

In Athens he began his studies at the British School of Archaeology. He and another student were put in charge of the British excavations at Megalopolis, in the centre of Arcadia. It was a disappointing experience. The theatre, the biggest in Greece, had already been cleared, and the plan of the Thersillou, the Council Hall, had been laid bare, so there was little to do but direct the workmen who were removing tons of earth. For recreation he and his student friend wandered through the country on mules, visiting Mycenae and Epidaurus, fishing for mullet and watching the spring flowers unfold. Delphi followed, and the excitement of seeing the French excavations there. When he had finished recording the results of his work at Megalopolis he returned to England. But Greece was in his bones and blood and Athens remained his spiritual home.

At this time Fred was collecting material for a novel on the Greek Revolution of 1820, to be called *The Vintage*, but first *Dodo* had to be resurrected. It was now submitted to Lucas Malet, whose criticism was kind but honest, even ruthless. She suggested where to cut, where to revise and how to give the characters vitality. Fred was inspired sufficiently by her observations to revise the story thoroughly and to write a second volume. He finished it in the autumn of 1892.

Methuen, the publisher to whom it was submitted, accepted it immediately, and the book appeared the following May. Fred, aged twenty-five, was again in Greece when *Dodo* came out, studying the precinct of Asclepios on the slopes of the Acropolis. The knowledge of his forthcoming novel had spurred him to write copiously, and when he returned to England he had a number of short stories tucked away.

'*Dodo* is out,' Minnie wrote excitedly to Maggie, 'and I have sent you a copy. If Fred wishes to present you with it himself, I will retire. Your father had the first copy and has positively read some of it.' Another letter soon followed. 'I have been reading *Dodo* again, and it's binding. I think it is cleverer than I ever thought. Now the world's eye is on it, and it is that majestic thing, out.'

It does not seem that the Archbishop, the most unliterary of men, was exerting himself unduly to finish *Dodo*. It was surprising that he had started the book at all, and the more he read the more puzzled he became that a son of his could write such nonsense. Still, parts of it were quite amusing, and it showed a certain application on Fred's part to have written so much and succeeded in getting it before the public in hard covers. After a month, thinking more about the book, he wrote to Adeline, Duchess of Bedford. 'I have just met Lord Halifax who says everybody is talking of nothing but *Dodo*, that it is most diverting. I cannot understand the source of this apparent knowledge. Fred is going to see the original, they having exchanged letters. What a cross-built world!'

Fred had come home to find himself famous in the literary and social worlds and in the lending libraries. *Dodo* became a sensational bestseller; the first edition sold out within a month and a second appeared in June. There were three more in July, two in August, two in October, the tenth and eleventh in November, the twelfth in March 1894, thirteenth in August. By 1915 there had been nineteen reprints. In September 1893 Fred had a note from Sir Walter Besant, president of the Society of Authors, to whom he had applied for membership. 'I congratulate you on the great success of *Dodo*. People are all talking about it, which is the only proof, real proof, of success. I am sure the council will welcome you as a member.'

Minnie reported an unwelcome complication. 'Fred banged off to London this morning,' she told Maggie. 'Both Gosse and Methuen had sold *Dodo* to American publishers. He intends to square it all without making anyone angry or apologising. I don't believe he can.' But Fred evidently did, for there is no further record of any disagreement.

Readers of *Dodo* went to great lengths to uncover the identity of the person who had sat for Dodo herself. The consensus of opinion was that Margot Tennant was the model, and though Fred denied the charge she remained the obvious claimant.

Margot Tennant, later Countess of Oxford and Asquith, was one of the wittiest hostesses of her day, and later the author of some racy autobiographies. She herself believed that the author had had her in mind, even though at that time they had only met once, briefly. Her belief was confirmed when Arthur went to see her to apologise for his brother. At the time of publication she purported to be distressed by the portrayal, calling Dodo 'a pretentious donkey with the heart and brains of a linnet'. She probably enjoyed the furore; whatever was being said about her at least ensured that her name was bandied about over dinner tables and in opera boxes. Nevertheless, her friends and husband-to-be were careful not to talk about *Dodo* in her presence. Years later Lord Asquith told his wife that Lord Rosebery had used the character Dodo to warn him against her before they were married. Rosebery had said, 'If you want to know what Miss Tennant is like read *Dodo.*'

To put an end to the speculation Fred wrote to Margot Tennant, apologising for the publicity that his book had caused her to be bothered with, and denying that he had had her in mind as Dodo. Margot Tennant's reply was: 'Dear Mr Benson, have you written a novel? How clever of you!' But they later became friends and Fred was forgiven.

Later in 1893 came *Six Common Things*, a book of short stories which Fred had written in Greece. It was published by Osgood, McIlvaine, a rather obscure firm, who were putting out a series called 'Short Stories by British Authors'. The book slipped quietly into oblivion, though there was an American edition, revised and with the title changed to *A Double Overture*, which appeared the following year.

The Archbishop liked the book very much, except for one story called *Poor Miss Huntingford* which concerns a cynical and thoughtless young woman who tries to humiliate a humble governess at a smart luncheon party given by Mrs Maseby, the daughter of a rich soap-boiler. She is so aristocratic that she cannot even remember the name of her child's governess. The 'I' of the story tried to defuse the situation by taking the blame for a wine-glass that the governess had broken, only to make her embarrassment worse. Obviously Fred's father felt that there was insufficient understanding of the natural and God-approved gulf between the rich and the poor, and that both high and low should accept their station in life.

One of the best stories is an account of an adventure that Fred and Maggie had when they were children at Lis Escop: a small incident about a stickleback disappearing down a drain while the aquarium water was being changed, and the grief that suddenly engulfs the children. Without the slightest hint of sentimentality, the story vividly describes the intense happiness that children can find in the simplest things and the equal misery that can blight their childish joys.

The final story, *The Death Warrant*, is an extraordinary little account of how the narrator, discovering that he is going to die of cancer, faces death and the thought of what might come after, with resignation and courage. It might have been written by a very old man instead of a young one on the threshold of life.

In 1894 Methuen published *The Rubicon* in two volumes,

the main character of which is Eva, young and beautiful, but cruel. Though she is of aristocratic birth she is poor and has to marry Lord Hayes, who is rich, dull and twice her age. Soon she falls in love with Reggie, also young and beautiful, though slightly weak. He falls in love with her in spite of the fact that he is engaged to Gerty, young and beautiful, but strong. Eva is unwilling to compromise her position in society and gives him up, so Reggie goes to Aix, where Gerty is staying with her mother, who is taking a cure. There he learns that Lord Hayes has died suddenly and Gerty gives him his freedom so that he can return to Eva.

But Eva has realised that her selfishness has nearly ruined three lives and has sent Gerty a letter telling her that she never really loved Reggie but was only playing a game with him, and urges them to get together again. Then, after prostrating herself on her husband's grave she returns home and takes prussic acid, a bottle of which she remembers seeing in Lord Hayes's laboratory. There the story finishes abruptly.

The critics fell on the book with delight, eager to put down the young man who had been so ill-advised to have written a wildly successful novel without any help from them. Their comments were unjustifiably savage.

'All the gutter elements of *Dodo* are rehashed and warmed up again with no touch of novelty or improvement.'

'It is an absolute failure, the writing forced and uneasy, the character-drawing is crude and uncertain, sensual, earthy and unwholesome.'

'The worst-written, falsest and emptiest book of the decade.'

'A school-girl's idea of plot, a nursery-governess's knowledge of the world, a gentleman's gentleman's view of high life, a man-milliner's notion of creating character.'

It is clear that the malicious campaign was launched, not at an innocuous little story, but at the author of *Dodo*. No book by an unknown, however bad, would have suffered such an onslaught. *The Rubicon is* bad, that cannot be denied. The plot, such as it is, is preposterous, and the characters are paper-thin, but at least it conformed to the conventions of the day and was no worse than scores of others of its type. Inwardly, Fred was crushed, but not for long. His natural resilience soon reasserted itself, and he was able to join his father in laughing at the newspapers; though there was enough truth behind the over-blown rhetoric for him to wonder whether it would not have been wiser to suppress the manuscript of *The Rubicon*. Soon he had begun to write *The Babe, B.A.* and forgot all about the *Pall Mall Gazette, Vanity Fair* and their beastly companions.

That autumn it was planned that Maggie should go out to Athens with him, and later to Egypt. Maggie enjoyed Athens tremendously. She became very popular with members of the Legation, with the archaeologists, and with the Queen of Greece, who asked her if the English aristocracy acted as oddly as they did in *Dodo*.

At Christmas Fred and Maggie got up and acted in an entertainment – a home-made farce called *The Duchess of Bayswater*. It was designed for an audience of English governesses who had to spend Christmas in Athens; but before the opening night Fred learned that the audience was to be increased by two hundred sailors from the English Mediterranean Fleet which had just come into Piraeus. A larger hall had to be hired, and the sailors agreed to take part in the entertainment with songs and hornpipe dances. Then, at the last minute, and without warning, all the royals in Athens trooped in and took up the front row. The evening was a rowdy but good-natured success. The King told Fred the next day that he and Maggie ought to go on the stage.

Such light-hearted goings-on were typical of Fred's activities at this time. In particular he made quite a reputation as a comic actor. 'The life and soul of the party' is a cliché that was often applied to him in Athens. His charm and wit enlivened many a dull dinner party; his interest in other people, his skill at sports and the vitality of his presence ensured his popularity in any kind of society. In Viola Bankes's autobiography *Why Not?*, published in 1934, she said he had the most original things to say on every subject. He was always the last to arrive at a party, and seemed to appear with a sudden rush, out of the floor, almost before he was announced. In all the vicissitudes that befell him, she said, he never failed to joke, his amazing blue eyes always smiling.

Since Cambridge days there had been nobody to stir Fred's heart as Vincent Yorke had done, but in Athens the flame of friendship burned strongly again. Up to then Fred had preferred clean-cut, clean-limbed athletes, but now he was bowled over by a charming but effeminate young man named Regie Lister, a Secretary at the Legation. His lack of masculine qualities was more than compensated by his capacity to evoke love from everybody he met. He had a genius for friendship, and for enjoying people and places with a zest that equalled Fred's. They became inseparable. In the morning Regie would visit the museum where Fred was studying sculpture, and in the evening they would dine together or attend a party or social gathering where they insisted on playing charades and childish games. Occasionally they would leave Athens for a few days to explore the Peloponnese. These trips led to adventures with shepherds and their savage dogs, sleeping with goats in a shed on the Langarda Pass, losing their mules and drivers, and experiencing the horrors of indescribably awful inns. Through all the discomforts Fred was happy because Regie was enjoying himself; and the two pilgrims worshipped at the shrine of Apollo in a state of youthful euphoria.

Eventually Regie was posted away from Athens and went from one capital to another, first Constantinople, then Copenhagen, Rome, Paris and Tangiers. During the next few years several months would elapse between meetings, but always it was as if they had never been apart.

While Fred was in Athens Lord Alfred Douglas stayed with him in his rooms for about a week. The weather was perfect and he passed most of his time sitting in the Acropolis. He greatly enjoyed his visit, finding Fred an excellent host and cicerone, and Regie Lister also made himself very agreeable. Fred tried to get Methuen to publish Douglas's poems. Methuen declined them, though with kind and encouraging words, and they were eventually published by Grant Richards in 1896.

Fred met Douglas again in Luxor. They, with Robert Hichens, author of *The Green Carnation,* and Reginald Turner, made a vivacious quartet, staying in the same hotel before travelling up the Nile together. They had a most lively and cheerful time, Douglas records. They all knew *Dorian Gray* almost by heart, and quoted bits of it to each other as they floated up the river. Rupert Croft-Cooke, in *Bosie,* called Fred 'one of the three queer sons of the Archbishop of Canterbury' and hints maliciously that the trip to Luxor was made for reasons the reverse of cultural.

Fred's involvement in the homosexual world seems to have diminished in the early years of the twentieth century except when he was on holiday on Capri. The trial of Oscar Wilde would have frightened him from too open an association with the figures of Wilde's world. Douglas had begun to show the true ugliness of his nature. There was too much public bigotry, too many dangers to face. It would have taken tremendous courage to stand out against the crowd, and he had his family and his father's position to consider. So Fred retired to the sidelines as an observer rather than a participant, knowing what was going on in the underworld of sexual deviation, commenting on it obliquely, but never openly acknowledging its attractions for him.

He knew, for example, all the details of the scandal involving the homosexual Lord Henry Somerset, who had departed for the Continent after his wife had discovered his association with young Harry Smith, and had put it about that her husband was guilty of a crime only mentioned in the Bible; and he was not ignorant of the story behind the theft of the Insignia of the Order of St Patrick – the 'Irish Crown Jewels' – from Dublin Castle by a group of homosexuals, and why the jewels were never recovered nor anyone charged with their theft.

Fred was also acquainted with 'Sydney Oswald', the pseudonymous name of Sydney Lomer (1880–1926) who translated the more than explicit *Greek Anthology: Epigrams from Anthologia Palatina XII* and published privately in 1914. The ninety-five pages are full of pederastic poems of which the following is an example.

Lo! Kypris all my heart makes mad
With love for maids; but Eros, dainty lad,
Bids me the love of youths enjoy.
Then which seek I? The mother or the son?
Lo, she, herself, declares the lad has won.
Henceforth I seek the daring boy.

Oswald knew Fred well enough to give him a signed copy of the book. It is still extant and Fred was sufficiently impressed to put his bookplate in it; though, to Fred's credit, he left many pages of the fustian outpourings unopened.

Sydney Oswald was one of a group of minor writers who celebrated both adult homosexuality and boy-love, and who wrote about it from about 1890 to 1930. They have been called Uranians and were responsible for a strong subculture of sentimental eroticism. Included in their company were Edward Carpenter, John Addington Symonds and Ralph Chubb. Two minor figures were the Reverend E. E. Bradford (1860–1944) and Captain Leonard Green (1885–1966). The latter was a friend of T. E. Lawrence. In 1922 Bradford wrote, in a letter to his friend Green: 'Do you know "David Blaize"? It always puzzles one. It pretends to be written from an old-fashioned puritanical point of view, and when David falls violently in love with a girl it is distinctly suggested that every rightminded boy does the same. Yet really I fancy that Benson inclines to platonic love?' It seems that even among the Uranians Fred was a somewhat mysterious figure. Michael Davidson, the openly pederastic author of *The World, the Flesh and Myself*, talked of the 'stealthy eternal adolescents' of the day purring over *David Blaize* and calls Fred the Nancy Mitford of the 1910s. 'In either mood,' he says, 'Society or homosexual, he was an enchanting novelist'.

Fred may really have found, as he always professed, that the sexual aspect of homosexual relationships was distasteful to him and to be generally deplored. There is no evidence of any intimate relationship with another man on that basis. Perhaps he gazed on male loveliness with appreciation and secret longing but disliked or feared the possibility of intrusion into his private life, or the irruption of forces he might not be able to control; though it is difficult to believe that a man so physically fit and with the sexual urges of the young could have remained virginal during those exciting years when life was unfolding around him.

Arthur's diary is full of simperings over the latest young man who came to tea and stayed to become a disciple, but Fred is silent in all his autobiographical writings about his sex life. The times were not propitious for honesty in such matters. The only significant factor we have to go on in considering Fred's sexual preferences is that throughout his life all his close friendships were with other men, such as Regie Lister, Philip Burne-Jones, son of the artist, Francis Yeats-Brown, author of *Bengal Lancer,* Eustace Miles, Vincent Yorke, and John Ellingham Brooks, with whom he shared a villa on Capri. We must also consider his family history; the atmosphere created by his parents, and that all his brothers and sisters seemed similarly afflicted with the inability to attain intimacy with a member of the opposite sex. Being more worldly than his brothers, more emancipated in outlook, more tolerant of human weaknesses, Fred was less inhibited, thus more likely to have had an adult and consummated homosexual life.

# CHAPTER SEVEN

or the next three years Fred alternated between Greece and Egypt, spending the winters in Egypt working for the Egyptian Exploration Fund. He was fascinated by both countries, representing as they did the different facets of his own character. Greece had cast a spell that transported him into the dawn of the civilised world and had brought the gods of love and wisdom into the open sunlight, so quivering with life that they seemed to have broken through the marble that enshrined them.

Egypt was a sinister mystery that appealed to another side of him, his imagination ever ready to be seduced by the malevolent behind the ordinary. The Sphinx's blank and stony face, the Pyramids, bleak symbols of slave labour, the hawk-faced gods and the creatures born of the mating of men and animals, all spoke of cruelty and religious mania. Yet at the heart of it all was an old, corrupting magic that gripped him, and that he could not ignore. His nightmares were dominated by the Nile and the terrible gods hiding behind the mimosa and the palm trees. The sounds, sights and scents of both Egypts, past and present, sank into his subconscious, to be released when, a few years later, he began to write *The Image in the Sand*. But while this layer of his mind was absorbing the darkness of Egypt, another part of him was bubbling over with what he had gathered in Greece; so that while the Egyptian book was lying dormant, *The Vintage* was spilling itself onto paper on the post-boats of the Nile and during the evenings in Pagnon's Hotel.

In the winter of 1895–6 Maggie was with Fred in Egypt, excavating the Temple of Mut in the horseshoe lake at Karnak. Amazingly, though suffering from rheumatism, congestion of the lungs and attacks of deep depression, she used her mental powers to brush her disabilities aside and to conduct the six weeks' exploration with enthusiasm and efficiency. Sitting on a white donkey and wielding a fly-whisk, she used her few words of Arabic with great effect on the workmen. At the beginning of 1896 she met Nettie Gourlay, with whom she formed a friendship that was to last the rest of her life. Nettie was thirty-three years old, plain and with little to say for herself, but Maggie discovered in her a fine and delicate mind and enthused about her in letters home. Nettie stayed with the Bensons on many occasions, especially after her widowed father had married a woman younger than she was, but she never completely became one of the family, as Lucy Tait was. Fred found it difficult to penetrate the long silences or sympathise with her growing invalidism. But to Maggie she was a soul mate and that was all that mattered.

At Karnak Fred was given two jobs: to oversee clearing away the earth, and to make a scale plan of the temple. He performed those minor jobs with the greatest good humour. The previous year he had been to Alexandria with D. G. Hogarth, the distinguished archaeologist, and together they had made a report on the prospects of research in that city. Fred's part of the report was a note on excavations in Alexandrian cemeteries.

In the evenings Fred and Maggie would settle down to writing, he to a story of Greece, and she to her exposition of her personal philosophy, later published as *The Venture of a Rational Faith*. Then they would play piquet. During this winter life was full and interesting. Maggie's growing intimacy with Nettie Gourlay was a source of deep joy to her, and there was also the excitement of discovering a statue of the Rameses of the Exodus, a Saite head, the figure of a scribe and, most important of all, the image of Sen-mut himself, the architect of the temple and intimate of Queen Hatshepsut. There were expeditions down and across the Nile, journeys by donkey or horse far into the desert, and frequent meetings with visitors to Luxor. Maggie's health problems, and letters from their mother complaining about the Archbishop's tiredness through overwork and his refusal to slow down, were the only clouds on the horizon.

But Maggie got better, the Archbishop's doctor seemed not to be alarmed by his stubborn patient's symptoms, and Minnie decided that her fears were unreasonable. 'Maggie is wonderfully better,' Fred wrote in a letter to his mother. 'She was always cheerful, happy and interested, and the most charming of companions. (Really my family are very nice.)'

Maggie was fully appreciative of Fred's constant companionship. 'He has been the dearest boy,' she wrote, adding that after she was well he was going to advertise himself as companion to an invalid lady. She would recommend him highly.

Meanwhile Arthur had become a Housemaster at Eton, bothered by occasional bouts of neurasthenia, but turning out in his leisure time, with typical Benson fluency, book after book of meditative essays and some verses; slick and shallow, but deeply satisfying to a large number of women readers. *The House of Quiet, The Thread of Gold, The*

*Leaves of the Tree, The Silent Isle, Where No Fear Was:* each book could have been given any one of the titles with equal aptness. Arthur was, of course, in real life nothing like the wise old philosopher he appears to be in the books. He could be grumpy, waspish, witty, sarcastic and quarrelsome. In addition to his published work he wrote a diary which in the end exceeded four million words.

Hugh had become an Anglican clergyman attached to the Eton Mission at Hackney Wick in East London. Only Fred had not settled down to a conventional career. His father was concerned, but bore the cross of a lighthearted son nobly. His concern grew when Fred announced that archaeology had nothing more to offer him. Grants from Cambridge had dried up and King's had not given him the Fellowship that he thought his work deserved. Reports of his work at Chester and in Greece had apparently been disregarded, and Fred felt somewhat disgruntled.

It could only have been the Archbishop who suggested to Fred that he should try for a post as examiner or inspector in the Education Office. Fred was capable of serious work in a subject that deeply interested him, but such a respectable, not to say boring, occupation was the last to engage his full attention. In any case, he fully meant to make writing his career, so he was relieved rather than disappointed when his tutors' testimonials and his application form were rejected. Obviously, *Dodo* had a lot to answer for. He was now regarded as a lightweight and a dilettante.

In the summer of 1896 Fred returned from Egypt to Athens to say goodbye to all his friends, then went for a holiday on Capri, an island which so enchanted him that he began to form plans for another and perhaps more permanent visit. In August the family was reunited at Addington. On September 16 the Archbishop and Minnie left for an official tour of Ireland, and a frightful crossing was followed by a full and exhausting round of engagements. At Addington the others had gone their various ways, leaving Beth, as always, custodian of the home.

Fred was back at Addington early in October. One of the letters he wrote on October 6 was to Sir James T. Knowles, the editor of *The Nineteenth Century*, reminding him that he had been sent an essay on Loti's 'Jérusalem' more than a year before and asking when it was likely to appear. The letter was rather terse for a young tyro to write to an established man of letters, especially when he was addressed as 'Dear Mr Knowles', and it brought forth no response and no appearance of the article.

His parents had sailed for home on Friday October 9. They spent a day in Carlisle, visiting the Cathedral, then travelled to Hawarden in Cheshire to stay with the Gladstones for a few days, hoping to recuperate from over-travel and overwork. Fred was waiting for his parents' return when, on the afternoon of Sunday, October 11, a telegram arrived from Mrs Gladstone informing him that his father had 'passed over quite peacefully' in the morning, with his mother at his side. For a moment Fred thought that 'passing over' meant sailing across the Irish Sea, but then the truth struck him and he hurried to London on the first available train, and caught an early train to Chester on Monday.

At Hawarden he found Minnie shaken, silent, but strangely serene. He learned from Mr Gladstone that his father had died in church, during the eleven o'clock service while saying the General Confession. He had been taken out of the church and laid on a sofa in the Rectory library. Various remedies had been tried but all had proved useless. Later he had been dressed in his episcopal robes, and in his coffin he looked as noble and strong in death as he had in life. The body was eventually taken by train to Canterbury via London, with clergymen waiting at each station down the line to do him honour.

Minnie was now fifty-five years old, a squat, fat little woman, her round face redeemed from plainness by a lively expression and friendly smile. Since her marriage at the age of eighteen all her life had been dedicated to her exacting husband. She had written in her diary, 'I must not think of being at ease, but of suiting my ways to his feelings, and this without a shadow of thinking that my ways are better than his, though I like them better.' But she had quietly changed a great deal from the shy, inarticulate girl-wife of the first years of her marriage. At Truro she had recovered her health and had become a self-possessed hostess, managing the servants and household affairs with complete aplomb and entertaining guests of every kind with a wonderful range of conversational topics. She was not interested in ecclesiastical affairs, and had none of the conventional accomplishments, except that she was a great reader of poetry and fiction. She was a woman of curiosity, quick perceptions and ready sympathy. Her husband's death meant that for the first time in her life she was not answerable to another person and did not have to put on a false front. Now at last she could give her better qualities full rein.

Fred and Arthur once discussed in letters the character of their parents and their relationship. They came to the conclusion that Minnie was an instinctive pagan with the most beautiful ways: Edward was an instinctive puritan with a rebellious love of art. On the whole he hated and mistrusted people he didn't wholly approve of, whereas Minnie saw their faults and loved them. Arthur remarked on how few friends his father had, how they had drifted away over the years. He had a fine character, not a beautiful one, and had a tendency to bully people from good motives, as he believed. Edward and Minnie had little in common, and Edward was cruel, and a very difficult person to deal with, because he remembered what points were in his favour and forgot those which were not.

Fred reminded his brother how their father had expected obedience and enthusiasm. Minnie claimed neither, but got both. Edward cared about details, Minnie didn't. Fred wondered whether it would have been better for Minnie to have stood up to her husband's bullying, but Arthur thought his father was too difficult to stand up to because he could be so terrifying; his hard displeasure about trifles could be intolerable. They also remembered ruefully how clever Minnie was in choosing subjects of conversation at mealtimes which always rubbed Edward up the wrong way, and they concluded that it was a case of real and natural incompatibility.

# CHAPTER EIGHT

he Benson family had to leave Lambeth Palace and Addington Park, and quickly, for the sake of the next Archbishop. They had no private home of their own, but before they decided where they should live another foreign trip was arranged, so that they could recover from the shock of the Archbishop's death and plan for the future. Minnie and Lucy Tait went out to join Maggie in Egypt, where she had already planned to spend the winter. Hugh, convalescent after an attack of rheumatism, joined them, and Fred was to follow later. Only Arthur stayed at home, disdaining foreign travel as a cure for post-funeral melancholy.

Before Fred could join the family he had taken on the task of getting ready for publication his father's book on the life of St Cyprian, Bishop of Carthage, a work which had taken thirty years to write. It was eventually published in 1897. But he had time for his own affairs too. On November 30 he wrote to William Colles, his literary agent, sending him the typescript of part of *The Capsina* together with a synopsis of the rest of the story, and giving his opinion that it would be a better story than *The Vintage*.

Fred supervised the clearing of Lambeth Palace, sending into storage most of their furniture, pictures and carpets. A caretaker was put in charge, and during the December evenings he and a friend of his father's worked, in an almost empty room in a mournful and deserted palace, on the appendices and proofs of St Cyprian. It was a depressing experience for Fred. He had lived in Lambeth Palace since he was sixteen, and had loved it for its splendour and for the opportunities it had given him to join a wider society than he had hitherto known.

Fred took a month to complete his task then he was free to join the others at Luxor. Maggie was again excavating at Karnak, her third winter there, and Minnie and Lucy hovered nearby, reading their guidebooks and trying to resist the importunities of the souvenir sellers. Fred helped Maggie in unobtrusive ways and Hugh went out shooting quail. Sometimes they would cross the Nile and picnic in the desert. In the evenings they would play games. Maggie would write up her notes and Fred continued with his Grecian novel, *The Vintage*. Minnie encouraged her children in all their efforts.

Hugh was the first to leave the party for a tour of Palestine. Then Maggie suddenly went down with a severe chill. Her lungs became affected and the doctor had to visit her three times a day. Finally he diagnosed pleurisy and decided that a lung-tapping operation was necessary. The result of the operation was that her blood pressure fell alarmingly and she lapsed into unconsciousness. Minnie, Lucy and Fred sat by her bedside waiting for the end. It was only her determination not to die that brought about her eventual recovery.

When she was well enough to be moved, and the heat of Luxor became too oppressive for them to stay, the harassed party decided to return to Cairo and from there to spend a week in Helouan. But Fred, through too much swimming and sun-bathing had, according to the doctor, developed a slight sunstroke and was ordered to keep quiet for a few days. It was felt that the journey back to Cairo would not help his condition. It would be better to stay behind in Luxor, to keep out of the sun, and to occupy his time supervising the packing of Maggie's antiquities. He would then be able to take a swift post-boat that would reach Cairo quicker than an ordinary steamer, and meet his family on the quay there.

During the two days he spent on his own Fred felt light-headed and remote from reality. On the journey by post-boat he was suddenly struck down by intense pains after a meal of curried chicken. At Cairo a doctor came on board and examined him. Fred suspected that he had caught typhoid fever; the doctor confirmed this and called an ambulance immediately, and Fred was taken to Helouan on a stretcher. His illness was long and severe, and left him feeling very weak. Hardly had his temperature become normal, however, than Lucy Tait's shot up, and she too was declared a victim of typhoid. Her illness was so serious, in fact, that her sister and brother-in-law, Bishop Davidson, Dean of Windsor, were sent for. For a time it was touch and go for poor Lucy, but her constitution was strong and she recovered.

Before the exhausted family left Egypt a malign Fate had one more try. Fred nearly stepped on a black cobra which he failed to see curled up on the floor of the hotel billiard room. Such a near catastrophe sent the family home reeling with relief.

For Minnie that spring had not proved to be a time of relaxation and renewal, but a period of intense stress and tension that lasted sixteen consecutive weeks. She had had to face the possibility that either Maggie, Fred or Lucy, or perhaps all three, might die in a foreign country, but she had come through the ordeal with her usual steadfast courage. Back in England she and Lucy Tait were faced with the ordeal they had dreaded, that of finding somewhere to live. While looking for a suitable house they went to stay with Lucy's sister and her husband, who had now become the new Archbishop of Canterbury, at Farnham Castle. Beth also greeted them there. She was now in her eightieth year, as full of love as ever, longing to have all her family round her again, looking forward to peace and quiet.

Maggie had gone to Aix for her rheumatism and Fred to Capri to complete his convalescence. He went by way of Athens, 'finding a little boy to play with, a nice young officer,' according to Ben, as Minnie came to be called. Fred had been worrying that his heart might have been weakened by his illness, but his English doctor had reassured him and told him to stop feeling his pulse. 'Oh, he's his mother's own boy,' Ben said fondly. Fred returned to England in July where Minnie and Lucy had found what promised to be a bulwark against the tide of misfortune. They had rented for a year a stately but comfortable Georgian house in St Thomas's Street in Winchester, a house with big rooms and a fine old mulberry tree in the garden. It was close to the Cathedral, and nearby were the river, the golf links and a County Club. The surrounding countryside was very beautiful, the town placid and drowsy. The Bensons moved in on a particularly hot day in August. Fred was in charge of the arrangements, but his efforts were impeded by two parrots, one of which made a noise like a cork coming out of a bottle to remind the workmen that they were thirsty; the other bit a removal man's finger. Taffy, the Welsh collie, did not help matters by lying in the hall and growling as furniture was carried past him, and Maggie's Persian cat scratched a visiting Canon. When all the furniture was in place, the pictures hung, the Archbishop's books on church history and lives of the saints installed behind the glass of the bookcases, and Maggie's Egyptian relics arranged, the interior of the house looked like a miniature Lambeth Palace.

It was around this time that 'Minnie' became 'Ben' to family and friends. Minnie had been Edward's name for the young Mary; Ben was Lucy Tait's. Now that the Archbishop was no longer there, and Lucy had in many ways taken his place, it felt natural for 'Minnie' to yield to 'Ben', and the children apparently found no difficulty in adopting this nickname for their mother.

For a few months life in Winchester was ideal, and the family was only too glad to be free from the chaos and crises of foreign travel, excessive heat, sandstorms, and impersonal hotels. Peace descended on them, and to Fred it seemed as though they could willingly spend the rest of their lives in this medieval atmosphere, with no disagreeable experiences, no emotional upheavals, nothing to impede the slow slide to a comfortable oblivion. At first the middle-aged security of the town suited them all. Maggie grew stronger and regained her enthusiasm for writing an account of the Karnak excavations, and then her book of personal philosophy. Lucy Tait and Ben remained soul-mates. Fred was busy writing. Arthur and Hugh spent the first Christmas in the new home, and they all filled up the time with the familiar pursuits that had made their earlier years so enjoyable: word games, piquet and caricatures, and heated discussions and arguments about every subject under the sun. They also started negotiations to buy the house instead of renting it, and they drew up detailed plans for the garden.

But as the spring of 1898 approached a shadow began to creep over their content. Ben discovered that she was feeling bored. Before her husband's death she had been a figure of consequence in the clerical and social life of London. With two large establishments to administer, her life had been very full with ample scope to use her energies and enthusiasms. Now there was nothing but the small ripples of a backwater to fill her days; calling on new acquaintances, going for drives, choosing menus. The old life of which she had been the centre had gone for ever; the banners had been folded and the bugles were silent. She was wearied by leisure. Her occasional trips to London only heightened her sense of inadequacy. It also dawned on her that her own children no longer depended on her. They had grown their full wings and had developed on their own lines; Arthur at Eton, Maggie with her philosophy, Hugh with his spiritual concerns and Fred preoccupied with fictional characters and new friends.

During that chilly spring Hugh had decided to give up his curacy at Kemsing, and the luxury of the Rector's house in which he lived, and had joined Canon Gore's House of the Resurrection at Mirfield in Yorkshire as a probationer in order to experience greater spiritual discipline. Ben disapproved but did not seek to dissuade him. Beth did more than disapprove. Tartly she demanded to know who was going to wash his vests, darn his socks, make his bed and empty his slops. Maggie's health received a setback when damp weather affected her rheumatism, and she began to suffer from the fits of depression similar to those that had afflicted her father. Her courage in accepting her disabilities deserted her. She grew jealous of Lucy Tait, whom she imagined had taken her place as daughter of the house. Ben could do nothing to reassure her, but she refused to sacrifice Lucy whom she regarded, not as a daughter, but almost as a second husband; and the distance between Ben and Maggie stretched uncomfortably.

The estrangement was made worse by the work that Maggie was doing on a final version of her father's manuscript on the Revelation of St John, and she was also helping Arthur on a biography of their father. Soaking herself as she did in the Archbishop's life, character and opinions, she began to exhibit some of his less attractive traits, his masterful personality and spiritual bullying. Gradually she took over the running of the household and dealt with things as her father would have done. Ben gave way to this reincarnation of the Archbishop, but bitterness grew inside her that her new freedom had been snatched away so quickly.

Fred, perhaps typically, decided to run away from the problem. His book about the Greek War of Independence had appeared, and because of the interest in all things Greek that it showed he was asked to administer a fund initiated by the Duke of Westminster, and directed by the Red Cross, for the relief of Greek refugees from Thessaly. The Graeco-Turkish war of 1897 was short-lived, and had been disastrous for the Greeks. Thessaly, which had been acquired by the Greeks in 1881, was lost to the Turks. The Greeks had been routed but the Turks were observing the armistice terms scrupulously until transport arrived to take their soldiers out of the country. Only a small number of Turks were being kept back to hold the captured province. Until they could get away the victorious soldiers were houseless while the vanquished Greeks slept in their own beds. Great numbers of Greek brigands followed the Turkish army to take their pickings from their defeated countrymen; and there were Greek refugees, the very old and the very young, who had been left behind, unable to escape the onward march of the Turks.

That was the bizarre situation when Fred arrived in Volo; it was both confusing and dangerous. Fred, deputed to distribute relief to the Greeks stranded in various towns and villages, could not get a Greek guard and had to ask the commander-in-chief of the Turkish army in Thessaly for a Turkish guard to protect him from Greek bandits. The request was benevolently granted and Fred, plus guard and a Greek doctor from Athens, struggled for two months to cope with the problem of the destitute refugees. Food was scarce and smallpox was rife; vaccination was distrusted. The doctor had to employ much guile to persuade the peasants to undergo the ordeal by telling them either that it was an order from the King of Greece and that refusal was punishable by prison, or that Queen Victoria had sent the vaccine as a present or, as a last resort, that it was an elixir of life that would make the old and ugly young and beautiful. Somehow the various ploys worked and the spread of the disease was halted. Refugee camps were set up and soup kitchens organised. In an amazingly short time Fred had accomplished more than the organisers had hoped for. He wished he could continue the good work, but funds had run out and he was called home.

It was an extraordinary interlude for a man whose life, both before and after, lacked material discomfort, hardship and danger. The head of the Red Cross told him that King George wished to decorate him with the Order of the Redeemer, but Fred heard no more about it, and decided eventually that either the Order had been lost in the post or that the King had changed his mind.

Before returning to Winchester Fred stayed with a friend who lived on Capri. It was the beginning of a long love affair with Italy. On Capri he had the ecstatic feeling of totally belonging. The vineyards, olive groves, uplands, cobbled alleys, shining waters and sun-soaked sands put out a magic that ensnared him completely. Every part of the day, from dawn to dusk, brought its own special spell. He bathed and basked, climbed Monte Solaro, wrote another novel, played the piano, gossiped with feminine relish, ate and drank what he described as the food of the gods, and was as happy as he had ever been.

The friend with whom Fred shared the Villa Cercola was John Ellingham Brooks, a dabbler in literature and an open homosexual. He had been to Cambridge and read for the Bar, but lack of ambition had prevented him from taking up a conventional career. He had enough money to travel and cultivate his tastes. Before meeting Fred he had known Somerset Maugham intimately, and his lively talk of art and literature and of the glories of Italy and Greece had fired Maugham's imagination. He became dazzled by this experienced man of the world. Much later in life Maugham admitted to his friend Glenway Wescott that Brooks had been responsible for his first homosexual experience and they had had a short but happy affair in Heidelberg. After the trial and conviction of Oscar Wilde, Brooks had been one of the many homosexual men who had left England hurriedly. He remained on Capri until his death in 1929 from cancer of the liver.

When Fred knew him Brooks was a good-looking man with a Byronic forehead, curly chestnut hair and sensual lips. He had an annuity that was sufficient to allow him to live comfortably, playing the piano and translating into English the sonnets of Héredia, the French poet of Cuban origin who had died in 1905, and whose reputation rests on *Les Trophées*, a book of 118 sonnets. That was Brooks's life's work. It was never published. His only income from literature was five guineas he once got for a sonnet.

There is no reason to suppose that Fred had anything other than a platonic friendship with Brooks. He found him amusing and undemanding, perhaps slightly pathetic. There were other people on the island, English and American, in whose company Fred found enjoyment. One of them was Count Fersen, a somewhat mysterious Swedish nobleman who was rumoured to have been jailed for offences against minors, Norman Douglas, who was writing *South Wind*, a young Dutchman named Van Decker who scandalised everybody by dancing naked, except for a bunch of roses, at a party in his villa, an American artist named Coleman, Axel Munthe and the English vice-consul: all part of the homosexual contingent that had taken over Capri almost completely. Compton Mackenzie spent time on the island too, and was to chronicle the foibles of the inhabitants mercilessly in his barely disguised works of fiction, *Extraordinary Women* and *Vestal Fire*. The latter book was dedicated to Brooks, who had contributed most of the material.

In 1899 Brooks met an American girl from Pennsylvania called Romaine Goddard, later to become a well-known painter and practising lesbian. He was captivated by her because she looked like a charming boy. Two years later she returned to Capri and found Brooks on the verge of suicide, depressed because his annuity was dwindling and he was unable to support himself in the manner that Lotus Land demanded. Soon afterwards her mother died and she inherited a large amount of money. In June 1903 she and Brooks were married, 'in a fit of aberration on both sides', as Fred put it. In just over a year the ill-matched couple had broken up, and Romaine left Capri for Paris, there to become the lover of Natalie Clifford Barney. She salved her conscience by allowing her husband £300 a year. Brooks, saved from insolvency, remained on Capri for the rest of his life, frittering his time away and watching the value of his money slowly depreciate. In his sixties he was living in two shabby rooms on the Matromania Road with his dogs, books and piano, surrounded by the evidence of his failure as a writer. Some years before he had written to Fred to ask him if he would set him up in a new villa. Fred sent him enough money to tide him over his immediate difficulties but received no acknowledgement and did not encourage any further appeals.

When Brooks died Fred was sorry. The intimacy of their shared life on Capri was long gone, but the memory of it was warm. 'Somewhere beneath the ash of his laziness there burned the authentic fire,' he wrote.

Fred's love affair with Capri lasted until the beginning of the First World War. He was there when war broke out and had to make a hasty departure. During the Edwardian years preceding the war Somerset Maugham was also a summer visitor to the Villa Cercola and shared the rent with Fred while Brooks lived there rent-free. The relationship between Maugham and Brooks was cool. Though Maugham was involved with Gerald Haxton, and his friends knew of his obsession, he was still resentful of the fact that Brooks had introduced him to active homosexuality when all his life he had tried to conceal his true nature. He did not remember Brooks as fondly as Fred had. He wrote unflattering accounts of him in three books and a short story, Hayward in *Of Human Bondage* being the unkindest portrait. Both Fred and Compton Mackenzie felt that Brooks had been treated badly when the book was published during one of Maugham's stays on the island.

Fred was staying at the Villa Cercola in 1898 when he

received letters from home that hinted that things were not well at Winchester, and he had to tear himself away from his idyll and set his reluctant face towards England. There he found that Maggie's depressions were worse, resembling the dark moods of their father that had put the whole household under such a strain. A tendency towards masculinity in her nature was beginning to show and Ben was troubled by what she didn't understand. Winchester was by now proving unbearably dull. They all felt suffocated by its smallness, its petty gentility, its lack of challenge and refreshment. Ben had decided that they must leave before the family disintegrated.

Fred disliked the idea of another upheaval. He believed that a move to another house in another small provincial town would only be a temporary easement of their difficulties. Soon, he was sure, Maggie's depressions would return and Ben's enthusiasms would collapse. Arthur and Hugh, busy with their own affairs, would be no help, and Fred himself would again be at the centre of a gathering storm. He felt that he was drifting, with no ideas, no strong feelings. He did not want to leave St Thomas's Street, but he saw that it was imperative that they must.

They explored houses in Haslemere and Basingstoke which turned out to be impossible. Then an advertisement in *Country Life* brought them to the verge of interest, and Lucy Tait was sent to investigate a house called Tremans near Horsted Keynes in Sussex, in upland country between Ashdown Forest and the Sussex Weald. It was about forty miles from London and twenty miles from Brighton. Lucy returned with an enthusiastic report of its charm and beauty and described in glowing terms the avenue of pine trees, the gardens, yew hedges, orchard, farm buildings and barns, the bowling green and brook. The family's lethargy was soon transformed into an intense desire to see, possess and absorb this new prospect of happiness.

Tremans was all that Lucy had described. The lease was bought and the house became the headquarters of the Bensons for the next twenty years. The oldest part had been built in the sixteenth century by a kinsman of the poet Thomas Wyatt. The rooms were oak-panelled and there were great open fireplaces so that the smell of wood smoke mingled with the scent of wallflowers and lilacs. The gardens were on different levels, leading down to a brook, and in season were washed over by the colour of the daffodils.

The Bensons moved there in April 1899, with the statues, books, heavy furniture, animals and parrots, and all the other family possessions that had once filled Lambeth Palace. As usual, Fred had to take charge of the move as once again neither Arthur nor Hugh was available. Arthur gave as his reason the fact that his boarding-house at Eton took up all his time and energy, and he did not, in fact, see the new home for three months. Then, like every other member of the family, he fell in love with it. Hugh was too busy with his religious interests to help Fred.

Lucy Tait's money had helped to buy the lease of the house and she contributed towards its upkeep. She travelled to London one day a week to do good works among the poor of Lambeth and took a small *pied à terre* where both she and the family could stay during visits to London. This was in a row of Queen Anne houses in Barton Street, near Westminster Abbey. There was plenty of room at Tremans for the three brothers to lead independent lives, and for Nettie Gourlay, Maggie's friend, who was something of an invalid these days. Gladys Bevan, another great friend of Maggie's, was also welcome, and Maggie spent a lot of time at Miss Bevan's house in London where she helped her friend to arrange details for the Archbishop's Diploma in Theology for Women.

Gradually Maggie's health improved again. She became more active and as happy as her unstable nature would allow. She took over the gardens at Tremans; planning, planting, rebuilding the summerhouse so that it could revolve to catch the sun or miss the wind, and she built a wooden dovecote in the cherry orchard. She built a brick base for one of her Egyptian statues and put up a hen run. She also made herself responsible for all the livestock: poultry, turkeys, pigeons, and the peacock. Taffy, the collie, followed her slavishly. Ra, her black cat, killed rabbits in the wood. Another collie called Roddy was an inveterate poacher.

Maggie seemed to be blossoming both physically and intellectually, but Fred was wary of rejoicing too much too soon. He regarded the situation coolly, unable to get rid of a certain apprehension about her.

Ben had no such fears. She was now enjoying her life again. She wrote a great number of letters, had her trips to London, kept her diary, spent much time at her devotions, enjoyed visitors, and found an outlet for her religious convictions, giving advice and consolation to friends and strangers alike.

Tremans would have been a house of contented people but for Fred. Perversely, he went into a decline as the rest of the family emerged from darkness into sunlight. After a couple of months he was bored and restless. He felt that his life was shallow, lacking purpose, with no opportunity for initiative and, above all, he lacked masculine companionship. Arthur and Hugh could not fill that need as they were only occasionally at Tremans and he was not specially close to them. Fred was then thirty-two years old and feeling that he was missing out on life. The male relationships he had experienced at Marlborough, Cambridge, Athens and on Capri were not so far in the past that he had forgotten their intensity. Now he seemed to be settling into a dry middle age, and the prospect dismayed him.

After three months in the new house he was able to get away for a few weeks, and no holiday had ever been more welcome. He went in a party hosted by the Countess of Galloway, a family friend to Bayreuth which, at that time, was at the height of its brilliance. The ugly little town had witnessed the only true revelation of Wagner's genius. His operas were supreme, and his fanatical followers believed passionately that only in Wagner was the final incarnation of the spirit of music. Only at Bayreuth were the glories of the operas fully revealed: elsewhere they were but cardboard imitations. Pilgrims from all countries flocked to the shrine and worshipped with uncritical fervour.

Fred was quite prepared to be one of them, but he was soon amused by the silliness of the scene, the source being the imperious behaviour of Frau Cosima Wagner, widow and priestess. She ruled like an autocrat over a number of daughters and a son, Siegfried, all lesser luminaries but united in their joint ambition to convert the whole musical world to worship at the altar of Wagner. Through one festival after another she had almost reached her goal. Her will and energy were prodigious. Her creed was the canonisation of her husband, and she pursued her goal with such intensity and with such a total lack of humour that to an outsider it became ridiculous. Fred, who met her on several occasions, found the old lady as awe-inspiring as everybody else in Bayreuth did, though he was secretly amused at her pretensions and the fawning homage of her followers. He was half hypnotised by the carefully orchestrated Wagner worship yet there was still a part of him that noted the deficiencies of the performances, the blemishes of the productions, the monstrous Rhine maidens and obese baritones; and he could retire to a corner of his mind and giggle quietly.

Back at Tremans memories of Bayreuth soon faded. He grew increasingly dissatisfied with life but was unwilling to alter the situation because he had once made a promise to his father that he would live with his mother if she were left alone. There was a barrier growing up between him and Ben, born of her anxiety and his depression. Both felt a sense of estrangement which neither found easy to bear. So Ben brooded and Fred quietly sulked, and the first year at Tremans dragged to an unhappy end. It was Ben who brought matters to a head. While Fred was away on a visit she wrote him a letter, full of love and understanding, absolving him from his promise, setting him free 'body and spirit and financially,' Fred wrote. Her letter may have meant that she intended to make him an allowance, though, considering the income that Fred was making from his books that does not seem likely. It is more likely that she was willing to give up his contribution to the household expenses, seeing that he would no longer be living at home.

Fred needed no prompting when he received the letter. With their former comfortable relationship restored he left Tremans in the autumn of 1900 and, strangely, for the first time he was able to regard the house as home. For the next eighteen years he returned to it gladly and frequently. He moved to London, where he took a small flat at No 395, Oxford Street, had his evening meal sent in from a small Italian restaurant round the corner and braced himself for a completely new life.

# CHAPTER NINE

rom 1900 to the outbreak of the First World War Fred's life was fuller than it had ever been before or was to be after the war. He was eager for every experience it was possible to get in the great world of London and beyond. He opened his arms to everything that would amuse or thrill him or give him material for his novels. His physical activities were phenomenal; he played golf and racquets, went to Switzerland for the skating in winter, fished, and followed the season diligently, dining in society, going to the theatre and opera. He spent the summer on Capri, and the autumn in Scotland.

With money coming in from his novels freedom seemed to go to his head. For a time music was the greatest of his enthusiasms and he haunted the Queen's Hall. Tchaikovsky was his idol at that time, and he would listen entranced to Henry Wood or Hans Richter conducting the Sixth Symphony. Later there were passing fancies for Debussy, Fauré and Stravinsky. They attacked him like measles but when the attack was over the giants of Bach and Wagner reclaimed him and kept him enchained for all his life.

There was one Christmas at Tremans when he irritated Arthur by strumming on the piano in a loud, coarse way, fretting, as Arthur said, to be back with his moneyed friends in London. Arthur never approved of Fred's friends – he called them flashy – a wealthy literary set who spent a lot of time in Venice. Percy Lubbock gave him some information which he did not like; he described the silliness of the Anglo-Venetian set, which was led by Lady Radnor, the idleness, the sentimentality about bronzed gondoliers, and he implied an even nastier background. Arthur complained that Fred led a mysterious life about which he would say nothing, and he wondered what it was all about. Fred was indeed much criticised, not least by his family, for the relish with which he enjoyed his friendship with some of the most extravagant and outrageous hostesses of the day. Edwardian society was made up of sets and cliques, coteries and climbers; the smart set was composed of the rich, the vulgar, the parvenus and the insensitive. Servants were treated with indifference, shopkeepers were nodded to condescendingly, the working class did not exist except as people to avoid in the street. And it was by this world that Fred was swallowed. He had to serve no apprenticeship to be accepted. He was the son of the late Archbishop of Canterbury but, better still, he was a best-selling novelist whose work had been touched by scandal. Invitations poured in and few were refused. But while he thoroughly enjoyed the spectacle on one level, he didn't lose his critical faculty, and was to parody in his books some of the grotesque individuals he met.

Soon Fred decided that he must have a manservant to see to his clothes and attend to his appointments. Ben was both amused and horrified. One of her sons – with his own servant! Of course the family had been used to servants since the Wellington days, but they had been of the faithful retainer type. Cooks, housemaids, gardeners – they were common enough in middle class families, and Maggie had McPherson, her own personal maid who had accompanied her to Egypt. But for a man to have his clothes laid out, his shoes cleaned and his linen starched by another man was too much for Ben. 'My!' she wrote to Maggie, 'A footman! Well, he finds things take more time than he knew, and also let him try his own little experiment.'

But the idea of Fred and his servant stuck in her throat and she squirmed when Fred said that he was going to bring him to Tremans. She did not voice her misgivings to Fred, though, as she put it, a strong young man with all his income to make should not go about with a man. But time would tell... Three months later she felt easier about the situation. She heard that Fred would be bringing a friend named Steel home for Easter, and that Sidney, an amiable young man, she conceded, would be with them. He wanted the cook to teach him 'single breakfast cookery.'

The following month Sidney was at Tremans again and she had to explain to him that it didn't do to smoke in the servants' hall with the door open. She told Maggie rather sniffily that 'his little servant' was nice in his way but she had to watch her p's and q's and she would much rather he didn't go, partly because of the cost of his board and lodging. In June she was definitely put out. 'He hadn't been mentioned so I hadn't expected him.'

After that Sidney disappears from view, and we don't know whether Fred decided that a personal servant was beyond his means or if Sidney remained in Fred's service but sank into the background and did not merit any mention in letters or conversation. Fred certainly had a valet in the war years, a man young enough to be called up for military service. He was quickly replaced.

There is no doubt that Fred's head was turned by the

attention he received from the society leaders of the day. He exploited his natural charm shamelessly, became a brilliant raconteur, flattered where flattery was needed and was indispensable when luncheon and dinner parties had to be livened up, or when weekends at stately homes needed a personable young man as escort, partner at games or harmless flirt. In old age he was described by Sir Steven Runciman as 'the best company I have ever known', giving as the reason Fred's devastatingly observant eye, together with a gift for balancing his almost slanderous anecdotes with just enough discretion.

However superficial Fred's life seemed to be, there was another side of it that his society friends knew nothing about. They would have been amused by his determination to keep fit by skating almost every morning and afternoon and passing all three tests of the National Skating Association, and would never have understood his efforts to become a good writer by serious study of the styles and methods of other novelists. So they were not told and Fred led his double life, enjoying both sides of it.

He began with the English classics, and Dickens in particular. He admired Dickens enormously, especially the vitality of his creations, but realised that the broad canvas and the detailed pictures, the crossings and interweavings of a host of characters were not for him. He found Jane Austen's characters, though as skilfully drawn, were more ordinary than Dickens's; they could be seen in the street, in a milliner's shop or at a vicarage tea party. Her books soothed him, though he didn't want to write soothing books. Mrs Gaskell, Anthony Trollope and George Eliot all wove their individual spells, and Emily Brontë had written the novel which for him stood head and shoulders above all others in the English language. For a long time he was obsessed by Robert Louis Stevenson. RLS to him spelt perfection – or did so until his critical faculties stirred uneasily and he began to find hints of journalese in the splendid words. He tried to be interested in Maurice Hewlett but could not get on with him and Hall Caine astounded him with his grandiose solemnity. He found Marie Corelli's books vigorous, but nothing more. He revelled in H. G. Wells's direct and lucid style, but was disillusioned when Wells's political and sociological ideals took precedence over his science fiction.

At last he came to terms with the methods, styles and personalities of all the authors whose books he had been reading in such prodigious quantities, thought over seriously what he had learned, and came up with some solid convictions that he could use as guidelines in his future writing. He had always instinctively felt that a fictional character should be revealed by what he said rather than by what his creator said about him. Direct speech was the way by which vividness and reality could be created, and not by editorialising, discussion, comment or analysis. Analysis and dissection killed a character off; life blossomed only by speech.

Fred had already rather crudely experimented in that direction in *Dodo*. The result had not been entirely successful but the originality of the idea had at least been tested and approved by the reading public. Over thirty years later he wrote, as part of a symposium of authors discussing 'The Book I Shall Never Write':

> The book which I mean to write and never will has neither narrative nor description of any kind in it, and I don't think even the names of the characters ever appear. They reveal themselves, their marvellously complicated and wonderful natures, and the whole dramatic situation with its astounding dénouement entirely by what they say. The book will be of immense length, and nobody will be able to lay it down till he has finished it. The social, economical, political, mental, physical, and spiritual life of England will stand still for that period.

Though humorously expressed, the general idea was meant seriously. Fred ignored his guidelines frequently, but he always paid special attention to dialogue, giving each character his own vocabulary and his own way of phrasing it, keeping narrative and speech apart, each having its own identity.

Fred loved exercising his craft and, in between his skating sessions and his frivols with his friends, he was never happier than spending long solitary evenings, often till well after midnight, sitting at his desk, filling sheet after sheet, spurred on by incessant smoking and frequent glasses of whisky and soda. His early writing was fatally fluent and his willingness to rethink and revise not nearly strong enough. He let his characters run away with him and failed to discipline their excesses.

His evening was broken by the arrival of a waiter from the nearby Italian restaurant bringing him a risotto and a bottle of wine, and after a bath and the meal he would resume his delightful and satisfactory scribblings, and would go to bed tired but happy and spend a dream-free night. In the morning he would read over what he had written the night before with largely uncritical approval. He claimed that his conscious mind was quiescent during his most creative periods, and that some part of his brain, not quite identified with his conscious self, took charge, stimulated by the favourite conditions he had built up – the solitude, the cigarettes and drink, perhaps an occasional break for a tune on the piano.

The author draws from himself, Fred said, and when his characters take charge and say what they want to say, then he is writing his best work. Though nominally the author is steering the course the story is taking, he has to unlock the door of a secret storehouse which holds the mysterious qualities which separate competence from great talent.

# CHAPTER TEN

uring the early years of his independence Fred found a welcome in both high and low places, though he doesn't specify the latter. All his weekends were spent out of London, and Tremans did not see him as often as Ben would have liked. But she was tolerant; the newly born butterfly must be allowed to spread its wings in the sunlight. Fred began to spend more and more time with one hostess in particular, Lady Charles Beresford. She lived at Park Gate House on Ham Common, though in the winter months she took a house in London to be nearer the centre of things. Due to some indiscretion in the past, the details of which were kept as secret as possible, she had been ostracised by the official Palace-led society of the day and had retaliated by starting a new society of her own. It was very successful and content with its own boundaries. It included ambassadors, City merchants and actresses who were even then considered slightly demi-mondaine. Fred moved comfortably between the two worlds, fascinated particularly by the extraordinary behaviour of Lady Charlie.

Lord Charles, handsome and debonair, was adored by other women and he often adored them, but as his wife didn't love him she remained unconcerned, though being middle-aged and stout herself she disliked all members of her sex who were young and beautiful. She could be as harmless as a dove and as venomous as a serpent. Her sole purpose in life was to be amused.

Fred was enthralled by everything about her; her absurd appearance, her inconsequential conversation, her vitality and her complete disregard for convention. She emphasised her stoutness by dressing in pale blue or pink little girl gowns studded with fake turquoises, her auburn-wigged head surmounted by a hat as wide as an umbrella. Her makeup was equally bizarre; eyebrows drawn in charcoal (though she was quite likely to put one on and forget the other) or made of fur and stuck on with adhesive. The powder on her cheeks was like icing on a pink cake and flew off in clouds, and the carmine on her lips came off on everything she ate. As her doctor had recommended exercise she rode a tricycle and sometimes got as far as a hundred yards down the garden path. By then she would be tired and get one of the gardeners to return the machine to the house.

Her talk was completely lacking in logical sequence. It could be amusing, or shrewd, irritating or ridiculous. She drifted from one subject to another, interrupting herself as well as other people, breaking off to admonish her dog or speak to a servant, pouring out an endless stream of nonsense. Fred had heard that kind of conversation before. At Cambridge Nixon and Browning had been adepts, and his Dodo had revelled in it, but in Lady Charlie's amazing loquacity it had reached its highest point. He was so fascinated by it that his own style was influenced, and thereafter almost every book contained a character whose way of talking had its source in Lady Charlie's surrealist meanderings.

The Beresfords took Fred to Bayreuth to the Wagner Festival; his second visit. Now, two years later, he found things very different. The Munich Festival, a great success the previous year, had stolen some of Bayreuth's thunder. There was more open criticism of the opera productions, and people who complained of boredom were not immediately ostracised.

Fred remembered this second visit for a comic interlude. One of the Rhine Maidens, a buxom creature with a hearty voice, fell in love with Lord Charles, and arranged for a love note to be placed on his stall seat before every performance his party attended. The notes were written in German, which he didn't read, but Lady Charlie did. She would scurry into the theatre in order to be first to pick up the letter and find out what new and endearing epithets the lovelorn lady had used. Her husband was not a whit embarrassed by the situation, making fun of both wife and temptress; and he taunted Fred with the prophecy that when he was over fifty he would not be at all likely to receive such amorous propositions. All such nonsense was grist to Fred's mill. When Wagner palled there was always a Beresford doing or saying to lift his spirits.

Fred spent some of the winter months in Switzerland for the skating, to work towards his gold badge. He often stayed at the Bear Hotel at Grindenwald. When he got tired of skating he would go off alone on a toboggan, far away from the village, and find pleasure in the solitude of the silent fields, the pine woods and, beyond, the northern face of the Eiger. In *Mother* he wrote that he felt the aloneness invade his whole being and take possession of him, shrinking him to an atom of nothingness. Family, friends, worldly pleasures and problems all ceased to exist. It was like losing oneself in a new beginning. When he had climbed up through the pine trees, reality would assert itself and he would discover that he was hot and hungry; and he would sit under a tree with his lunch. He remembered vividly on one occasion a sudden lapse into childishness.

He scooped out a hole in the snow among the roots of a tree and hid in it a piece of chocolate, a cigarette and a small coin. He smoothed the snow over the hole and wondered idly who, if anyone did, would find the articles and what they would think. There was then another climb before it was time to descend, sliding downwards on his toboggan through the wind-stirred silence and coming to a relaxed halt in the familiar valley.

After his Swiss holiday Fred returned to Paris in the New Year of 1901 to spend a short time with Regie Lister, now second secretary in the British Embassy. On January 22 he arrived at the station and saw Regie's white, strained face and heard the words, 'The Queen is dead...'

Queen Victoria was nearly eighty-two years old. She had been ill for some time but nobody expected that she would ever die. She had been on the throne since 1837, before any of the Bensons, except the late Archbishop, had been born; only Beth could remember clearly the accession of the frightened young girl who for the next sixty-four years was to preside, sometimes majestically, sometimes querulously, over the British Empire. For Fred and his brothers and sisters, through infancy, childhood, and adulthood into middle age, the queen had been imperishable, and now she had perished. It was as if an unforeseen earthquake had shattered the natural order of things.

The Queen had once visited Wellington College and had taken tea with the Bensons, but that was before Fred was born. He had only once been in her presence when the family, on holiday on Deeside, had been invited to Balmoral. He had been impressed by the tiny old lady with the beaky nose, prominent eyes and beautiful voice who represented everything that was stable and secure. To him, as to millions of others, she was a symbol of simplicity, dignity, majesty, and loneliness. When Regie had told him the news they drove to the Embassy, Fred in a stunned silence. He cut short his holiday and returned to England to be present at the funeral in St George's Chapel, Windsor, where he was to represent his mother.

He found the service a very moving experience, a mixture of pageantry and simplicity; though, with his usual quirky eye, he found something to smile about. The guests in the Chapel had to wait for a very long time before the coffin arrived because the train carrying it from London was very late, and many of them found the waiting difficult: there were agonised expressions and much shuffling of feet. He wondered why a large block of seats in the nave was empty – had the occupants-to-be decided to stay away? It turned out later that a batch of invitations had gone astray. When the bier did finally arrive at Windsor station one of the horses harnessed to the gun carriage which was to bear the bier to the Chapel became frightened and tried to bolt. So all the horses were unharnessed and the bier was carried by sailors on foot.

The service itself went without a hitch. Following the coffin were the new King of England, the Emperor William II of Germany, sons and daughters with wives and husbands, nieces and nephews and grandchildren of the dead Queen. Fred was particularly affected when the coffin was laid down and the sceptre and orb and crown, symbolising her royalty, were placed on it. That seemed to him the supreme moment of her greatness.

# CHAPTER ELEVEN

or the next five years, up to the summer of 1906, life at Tremans passed like a long summer afternoon for the Benson family. Fred was a frequent visitor, and now that he no longer had to endure the feeling of suffocation that had driven him away, he enjoyed his family all over again; his relations with his mother were particularly harmonious, and he was able to see Maggie's problems with a greater understanding.

Maggie had benefitted most from the move to Tremans. Her health had improved dramatically. The depressions and many infirmities which the damp, low-lying town of Winchester had visited on her disappeared; her spirits soared and her activities in the house and garden increased. For the first time for many years she enjoyed health and contentment. That it was to be the final flowering was not foreseen by anybody.

At Winchester she had been an invalid looked after and protected by Ben; now, with her vitality restored and her brain teeming with ideas, the position changed. She took over the reins and directed the course of household events but still demanded her mother's tenderness and protection, and Ben was puzzled how to reconcile the two opposites in Maggie's character. But because they loved each other deeply, they succeeded in coming to terms with their needs, and to soften the strain they each had other people to turn to. Ben had Lucy Tait's devotion to sustain her, and Maggie had her acolytes, Nettie Gourlay and Gladys Bevan; and when she had finished her work on her father's books his awkward spirit left her.

Ben was now over sixty, stouter than ever and continually failing to control her size by dieting. She felt rheumatic pains in damp weather and her eyes grew tired easily, but her vitality, eagerness and youthful mind were not impaired by the passing years. To her children she always presented an interested, critical and humorous front. If she had any worries she refused to acknowledge them to anybody but Lucy Tait. She could talk to Lucy freely, grumble about her ailments, her failure to control her weight, any misgivings she might have about Maggie, analyse passionately all the weaknesses (most of them imaginary) of her own nature, and resolve to do better in future. Lucy smiled, agreed, consoled.

In 1903 Arthur resigned his mastership at Eton, after deciding that teaching took up too much of the time he wanted for writing. He had been a good but unconventional teacher; one of his odd practices had been to go round the dormitories every night and tickle the boys in their beds. He went to live in Cambridge, intending to give himself up completely to writing and editing. In collaboration with the second Viscount Esher he edited selections from the correspondence of Queen Victoria, which were to appear in three volumes in 1907. Six more volumes came later, from other editors' hands. Then chance took a hand in Arthur's affairs, and the course of his life was drastically changed. A friend, Stuart Alexander Donaldson, the Master of Magdalene College, then a small College with only thirty or so undergraduates, mentioned to him that the College ought to elect a Fellow but would find it difficult to pay whoever was appointed. 'Why not take me?' said Arthur promptly. 'I can afford to accept a fellowship without emolument.' The Fellows of Magdalene unanimously decided that he would be a distinguished addition to their number and he was elected in October 1904, taking office the following year. For two years he lived in rooms in College, then in 1907 moved into the Old Lodge, which formed part of the College buildings. Arthur added to it so that it became a spacious and comfortable house, and he remained there for the rest of his life. Donaldson died in 1915 and Arthur was elected Master of the College, a post he held for ten years, until he died in 1925.

During his Cambridge years his books of essays appeared regularly. They were urbane in tone, tenuous in substance; too light for philosophy, too reflective for journalism; written easily and with pleasure, but unlikely to last. His critical works on Rossetti, Fitzgerald, Pater and Ruskin are more acute and deserved the success they achieved.

The only time that Arthur disappointed Ben was when he failed to be offered the Headmastership of Eton on the retirement of Dr Edmond Warre in 1905. His name had been mentioned by many of his friends, who hoped that he could change the old-fashioned teaching of the classics and introduce more history and modern languages, but Arthur refused to apply. Afterwards he bore his Eton colleagues a grudge because they hadn't put his name forward without his consent.

While Fred was 'playing with his earls and countesses,' as his mother put it, and Arthur was settling happily into his scholarly backwater, Hugh was struggling with his conscience at the House of the Resurrection at Mirfield, beginning to wonder if the Anglican Church was his final resting-place. There were stirrings in him that hinted at a change of direction, to the first steps along the road that would lead to

Rome. He wrote a number of short stories, published under the title *The Light Invisible*, the setting of which were the house and gardens at Tremans, the protagonist an old Catholic priest who clearly had the author's sympathy. Hugh's first book was probably his best.

Hugh kept Ben informed of every step he took towards his final conversion and she, wise woman, did not attempt to dissuade him. She believed that the Divine Will was at work, and who was she to question it? If the Archbishop had been living at the time it is not difficult to speculate on the thunder and lightning that would have shattered the household calm. That a son of his could go over to the Antichrist would have been impossible to contemplate.

Hugh could not have been ignorant of what his father would have felt and what his mother did feel, but his longing for the shelter and security of Rome outweighed any other consideration. There was that in Hugh's makeup which demanded the right to individuality but needed to be curbed by benevolent authority. In the autumn of 1903 he went to Rome to the College of San Silvestro and was ordained nine months later. He met the Pope in the Vatican. Each happened to drop his skull cap, and as each bent they nearly cracked their heads. This caused some irreligious chuckles.

Tremans contained a small room already licensed as a chapel where the family could celebrate Holy Communion. When Hugh finally became a priest he appropriated the room so that he could say daily Mass there; otherwise, he told his mother, he would not be able to stay at Tremans. He introduced a plaster cast of the Blessed Virgin and of other saints which he painted with more enthusiasm than skill, and, in order to use up Maggie's paints, he extended his art to the leaded window panes with more saints. These became known to the servants and tradespeople as 'Mrs Benson's Dolls'. He was insistent that the Anglican linen should not get mixed up with the Roman linen in the oak chest which served as an altar, and warned Beth to be careful where she put her bundles. He found a boy from the village to act as server, and every morning Tremans was alive with the sound of two services going on simultaneously, Anglican hymns and prayers from the ground floor and bells and incantations from the chapel.

Fred was to remember an occasion when he and Hugh were playing croquet on the lawn below the chapel when Hugh suddenly realised that it was time to say his prayers, and vanished. Fred heard a garbled murmur from the chapel, then in an incredibly short time Hugh reappeared. He looked suspiciously at the lie of the balls and accused Fred of having moved one of them while he was away. Fred observed ruefully that Hugh's religious observances had not produced an increase in brotherly love.

Still, Hugh's defection to Rome, for so the family regarded his move, made him very happy, and he flung himself into his religion and his novels with great zeal, finding everything the greatest of fun. After four years in Cambridge, for three of them a curate at the Catholic Church, he decided that parochial work did not suit him. All he wanted to do was preach and write, and his novels had brought him so much money that in 1908 he was able to buy a small manor house at Hare Street near Buntingford in Hertfordshire. Then began for Hugh seven years of intense activity. He was at the peak of his physical powers, and fizzing with such enthusiasms and nervous force that he negotiated pitfalls and setbacks with ease.

He was in deadly earnest about his religion, and the duties and observances attached to it, but at the same time he seemed to find life a joyous adventure, so that he took pleasure in all the serious things. 'Oh, isn't it fun?' was one of his frequent exclamations. He enjoyed writing, and thought, as he finished each book, that it was the best he had done. He was as uncritical of his work as Fred was of his, and never gave another thought to a book when he had set down the last word. It had been amusing, and now he was going to find the next one just as amusing. The purpose behind the books was to propagate the Roman Catholic religion, and by doing so save the souls of all his readers. But his novels failed to last because they were slapdash, over-emphatic and shrill, and because they had no heart.

That applied to Hugh himself. He had charm, vitality, eloquence and fervour, but he had no heart for anything or anybody but God. He couldn't understand human love or enter into intimacy with another human being. He loved children in general, his mother and Beth; and Arthur was his closest man friend. Apart from that love meant nothing to him, and sex even less. His life was so full that he had no energy left for emotions. If he couldn't be lover or friend, neither could he be enemy. In all, he was an exasperating person, dogmatic and egocentric.

Hugh was careful to maintain his family ties, paying regular visits to Tremans, and occasional ones to Cambridge to see Arthur, but when he was at Hare Street he left it as little as possible. He once confessed to Arthur that he did not know the name of a nearby hamlet. He gardened, carved, painted, stitched tapestries, read voraciously, dealt with an enormous correspondence, smoked almost as heavily as Fred. When he was not doing any of these things he was compiling a prayer book or writing a mystery play; or he was talking at street corners, or preaching a course of sermons in America, Rome or London; instructing converts, writing verses, or investigating psychic phenomena.

This busy and happy period was shattered by the most

traumatic experience of his life when he met Frederick Rolfe, self-styled Baron Corvo, who had shortened his first name to Fr. so that people would think he was a priest. For about two years Hugh's life was turned upside down, and he emerged from the ordeal broken and embittered.

Early in 1905 Hugh read Rolfe's book *Hadrian the Seventh*, published the year before, and he wrote to the author through the publisher, Chatto and Windus, praising it extravagantly and offering to be of service to Rolfe. The book was not Rolfe's first, but was probably his masterpiece. In it he was able to pour out all his venom against the Catholic Church which had rejected him, and to indulge his wishful thinking in creating the character of George Arthur Rose (his *alter ego*) who was elected Pope.

At first Rolfe's response to Hugh's friendly overtures was one of suspicion; he had little time for Catholic priests and in general his friendships tended to founder quickly. But the correspondence between the two men continued, and after six months they met and became friends: Hugh an admiring and uncritical fan, and Rolfe happy to receive the praise which he had always considered to be his due. Later in the year they went on a walking tour, taking with them the minimum of luggage and staying at the most obscure of inns. Rolfe told Hugh of his rejection by the Church, his abysmal poverty, the plots against him, the friends who had betrayed him, the whole catalogue of his paranoid fantasies; and Hugh was dazzled by the wildness, the frenzied words, Rolfe's passionate commitment to the Church he could not join. Hugh could only respond with talk about his literary plans and of his interest in the occult, a subject that also fascinated Rolfe.

With little experience of the world outside his home and the pulpit, Hugh displayed an almost childlike innocence in his dealings with the unbalanced Rolfe. His infatuation blinded him to the man's excesses. His feelings were not shared by Arthur, when they returned to Tremans at the end of their tour. Arthur disliked Rolfe intensely, and Rolfe responded by being argumentative and rude. Ben disliked the visitor also, but her loyalty to Hugh made her refrain from criticism. She did suggest, though, that if he were to come again it would be better if Arthur were not present.

During their walking tour Hugh and Rolfe had decided to collaborate on a book. Rolfe was particularly enthusiastic because he saw it as a means of getting his name before a large public. His own books had achieved relatively small printings, while Hugh was well-known and successful. An added benefit to Rolfe would be his association with a highly respectable Catholic convert and priest, thus improving his own chances of acceptance by the Catholic hierarchy. The subject of the book was to be Saint Thomas of Canterbury. A synopsis was agreed on in

August 1906, and the division of labour settled. Hugh was to do most of the writing and Rolfe the research. As a medievalist, this appealed to him greatly. He was to get a third of the royalties, though both their names would appear on the title-page.

Predictably, things did not go smoothly. Their styles didn't match, and each criticised the other. There were recriminations about late delivery of material, or whose turn it was to do what. Late in 1907 the project began to flag and Hugh's feelings for Rolfe cooled. An end to the collaboration came when Hugh learned some of the details about Rolfe's private life and decided that it would not be desirable for their names to be linked. Cardinal Bourne, Archbishop of Westminster, spurred on by Arthur, persuaded Hugh that it would be folly to keep associating with such a dangerous man, and Hugh agreed to tell Rolfe that their names could not appear together on the book. The financial arrangements would still stand, and Rolfe's help would be acknowledged, but that was as far as he was prepared to go.

Rolfe objected strongly to this proposal. Hugh then offered him all the material so far written to do with as he liked. That offer was rejected too, and from that time Rolfe became Hugh's implacable enemy. His persecution mania built Hugh up into a devil incarnate, a man who 'showed the cloven hoof', and who was living proof of the wickedness of Catholic priests. Rolfe sent letters of calumny to all and sundry, including Arthur, and Hugh's bishop. To Hugh he sent abusive postcards. Hugh did all he could to bring about a reconciliation but Rolfe refused every friendly gesture.

The relationship ended in farce. Hugh drew Rolfe as the frightful Enid ('a devil's changeling') in his novel *Initiation*; and Rolfe, with rather more panache, changed Hugh into the Reverend Bobugo Bonsen in *The Desire and Pursuit of the Whole*, calling him a 'stuttering little Chrysostom of a priest, with the Cambridge manners of a Vaughan's Dove, the face of the Mad Hatter, and the figure of an Etonian who insanely neglects to take any pains at all with his temple of the Holy Ghost'.

Rolfe was to die in poverty in Venice in October 1913, where he had for many years maintained his manifold feuds, borrowed money constantly, and acted as a procurer of boys for a group of English paedophiles. Hugh's comment on his erstwhile friend, given shortly before Rolfe died, was, 'The man's a genius, and I love him. If he'll only apologise I'll ask him to come and live with me; he's quite destitute now, but he is welcome to everything I've got.'

There is no doubt that Rolfe, vindictive and megalomaniac as he was, was badly treated by Hugh, who showed weakness and duplicity in his dealings with his difficult collaborator. The combination of gullibility and perversity was typical of Hugh.

Maggie's troubles began in the late summer of 1906 with moods of great depression which came and went without reason. Her joy in her work at Tremans was less fervent, and she lost heart easily. She exhibited signs of nervousness and grew increasingly anxious about her health. The family put the symptoms down to overwork and the sultry summer weather, and didn't think that there was anything seriously wrong with her. Her letters to Fred and the others were full of family gossip; they gave no hint of an underlying malaise, except that in a letter to Arthur she wrote that one thing she desired was to *want* some day to die, 'to lay me down with a will'. In June she told Gladys Bevan that there was nothing wrong with her except tiredness. In September though she admitted that she got into fusses about detail and unnecessary paroxysms of anxiety, and eventually she confessed all to Arthur. She told him about her black moods, how she had worried her mother by telling her about them, and how she had developed a hard and critical attitude towards her home and family.

One morning Ben went into Maggie's bedroom where she was having breakfast in bed and found her in the grip of a fierce emotion. When she asked tenderly what was the matter Maggie replied, 'Oh, I am killing it!' Ben realised that a dread struggle had begun, a struggle with fear, darkness and the unknown. Ben's agonised recognition that Maggie was doomed was confided only to her diary. 'Deliver me from fear,' she cried in silence.

Maggie's condition had deteriorated by Christmas though she fought against the demon and there were times when she achieved serenity. She finished her book *The Venture of a Rational Faith*, saw her friends and wrote cheerful letters. In February 1907 she went to Cornwall for a month with Nettie Gourlay and another friend, Beatrice Layman, to recuperate from a bout of pneumonia, and she wrote ecstatic letters about the beauties of the early Cornish spring, and she sketched contentedly for hours. From Falmouth they went to Fowey – 'a beautiful and queer place – it isn't a bit like England'. To Arthur she wrote, 'I believe the mists will disperse – I think they must...'

She stayed in London at Gladys Bevan's house in Evelyn Gardens for a few days and went to see Fred in Oakley Street. She spoke to him quietly of the thick cloud that surrounded her and the terror she felt, but still insisted that there was nothing really wrong with her, and. that one day she would be happy again. 'I wanted to see you again first,' she said, and Fred, with a stab of foreboding, wondered why she had said 'first'.

More than one doctor had told her that her trouble was temporary, but Maggie only half believed them. She could not accept

that the terrible things that had taken possession of her mind could have a
physical basis, and that one day they would go away like an attack of
measles. In the faces of people she passed in the street she saw evil behind
the innocent expressions, beasts and demons lurking behind the human
masks. Life was a void; every thing and every person was crumbling into
a dust that would dissolve into nothing. There was nothing she could
cling to. There was no hope. Neither friends, family, not even her
religion, could help. She knew she was going mad.

Back at Tremans she recovered for a little while, and she
was able to write to Fred telling him about the animals and birds, how
well Beth was and how pretty the garden was looking with its cherry
trees, tulips and forget-me-nots. Ben and Lucy had been away but when
they returned they soon realised the remission had been temporary and
she was really very much worse. The crisis was at hand. Ben sent a
telegram to the family doctor in London, Ross Todd, and he arrived at
Tremans the same evening. During the day Maggie had been quiet and
listless and Ben had decided that she would not worry any of her sons.
Resting in her room before dinner, with Beatrice Layman trying to
comfort her, Maggie may have known what was about to happen for she
suddenly began to quote Browning: 'If I stoop/Into a dark tremendous
sea of cloud,/It is but for a time...'

Doctor Todd persuaded her to dress for dinner, promising
her that he would look after her, and she sat at the table obediently. But
during the meal there came a complete collapse. The quiet, self-con-
trolled Maggie turned into a homicidal maniac. What actually happened
has never been described in detail or explained. Maggie may have tried to
injure herself, but it is more likely that she attacked either her mother or
Lucy with a knife. Neither Fred nor Arthur were explicit in their later
accounts; the horror of the situation was, even after many years, too
shocking.

Maggie was restrained by the doctor. Then she collapsed.
Ben wrote to her three sons that evening. 'We are in very deep waters,'
she said, and they hurried home. They found Ben shaken, but calm and
resolute, with no feeling of outrage. All her fears of what might happen
had gone because she now knew the worst. Her faith came to her aid and
she accepted without question what she believed God had ordained for
her.

Maggie was moved to a private home for the insane, run by
Sisters of Mercy at Burgess Hill nearby. Fred went to see her there in
order to get the papers that would certify her as insane signed. He found a
stranger. There was a gulf between them that he had no way of crossing.
She did not respond even when he took her hands and tried to talk about
pleasures they had shared. Just for one moment she came out of her

darkness when she asked him if he had come to take her home.

For the next ten years Maggie was never out of medical care. After the fierceness of the first attack had abated her condition improved so much that the family hoped for a full recovery. She was moved to a private asylum at Roehampton called The Priory where, although she had periods of sanity, she developed a new delusion; that her mother was conniving with doctors to prevent her from going home. Nothing could convince her that Ben and Lucy would welcome her back. Ben's visits to Roehampton led to bitter accusations and she was advised not to go again. Instead, she wrote Maggie long and loving letters in which she tried to reassure her of the love that was waiting for her at Tremans. But the antipathy towards Ben and Lucy persisted. Maggie would write back insisting that Ben was telling lies and would scribble furious little comments on the loving screeds. After Ben's death Fred found a number of Maggie's angry and accusing letters and destroyed them. They were too painful a reminder of his mother's sorrow and Maggie's disordered mind.

# CHAPTER TWELVE

eth's long life was drawing to a close. Her health began to give cause for concern in late 1910, when she was ninety-two years old. When, after the Archbishop's death in 1896, the family was dispersed for a time, Beth had returned to Yorkshire to stay with relations, but she had rejoined the family when they settled in Winchester. She could not read or write with any fluency; she had only had simple teaching at a dame's school, where she had spent most of her time sewing, but she would occasionally and with difficulty write a short letter to Hugh. When he lived at the House of the Resurrection at Mirfield near Bradford and had to submit to the vows of poverty, chastity and obedience, he was allowed to receive gifts of clothing and small luxuries. Beth was the chief provider of the things he needed. 'I can't bear to think of the greedy creatures taking away all the gentlemen's things,' she lamented.

'Beth is nearer to me than almost anyone in the world, I think,' Arthur wrote after a visit to Tremans in 1903. 'Her whole life from morning to night is spent in doing some kind of work and looking after someone...I think her life is one of the most beautiful things I know.' Two years later he wrote in his diary: 'Dear old Beth comes trotting up with a rose which she has tied for me.' And Maggie said, 'Beth is wonderfully busy, so that she has no time for reading.' Fred thought of her too with tenderness and gratitude.

Every mention of Beth, in letters and diaries, comments on her solicitude and her simple goodness. When she was free from nursery responsibilities she developed a gaiety and a childlike zest in the little incidents of life, loving to be made fun of and reminded of her old strictness; and when she was too old to do housework she took on all the darning of the household linen and the family's clothes. Then the time came when she was too old and tired even to use a needle, and she took to her bed, occasionally finding enough strength to get up to lie on the sofa. Her room was a little gallery of family pictures and photographs. A nurse looked after her and Ben spent as much time as she could by her bedside reading to her. When any of the brothers went to see her she brightened immediately and sent the nurse out of the room so that she could talk to her gentlemen alone.

When she was remembering the past Beth was alert, but her perception of what was happening in the present was vague, and she didn't realise what had happened to Maggie, except that she could not come to see her. She was consoled, however, when Maggie sent her love. Then she had a stroke which for a time disabled her, but some power came back to the affected side, and there followed six months of semi-consciousness before she slipped away, on a May day, in Ben's arms. She was ninety-three. Her whole life had been devoted to the family, and they regarded her almost as an institution, changeless and immortal.

All the family, except Maggie, gathered for the funeral. They had not seen each other for some time. Fred was full of stories about his eccentric friends, and Hugh brought the news that he was to be gazetted a Monsignor. They followed the cortège to the church at Horsted Keynes and Ben tossed a sprig of orchids on the coffin as it was lowered. Arthur could not help noticing a choirboy near him with a 'wide-open, fearless eye' gazing down into the grave. He also saw with distaste a nephew of Beth's who had not been seen for twenty years, a red-nosed man in a frock coat who broke down into paroxysms of pretended grief.

When Fred was in London he would go down to Roehampton once a week and spend the afternoon with Maggie. When the weather was fine they strolled in the Priory garden and he would have tea with her in her room. Fred found that, though her delusions were still present, beneath them there was a clarity that could still be reached. It was as if a veil which hung between her and the normal world was very thin, and Fred set out to break through it. With his cheerfulness and charm, and his affection for her shining through everything he said and did, he did more to keep her spirits up than anyone else. Her memory had been unaffected, and she and Fred would talk endlessly about their childhood days, their games and their collection of plants, butterflies and birds' eggs. She would send him notes reminding him of things they might have forgotten to talk about and provide things for tea which she thought he might like. But over all their talks and in all her letters there hung a great sadness. There was no spring in her mind, nothing could shake her conviction that lies were being told about her and plots being formulated. She couldn't understand why she could not go home, even though she insisted that her breakdown had been engineered by malevolent influences at Tremans.

Once, and once only, in the summer of 1913, did she go home. At that time she had been transferred from the Roehampton asylum to live under the care of a doctor in Wimbledon. She escaped from the house and made her way to Victoria Station, and found a train which took her to Horsted Keynes. It was two miles from the station to Tremans, but although she was physically feeble she managed the hilly walk. She arrived exhausted as dusk was falling, walked past the open kitchen door and saw Mary, an old servant. 'Mary, I have come home,' she said. Ben had been warned by a telegram from Dr Barton, the Wimbledon doctor, that Maggie had disappeared, and was not surprised when she saw her daughter. Arthur was staying at Tremans at the time with Geoffrey Madan, the young man he was then in love with. It was an awkward situation. Madan had been put in Maggie's old room and had to have all his things transferred elsewhere. They were surprised at Maggie's apparent normality, though she ignored her friend Beatrice Layman and refused to speak to the gardener. The next morning, after Maggie had slept peacefully, Ben took her round the house, pointing out all the old familiar things and Maggie grew animated, her enjoyment evident in her delighted remembrance. Then Dr Barton, who had arrived late the night before, decided it was time to go. As they put her in a cab her mood changed. She flung the usual accusations at her mother and begged not to be sent away. Her intellect was as sharp as ever, Arthur noted, but her emotions had become atrophied or perverted. She was never to see Tremans again.

There was one brief period when Maggie improved so much that she was able to travel to London with her nurse and visit Fred at 102 Oakley Street, a large house in Chelsea he had taken in 1905. Fred took her to St Paul's Cathedral, Lambeth Palace, Hampton Court and to museums and picture galleries. She even went to the theatre. She wrote to Arthur, saying, 'Fred has been good in coming to see me. I went to a little play of his last week – it was amusing.' This must have been *Dinner for Eight,* a one act play which was performed at the Ambassador's Theatre in London on March 23 1915.

On such occasions Maggie seemed to have recovered some of her former vivacity, laughing over reminiscences of times past, showing an incisive interest in the affairs of others, making caustic comments on life in general. 'How one longs for the old days, imperfect as they were,' she wrote, 'but one has no confidence that one would live them better.'

Gradually Maggie weakened physically. She grew tired easily and her heart showed signs of weakness. The visits to Fred in Oakley Street became less frequent. In August she had a heart attack. For a time the delusions went away and she saw people and things as they really were. Ben was surprised and delighted to hear that Maggie wanted to see her. She went to Wimbledon immediately, accompanied by Fred. For two days they talked again as members of a family, without accusations or hostility. No longer the enemy, Ben was happy to put aside the years of miserable separation and to join with Fred in humorous stories and recollections of the past. 'She was just her old self,' Ben wrote, 'and most affectionate.'

But Maggie's convalescence slowly flagged; the clouds thickened and the delusions returned. She began to lose hold of life. When Fred saw her in the spring of 1916 he knew that she could not last more than a few days. All the members of the family went to see her and she talked to them cheerfully. On her last evening she saw Ben and Fred, and then Ben alone, treating her as if there had never been any dislike or suspicions. They didn't speak of estrangement, but only of love and regret for the missing years. She made her mother promise to come again the next day 'before I die', and she asked her nurse to call her early so that she could continue her talk with Ben. 'Well, I *have* had a happy day,' she said before she fell asleep.

She died during the night. Her body was laid in the crypt of the Chapel at Lambeth, and she was buried beside her sister Nellie at Addington. A fitting epitaph came to Arthur as he was standing by the grave. 'My soul is escaped even as a bird from the snare of the fowler; the snare is broken and we are delivered.'

If the death of Maggie was poignant, Hugh's was touched by farce. His health declined noticeably in 1914, after the outbreak of the war, when he began to suffer from breathlessness and pains in the chest and arms. At Ambleside, where he was staying with cousins, he saw a doctor who put his trouble down to simple indigestion. Hugh cut down smoking and promised Arthur that he would see the family doctor, Ross Todd. Now 'false angina' was diagnosed and he was told that he must cut down his work load considerably. On October 4 he preached at Salford, then went to Ulveston to conduct a mission and, though the pains returned with greater severity, preached again at Salford a week later. Days of sleeplessness and acute pain followed, and he caught a chill which turned into pneumonia. Congestion of the right lung caused his condition to deteriorate rapidly, and it was thought necessary to give him the last rites. Hugh was staying with Canon Sharrock of Salford Cathedral, in the Bishop's House, and the canon gave him Holy Viaticum. Hugh made all the responses and even corrected the canon when emotion caused him to stumble over a word.

Soon afterwards Arthur arrived in response to a telegram and was reassured by Hugh's insistence that he felt better. 'Mind,' he said, 'I don't think I'm going to die! I did yesterday, but I feel really better.'

Ben telephoned to Fred, telling him the news, but suggesting that as Arthur had already gone to Salford it would be better if he stayed away in case Hugh should worry that the family believed he was about to die. So Fred stayed in London.

Hugh was a difficult patient, excitable and uncooperative. His mental faculties were as active as ever and his piety was as strong, but the strain on his heart from the pneumonia was beginning to tell. Hope was abandoned that evening, and Hugh too seemed to realise that there was little time left. The next morning the canon and Arthur were summoned to Hugh's bedside. Hugh joined in the responses to the prayers for the dying which the canon recited, stopping him once or twice in order to give Arthur some last minute instructions about his estate. He was conscious almost to the last moment, seemingly without pain, though he found difficulty in breathing. 'You will make certain I am dead, won't you?' were almost his last words. He died with a sigh, just as though he were slipping into sleep.

The next day Fred travelled to Hertfordshire to Hare Street to find Hugh's will and see what special instructions he had left for his burial. He found it on top of a pile of papers on Hugh's desk and wondered if his brother had had a presentiment about his coming death. His wishes were unusual. He wanted to be buried in a brick vault in his garden and a chapel to be built over it. The coffin was to be made of a light wood so that, if by any chance he was buried alive, which had always been his secret fear, he could break the top and use a duplicate key to the vault which was to be placed in the coffin and so make his escape. If this plan was not practical, a vein in his body was to be opened before he was buried. Fred saw that the latter was done, and the breakable coffin and the duplicate key were not required. Later a chapel was built over the grave.

# CHAPTER THIRTEEN

n June 1909 Fred, aged forty-two, met a young man of twenty-three with whom he was to establish one of the firmest friendships in a life full of romantic interludes. He had been staying with the raffish Countess of Radnor in her flat in Venice for several weeks, and followed that with a visit to Lord Stanmore in the castella at Paraggi, a little castle which stood in a pine-shaded garden immediately behind rocks which plunged straight into the sea, a mile or so from Portofino. One afternoon a boat came across the bay, carrying the family from the nearby castella at Portofino. The passengers were Montagu Yeats-Brown, late consul at Genoa, his wife, and their youngest son Francis. Francis had been an officer in the King's Royal Rifle Corps; later he joined the Bengal Lancers, the 17th Cavalry. He had been educated at Eton and Sandhurst, and had been in the Indian Army for three years.

Immediately Fred and Francis sensed an attraction and in no time they became inseparable. On June 19 Francis wrote in his diary: 'I have made great friends with E. F. Benson. He is a most remarkable man: living vividly in the present: and talking cleverly. His manners are truly perfect: he has square shoulders and looks boyish. His forehead is magnificent: he is strong and well built. He likes his work, but perhaps he likes the world still better.' He was not sure what to make of his feelings for Fred: 'fear: awe: love: God knows what.'

When Francis confessed somewhat shyly that he wanted to be a writer, Fred responded with alacrity. 'He gave me much excellent advice on writing,' Francis wrote. 'First to get the story clear in one's head. Then to alter one's style for descriptions, conversations, dreams, etc. To write quickly but correct much and often. To observe carefully: to listen carefully to conversation. Writing is a trade which must be learnt.'

Soon he and Fred were taking long walks every day and swimming from Francis's red-sailed cat-boat. When Lord Stanmore left they had the castle at Portofino to themselves, for Francis's parents had returned to England. They slept in hammocks slung between two trees in the garden. Every morning they got up at six, had a light breakfast, then settled down to writing for two to three hours. Fred was working on a novel, as usual. This was *The Osbornes*, which he finished in about six weeks. After another and more substantial breakfast they worked again. Then there was the long ritual of swimming and sunbathing and, after a lunch of figs and wine, a session of sailing or rock-climbing. At four o'clock they would rest for an hour. A three hours' walk at a fast pace through the mountains of Liguria finished off their physical exertions for the day. After dinner on the terrace beneath the lights of stars and fireflies Fred would read aloud what he had written during the day. They eventually retired to their hammocks and talked about art, life and literature.

For the rest of his life Fred was to remember the happiness of those few weeks, the precious hours of intimate talk, the pleasurable exhaustion of a body exercised to its limit, the drowsy content of falling asleep in the open air with the scent of flowers and the murmur of the sea below, and the nearness of a friend with whom he felt in total accord.

Fred had opened a new world to Francis. He had great literary ambitions but so far they only amounted to a few articles published in Indian papers, and he had never before met a professional writer. Many years later he wrote, and re-wrote with Fred's help, *Bengal Lancer*, the story of his life in India. It was twice rejected, then Fred strongly recommended the book to a new and enterprising publisher, and Francis was grateful for his interest. However, although the publisher enjoyed reading the book immensely, he rejected it on the grounds that it contained too much about Yoga and too little about the life of Englishmen in India. Eventually Gollancz accepted it and brought the book out in 1930. It was a runaway success.

In 1912, when Francis had returned to India, Fred visited him there and stayed for several months. While there he fell ill, and pains of increasing severity caused him to return home. He was found to have a tumour on a kidney which was so far advanced that an operation for the removal of the kidney was inevitable. This took place in May 1913. After convalescing at Tremans he was deemed to have recovered. Fred was never again as strong as he had been. He had to cut down on skating, tennis and golf for a long time, but his natural resilience kept him cheerfully resigned to a less active life. He also cut down on the amount of whisky he drank, but his consumption of cigarettes remained unchanged.

Fred was at the Villa Cercola with John Ellingham Brooks in July 1914 when the excursion steamer from Naples landed at the Grande Marina, disgorging tourists, letters and newspapers. He brought a copy of *The Times* and Brooks opened it. 'Hullo,' he said, 'an archduke has been assassinated. Franz Ferdinand.'

'How awful,' said Fred. 'Who is he, and where did it happen?'

'He's the Emperor of Austria's heir,' Brooks said. 'He was attending manoeuvres at Sarajevo.'

'Never heard of it,' Fred said. 'I want to see the tawny lily in flower on Monte Solaro. Will you come with me?'

'Too hot,' Brooks said. 'I must water the garden.'

Fred looked at an atlas and found that Sarajevo was in Bosnia. It all seemed very far away. The lilies on the mountain side were much more important.

Soon, however, the shadow cast by the oncoming catastrophe reached the island and Fred realised that war was inevitable. He could not remain uninvolved in this paradise while people at home were in danger so he returned to England, leaving Brooks to sit out the next four years as an ageing exile.

That Christmas Fred was at Tremans. There was no Hugh to raise the temperature with arguments, but Arthur was there and the two brothers got on each other's nerves, particularly as Fred affected to have inside knowledge about the war and dropped dark hints about what people in high positions had confided in him, though he was careful not to name anyone. It was a rather juvenile way of showing off – the unworldly academic was expected to stand in awe of the man of the world. The holiday was uncomfortable for all, with a lot of tight lips and eyes raised to heaven.

Fred was forty-seven years old at the outbreak of the war, too old to enlist as a soldier, but not too old to do interesting and vital work in another sphere. He became attached to a branch of the Foreign Office; his job was to collect material about the enemy's position in Turkey, where the Germans had gained complete control of every aspect of Turkish life. Turkey had been deluded into helping Germany by promises to restore the Ottoman Empire which would include Egypt and the Volga provinces and stretch to the boundaries of China. Fred studied the maps which the Germans had distributed throughout Turkey showing the extent of the fictitious empire; the propaganda designed to lull the Turks into acceptance of temporary serfdom was diabolically clever.

By the end of 1916 he had amassed a large amount of information about German activities, and by the following summer had all the material he needed to expose the German plans. All he needed was the time and the place where he could write undisturbed; and the sun-washed house in Capri leapt to his mind. It would be the ideal place; all that was lacking was the opportunity. Fred waited patiently, sure somehow that something would happen. Then a friend in the Foreign Office wanted something taken to Rome, and at the same time another friend in another department wanted some information that could only be gathered in Rome. So Fred had an official reason for travelling abroad in wartime, and all possible obstacles to moving about in dangerous waters were swept aside.

The mission to Rome was successful. One of Fred's tasks was to find out whether the Pope was pro-British or pro-German, and from the conversation he had in various quarters it was clear that the Pope was not on the side of the Allies. Fred delivered his mysterious package to the Embassy, and in return received a bag of dispatches to be given to the Foreign Office. He sent off to London an account of what he had done and learned, then he made for Capri with all possible speed.

There, although Italy had abandoned her neutrality and had officially joined the hostilities on the Allied front, it was difficult to realise that there was any war at all. Newspapers were often late or failed to appear at all, and, as they were the only source of information, news of battles, advances and retreats were out of date or inaccurate. So Fred could concentrate on his book and ignore the discomforts he had not hitherto experienced; the scarcity of meat and the inedibility of wartime bread. But fruit was still plentiful, and figs and peaches took the place of bullet-like chops and toast that tasted like wood shavings. The sun still shone, the lizards still basked on the whitewashed walls of the Villa Cercola, and for a few weeks Fred was transported back to the happy days of pre-war Capri. He laid down his pen reluctantly when there was no excuse for writing any more and prepared to return to London.

Fred was a very inefficient packer of bags and suitcases. When he had finished trying to cram everything he had brought with him and the things he had acquired there into his cases, he found that there were still shoes and shirts lying around, also his manuscript and the bag of dispatches. He was forced to look for an extra suitcase and found one that he had left behind years before in the villa's boxroom. The overflow went into it comfortably and Fred was pleased with the way he had managed.

It was not until he was standing on the platform at Rome station, waiting to verify the number of his berth on the sleeping-car, that he became aware that there was something very wrong about his luggage, for one of his cases was attracting pointing fingers and hostile stares from a crowd of Italians.

It only took a moment for Fred to connect the menacing attitude of the onlookers with the labels on the suitcase. One had an hotel label but the case from the boxroom had a luggage label from Trieste, a port in the enemy's country. Fred had sailed to India from Trieste in an Austrian-Lloyd steamer, an innocent enough journey five years before, but now he gave the impression of a rather stupid spy with a forged passport who had forgotten to change his luggage labels.

All kinds of possible disasters flashed through Fred's mind as he picked up the suitcase and made his way as nonchalantly as possible to his berth in the sleeping-car. There he mutilated the labels with fingernails and penknife until there was no trace left of the offending name. As the train moved out he hoped that the incident would lead to no embarrassing complications. It didn't and Fred arrived back at the Foreign Office with his reputation intact.

Fred's work for the war effort was done on an *ad hoc* basis, and he received no remuneration for his political books. In 1917 he decided to attest under the new scheme which asked men under fifty to offer themselves for National Service. Charles Masterman, director of Wellington House Propaganda Department in Buckingham Gate, heard about this and wrote to Fred in May 1917, hoping that his attestation wouldn't interfere with his work for national propaganda. He had already asked Fred to write the book about Turkey and went on to ask for a book about German crimes. This would be for circulation among neutral countries, so that they should not turn with sympathy to Germany and demand soft terms when the time came to discuss peace. 'You have generously offered to do this work without remuneration and I cannot imagine *any* work more suited to the special talents you can give to the service of the nation,' he added.

So Fred put aside any other plans. *Deutschland uber Allah*, written on Capri and brought back in the famous suitcase, was seen through the press in 1917. It was a short work of about fifty pages, and Fred expanded the theme in *Crescent and Iron Cross*, published the following year.

The book had two aims – to expose Turkish cruelties by examining the history of Ottomanisation from the thirteenth century when the Osmanli Turks moved westward into Europe, and to underline Germany's compliance with the evils committed by the Turks. The Turkish Empire reached its expansionist limits in the seventeenth century, occupying land from the Adriatic to the Black Sea, but when Turkey declared war on Russia and was soundly beaten in 1878, her expansion into Europe was reversed. By 1914 Turkey in Europe was limited to an area by the Sea of Marmora which included Constantinople. In Asia it comprised Armenia, Kurdistan, Syria and Mesopotamia.

During the reign of Abdul Hamid, which began in 1876, the first of the Armenian massacres took place, and when he was deposed and the militarist 'Young Turk' party took power, the horrifying killings continued. Fred's account of the sufferings of the Armenians and others, the torture, rape and pillage, is very vivid and moving. Germany, after being snubbed by Abdul Hamid, slowly and methodically achieved

THE MASTER'S LODGE, WELLINGTON COLLEGE,
HOME OF THE BENSON FAMILY

FRED'S FATHER, EDWARD
WHITE BENSON,
ARCHBISHOP OF CANTERBURY

MINNIE BENSON AT 19,
NEWLY MARRIED

MINNIE, NELLIE, MAGGIE, BETH,
AND FRED, AGED 2, 1869

FRED, AGED 9, AND HUGH,
AT LINCOLN

FRED, AGED 15, ARTHUR
AND HUGH, 1882

FRED'S COLLEGE, KING'S

FRED AT CAMBRIDGE

FRED, AGED 26, AFTER THE
PUBLICATION OF DODO, 1893

FRED WITH FRIENDS AT VILLARS–SUR–OLLON, 1910

FRED JUDGING A
SKATING COMPETITION AT
VILLARS–SUR–OLLON, 1910

FRED 'CURLING'
IN SWITZERLAND

FRED'S HOME AT 102,
OAKLEY STREET, CHELSEA

ARTHUR, HUGH AND FRED
AT TREMANS, 1913

TREMANS, THE BENSONS' HOME

BEN, AGED 75, AT TREMANS

LAMB HOUSE AND GARDEN ROOM, RYE

FRED AT BROMPTON SQUARE, 1920S

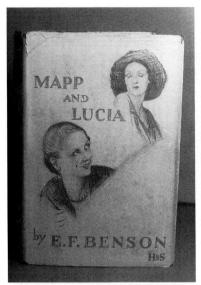

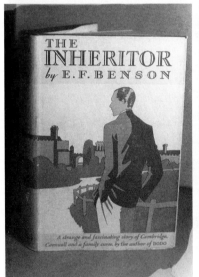

FOUR EARLY JACKETS

ultimate supremacy, ignoring the Armenian massacres. When Turkey had become totally subject to Germany, both militarily and economically, Germany was able to make use of all the Turks' ill-gotten gains. The final section of the book deals with Fred's suggestions as to how the protected territories should be apportioned after the war. He concludes that Ottomanisation is desirable as long as it remains firmly within the Turkish borders. The Osmanlis could retain their customs as long as they imposed them on no one else.

Fred had not finished with the tangled affairs of Europe. After dealing with Germany and Turkey he turned to Poland and its nineteen political parties, all at loggerheads, and the involvement with them of Germany and Russia. He wandered miserably among the obstacles for weeks. Experts to whom he showed his first tentative drafts all disagreed, each turning the facts and arguments of the others upside down. Finally things began to clear; facts were sorted out and confusions disentangled. He published *Poland and Mittel-Europa* in 1918, another brief tract. Then, as he had done with the Turkish book, he expanded his study and brought the story up to February 1918; his original tract became the first chapter of *The White Eagle of Poland*, which appeared later in the year.

With his work for the Foreign Office, his own writing, which was as prolific as ever, and his socialising, Fred did not have much time for other activities, but he managed to do some work, as Honorary Secretary, for Lady Sclater's Fund for Wounded Soldiers and Sailors, and for this he was awarded an MBE in 1920.

# CHAPTER FOURTEEN

n September 1915 Fred gave up the lease of his house in Oakley Street and moved to a large house in South Kensington: 25, Brompton Square, overlooking a disused graveyard full of trees at the back of the top closed end of the square. Between the graveyard and the house was a narrow alley used only by pedestrians, and beyond it a church, with the dome of the Brompton Oratory rising over its shoulder. Fred fell in love with the house at first sight. As soon as he opened the front door, the order to view in his hand, he knew that his search was over. Everything was perfect, or would be when the plans that were rioting in his mind had come to fruition.

There were four weeks before he must leave Oakley Street, and he and a friend spent most of the time measuring, arranging for carpets and blinds to be fitted, deciding where to put the furniture, and painting and decorating. Soon the house began to gleam with Fred's favourite colours. The hall and passage were painted a Giotto blue that reminded him of Italy, and the floor was laid out like a chessboard with black and white linoleum squares. The windows and staircase were also black and white. The dining-room had a yellow ceiling, and the drawing-room had soft grey walls and Bokhara rugs on the black floor.

More than ten years later Beverley Nichols dined with Fred and went into raptures about the house, saying in his usual whimsical way that the furniture seemed to have been put in its place by the gentle hands of Time; the pictures had almost grown into the walls; and the carpets had sprung naturally from the floors like some gracious form of grass. According to Nichols, Fred's face glowed with happiness as he showed his guest round the house. He was described as 'a smallish (Fred was five feet ten), pinkish, twinkling, urbane, grey-flannel-trousered man' who had finally come to rest in a quiet London square, having retained the sparkle of his eyes, his taste for Italian wine and, above all, his love of a sheet of white paper in the stillness of the night. Fred, who had not 'come to rest' at all, noted with amusement the slight cattiness behind Nichols's gush.

The arrival and unloading of the furniture vans from Oakley Street to Brompton Square caused chaos. The refrigerator blocked access to the dining-room and the grand piano would not go up the stairs. So it had to stay in the hall on its side and people could only just squeeze past it. In the evening of the first day a policeman arrived to complain about unshaded lights. The servants went to bed and left Fred alone to face his nightmare of unutterable confusion.

The grand piano remained at the bottom of the stairs for two days. Various methods of dealing with it were discussed with the removal man, and it seemed that a regiment would be needed to take out the drawing-room window on the first floor and, by means of block and tackle, hoist the instrument through it, assuming the stone window ledge would take the strain. At his wits' end Fred telephoned Harrod's, the firm which had originally supplied the piano. They sent down three men who, in half an hour, had manoeuvred the piano up the stairs without a bump or a scratch. After that, difficulties resolved themselves magically, and Fred soon felt that he was really home and not camped out in some borrowed squat.

During the war all Fred's political writing was done in his room in the Foreign Office during the day: in the evenings his time was his own. Social engagements were fewer than they had been because so many of the leaders of society had left London either to run hospitals for wounded officers or to escape from a city whose shortages had become boring; so Fred would return to Brompton Square, shut himself up in his study and forget the war for a few hours. During those four years he wrote several novels, but the most important, and the one he gave his heart to, was *David Blaize*. Never had a character taken him over so completely, never had he written with such lack of inhibition about himself. True, it was himself as a boy, but it was a true, clear picture of adolescent passions.

Fred had long wanted to write a chronicle about the time in a boy's life when, both impressionable and sentimental, he is without a gender of his own, feeling neither completely male nor female, but indeterminate. Such creatures, Fred claimed, are not bothered by sex, so their energies can be directed into other channels, and in particular into a devotion that transcends the physical. He wanted to write a story of school life that would be completely unlike *Tom Brown's Schooldays*, *Tim* or *The Hill* and the other traditional stories of bullies and cheats and captains of cricket who kiss the fevered brows of First Formers who are dying of consumption. He thought he could do it by depicting himself under the name of David Blaize as he really had been, or had wanted to be, all those years ago: yellow-haired, sunny-natured and of an unbelievable goodness.

Helmsworth Preparatory School, where we discover David Blaize at the age of thirteen, is, without doubt, Temple Grove, and the austere and terrifying Headmaster with the rolling gait is Waterfield to the life. The spiteful Mr Dutton is an amalgam of some of the ineffectual masters that Fred had known. Actual incidents from real life occur regularly; especially an embarrassing visit to the school from David's Archdeacon father, who participates in cricket practice, dives into the swimming pool with a loud belly flop, and preaches a long and boring sermon in chapel. David's interest in games and keeping stag beetles are a replica of Fred's, and Maggie appears as David's sister Margery. They live in a cathedral close, in a house with attics which contain gurgling tanks just as the Chancery at Lincoln did.

After Helmsworth comes Marchester, which is Marlborough, and the great friendship between David Blaize and Frank Maddox springs into being. Maddox is three years David's senior, black-haired and brown-skinned, a complete contrast to the Nordic David. David is the young Fred throughout, but Maddox is not Eustace Miles, Fred's real life friend at Marlborough, because in fact Miles was more than a year younger than Fred, and their positions in the school were the reverse of those in the novel. It is likely that Fred took Miles's essential character, his serious attitude to work, his prowess at games and his capacity for friendship, and grafted them on to a composite stock with elements of several boys he idolised at various times during his Marlborough days.

David Blaize, though he occasionally utters a mild expletive, smokes when smoking is the fashion (though he doesn't enjoy it), and uses cribs only to avoid impositions, is impossibly good for an adolescent. He won't sneak or lie, always says his prayers, and sails through school life candid and clear-eyed, loved by both masters and boys. Not a hint of impurity crosses his mind and he turns a puzzled face from any suggestion of immorality. Only once is he scared by the possibility of an approach that hints of sex.

That happens one day when David emerges from the shower and sits on a bench drying his hair with a towel, but is otherwise completely naked. Maddox comes in, looks at him and smiles in a way that gives David a sense of choking discomfort, and he leaves the bathroom hurriedly. Back in the dormitory he feels that he has escaped from some distant nightmare but cannot explain to himself what has caused it; though he vaguely guesses that Maddox was about to tread along a very miry road. In the meantime, Maddox has been sitting in front of his fire reviewing the intense friendship that has sprung up between himself and David, the good influence he has so far been on the younger boy and how he has shielded him from anything that might have sullied his innocence. He realises that he himself has brought danger near. If their friendship, so dear to him, is at stake, he must in future turn aside from all muddy places. After that there is a gruff little scene of reconciliation, and with sighs of relief the two boys resume the old relationship.

The rest of David's time at Marchester is a jolly one. Maddox makes him work hard and he gets his remove; he develops into a wily left-hand bowler, plays fives, racquets and golf, and goes on holiday with his hero who quotes Swinburne at him and confesses that his past has been rather beastly. Since the incident in the showers he has tried, not to corrupt David, but to uncorrupt himself. David had made him ashamed and that had been his salvation.

The climax of the story comes after Maddox has left Marchester for Cambridge and David is a prefect in the Maddox mould. He stops a frightened horse, which has thrown its driver and is bolting down the steep High Street, by clinging doggedly to one of its reins. But the wheel of the cart goes over him and he sustains severe internal injuries. He lies, hovering between life and death; for several days, but, being David, not afraid. Maddox hurries from Cambridge to be at his bedside and sits holding his hand all through the night while David sleeps and at last turns the corner towards recovery. It is a scene not far removed from the sentimentality that Fred was trying to avoid.

The important thing about *David Blaize* is that for the first time love between two boys has been described openly and tenderly. Fred had been re-living his own schooldays, pulling aside the screen of adult hypocrisy and revealing something of the difficulties that can disturb a boy's adolescence.

Ben loved it; it was the only book of Fred's that she ever approved of. The effect of the book on the reading public was electric. Fred's regular readers took it in their stride. It was a new departure for their hero but the style was typically his, and they were content, reading it with pleasure if not too much understanding. A large number of middle-aged men, in search of their lost youth, were attracted by the portrayal of an age before war and sex had destroyed the golden afternoons of their childhood. Fred had brought back the sights, sounds and smells of boarding schools all over the country; the games, japes, trouble with teachers, all tinted with the rosy glow of nostalgia. They remembered and were grateful.

A third class of readers, new to Fred, were those who fell in love with the two boys, instinctively responding to the underlying eroticism of the friendship that had almost trembled into something more disturbing. They represented a wide cross-section of the middle-class homosexual world, and Fred received many letters from them after

*David Blaize* had been published in 1916.

One that expressed well the rather inarticulate voice of the man of action was from a major in the army:

> I have just been reading *David Blaize* and think it lovely – the best school story yet written bar none. Here we have a continual stream of young officers to train as scouts and snipers and there has been a great run on David, as many as three copies of him on one course. Many of the lads who have come have few if any memories of anything but home and school as this is a young man's job. I think you would perhaps like to know the pleasure your book has given to these very fine and gallant lads who come to first army training school from the trenches.

It is unlikely that Fred had planned his book to be an army training manual, but he no doubt appreciated the motive that prompted the major to write. Another letter, also from a serving soldier, was a little more personal:

> Please excuse my temerity but I want to thank you for *David Blaize*. I've always loved *Sketches from Marlborough* but this is supreme. It *is* the place in all its essentials, how on earth did you manage it? I can't tell you how much I enjoyed it the first time – at eleven pm I began looking idly at the first few pages just to see how it started and my next conscious act was turning the last page at three in the morning. And the second time was just as good as the first. Other school tales can hide their dishonoured heads. I had your old study in 1901 or thereabouts – at least your name appeared on the list on the door. No 12, The Alley, I think. Bothering people with letters is not a habit of mine but this was a special case so I hope you don't mind.

A young American, due to enter Harvard the following month, wrote to Fred from Boston:

> I have written to you once before on the same subject I write to you now, and you answered my letter. I have just finished my second reading of *David Blaize* and I like it better this time than any time of many months ago. Despite your previous statement I wish you would write of David's life at college. This letter is supposed to convey to you my deep appreciation of the most beautiful book I've ever read. Have you yet discovered an English boy with whom I may correspond? I hope so. Please write something further of

David and Maddox. Send them to war if you wish, but don't kill them.

David and Maddox did not get sent to the war; it was eight years before they appeared again in print. Fred evidently took note of his correspondent's wish and did send them to college.

Many years later Ethel Smyth wrote to him. 'I've been reading and delighting in *David Blaize*. I always knew I should. I think it's frightfully well done – the sort of thing no-one but you can do. The balance between...oh, well, all moods are truly and well kept, I think. Congratters.' The allusion to 'balance' is mysterious but it is likely to refer to Fred's treatment of the finely balanced relationship between the two protagonists.

The most puzzling communication that Fred ever received was a postcard dated 8 November 1917. There were only four words on it, and it was unsigned. The words were: 'I know your secret.'

# CHAPTER FIFTEEN

p to the middle of 1917 Arthur lived in a world in which he felt completely at home. He was Master of Magdalene with a large salary of which he only took part, a substantial income from his writings, and a capital of £40,000 which a Swiss woman, an admirer of his work, had given to him with no strings attached. Though not frugal in his habits he was not profligate, but now he was able to spend freely: cheques to friends in trouble, many gifts to the College, paying for additions and extensions to the Chapel, Hall and Old Lodge, and the financing of fellowships and exhibitions. One of his greatest pleasures was having a chauffeur-driven car. He liked presiding at High Table and enjoyed the deference that was shown him by officers billeted at Magdalene. He was elected to the Council of the Senate, the innermost oligarchy, as he called it, and was an Alderman of the Cambridge Town Council. He was on the Board of Governors of Gresham's School at Holt, and was a Liveryman of the City Guild of Fishmongers, which supported the school.

His activities at Cambridge suited his character in a way that gave him great contentment. There were committees, syndicates, the minor squabbles that were a part of university administration, receptions and honorary degree ceremonies. He frequently grumbled at the hours he had to spend at such events, but would not have had things otherwise for the world. He was a person of great standing. If his sense of humour had been less highly developed he could have become unbearably puffed-up, but he was able to chuckle privately at the small pomposities of his enclosed world. He was still able to succumb to the boyish charm of undergraduates and the younger officers, courting them in his sexless way. At other times he relaxed in the company of old friends such as Percy Lubbock and Monty James, and they discussed with friendly malice the quirks and foibles of their colleagues.

But Arthur's idyll was not to last. Suddenly, and without warning, he began to have vivid and grotesque dreams in which he suffered accidents and was involved in disasters. Maggie, who had died the year before, returned to haunt his nightmares, and awful things happened to her that he was unable to prevent. He grew frightened; his broken nights seemed to be a danger signal. But what were they warning him of? Was he about to undergo again the frightening depressions of 1907 that had left him shattered for two years? As a kind of exorcism he began to write a biography of Maggie, and sorting through her papers and letters he learnt how their father's death had affected her, leading to the collapse of her sanity. Would he eventually be afflicted in the same way? He put the idea aside with a shiver of apprehension, but it remained curled up in a corner of his mind.

After a visit to Eton, his first since leaving the school, he went on to Tremans. Far from finding peace there, the dreams continued and now he was also brought low by severe headaches. Dr Ross Todd and a specialist diagnosed exhaustion through overwork and prescribed bromides. They didn't work. Arthur returned to Cambridge and tried to lead a normal life, but the attacks increased in frequency and violence and, (which was even more worrying), they began to happen during the day too. Sometimes he felt that his head would burst and feared that he would soon totally collapse.

He fell into an abyss of hopelessness, writing out his resignation of the Mastership, directing what should happen to his possessions if he never regained his sanity, and even composing his own epitaph – 'a rhetorician without passion, a quietist without peace'. In the middle of August 1917 he was taken to a nursing-home for the mentally sick at Ascot, and for the first few weeks he lay under constant sedation.

Then he had a series of hallucinations, the worst being that he emitted a horrible smell and that everything he touched was affected by it. He wrote to Fred asking him to go to Cambridge because his servants' wages had not been paid, and he imagined that they might be starving, even dead.

After some months he was weaned painfully back into social life and became friendly with some of the other patients, elderly men, many of them Jewish, and most of them doomed to stay in the institution for good. He rarely thought of the world outside. If he did he was assailed by feelings of guilt, that he had been proud and foolish and had ruined his own life. God had judged him and found him wanting, and he had got precisely what he deserved.

His neurasthenic condition was treated, according to the practices of the day, by rest, sedatives and massage, and they brought him some relief. In 1918 he began to write his diary again and looked forward to the day when he would be released. Then he had a relapse and closed his diary, not to open it for another two years. More months of depression followed, and for six whole years he was to wake up every morning with a sickening pang, wondering if he could get through the barest outline of a day, struggling with a sort of outrageous nausea with life and everything connected with it.

Ben died on June 18 1918, aged seventy-seven. It would have been Maggie's birthday. At the end Ben was frail and very deaf, but possessed of the same indomitable courage that she always showed. Fred had been staying with her shortly before, after he had finished his book on Poland. His suggestion for a visit was met with an enthusiastic response: 'Oh, Fred, a whole week! Lovely! Come to your foolish but ever-loving Ma.' She had wanted to read his manuscript and had looked up Poland in the atlas. It had been an enjoyable week and Fred had promised to return very soon. He left to the usual ritual of departure that had been a family tradition for years – a frantic waving of hands and handkerchieves as the car bearing the visitor disappeared round the corner of the house.

Ben had lived a life of great extremes. The daughter of a middle-class family of unexceptional stock, she had become second lady in the land, with a handsome, if difficult husband, many servants and a family which adored her. For fourteen years she had attended and given dinners and receptions at Lambeth Palace and Addington Park, mixed easily with diplomats, politicians and great divines, always admired and sometimes loved by them. Her letters had gone out to the great and the humble. She had spoken at meetings, her plump little figure aglow with humour and confidence. She had been revered by Gladstone and had had an affectionate relationship with Queen Victoria.

When this glamorous phase had ended with Edward's death she retired into obscurity, not altogether willingly, entertained on a much smaller scale, and continued to wield influence in correspondence. Hugh and Maggie died and Arthur was shut away in his own dark world, but Lucy Tait was always at hand and Fred was always cheerful and supportive. Three days after his fiftieth birthday – his Jubilee, she called it – she wrote to him, calling him 'Dearest of men,' and signing herself 'Everlovingest'. In the letter she admitted that she was anxious about Arthur's condition, how his attempts to make little jokes in his letters were pathetic, but continued to hope that he would improve. The letter was determinedly cheerful, but underneath there was strain and sadness. She was not to see him well again.

For a year after Ben's death Tremans remained unchanged. Fred hesitated to take any irrevocable step because there was a chance that Arthur might recover, resume normal life, and either stay at Tremans during vacations or even live there permanently if he retired from Cambridge. But it became apparent that Arthur was indifferent to his future. His mother, whom he had loved more than anyone else in the world, had died, and he felt that there was no rock on which he could find safety. As far as he was concerned Fred could do with Tremans whatever he wanted.

For nearly twenty years Ben had been the inspiration of Tremans; now it was just a house full of family furniture. Fred knew that he himself could never live there alone, haunted by spirits and associations that would cause constant pain. Lucy Tait felt the same way. For thirty years she and Ben had been inseparable; now there was nothing left for her at Tremans. She bought herself a smaller house in the neighbour-hood, and divided her time between her new home and Lambeth Palace, where lived her sister, the wife of the Archbishop of Canterbury.

Lucy Tait has always seemed to be a somewhat shadowy figure, but she had actually played a significant role in Benson affairs; on Maggie particularly she had had a most damaging effect, through no fault of her own. In age she was between Maggie and Ben. She was the daughter of Archbishop Tait, Edward Benson's predecessor, and was one of the four survivors of nine children, the other five having died of scarlet fever. She had come to live with the Bensons after Nellie's death in 1890, though she had been a frequent visitor for many years before that, and the Archbishop had been very fond of her. Gradually she and Ben had grown together and had formed an association of more than ordinary intimacy. They were rarely apart. Ben reached her final emotional fulfilment with Lucy, who was stronger-willed than she was, not over-intelligent but with a direct, sometimes acerbic manner. They slept together in the great Victorian bed in which all the children had been born.

They addressed each other in letters in extravagant terms. 'My own darling,' Lucy would write, and 'Goodbye, my own best darling, Your own Lucy.' But both of them, given their Christian beliefs and upbringing, would have recoiled in horror at any hint of carnality in their love. However, that hint must have once been there, when Ben had written in her diary: 'Once more and with shame, O Lord, grant that all carnal affections may die in me. Lord, look down on Lucy and me, and bring to pass the union we have both so blindly, each in our own region of mistake, continually desired.' Whatever had caused Ben to be horrified at 'carnal affections' was firmly and finally buried, and she and Lucy continued to enjoy their love affair, free from moral wrong, till the end.

Fred disposed of the remainder of the lease of Tremans, and the question next arose of what do with the contents. The house was cluttered with furniture, pictures and plate, old and unused wedding presents, Egyptian antiquities from Karnak, a library of his father's books, boxes and cupboards full of papers, the Archbishop's letters and dossiers of obsolete business matters, packets of Ben's diaries and letters, including the hundreds she had received from her children over the years, great-aunt Henrietta's collection of seaweeds, and miscellaneous bundles of ephemera that a large family had accumulated over sixty years.

It was obvious that much of the house's contents must go to auction. Fred's own house in Brompton Square was more than adequately furnished, and his sense of family tradition was not sufficiently strong for him to keep things merely out of sentiment. He sent a quantity of pictures and some furniture to Arthur's house in Cambridge and kept for himself a few articles he thought particularly beautiful: some miniatures, a Jacobean pulpit, an Elizabethan corner cupboard, the Egyptian relics, and that was about all. He kept the letters and diaries, thinking that nobody but he would ever look at them again. What was inflammable was burned on a bonfire in the orchard, vans carried away to Cambridge and South Kensington what was to be kept, and an auctioneer arrived to compile his catalogue, fix his labels to the furniture, tie up the books in ill-assorted lots and make bundles of the miscellaneous articles that could not be sold separately.

Mrs Taylor, the cook, had died some months before so the only members of Ben's staff to be kept on were Spicer, her parlourmaid, and Charles Tomlin, the house-boy, both of whom were to enter Fred's service. Charlie Tomlin was born in 1902 and was thirteen years old when he joined the Bensons as 'boy', and stayed with them for twenty-five years. He left school a year before he need have done in order to help his widowed mother to bring up five children, and at Tremans earned half-a-crown a week and his keep. He lodged with the coachman and his wife and was well looked after; the family kept a coach but only one horse. His duties left him very little free time, but he never complained. He had to clean the silver and the knives, (two very different operations), waited at table for the staff and cleaned the family's boots and shoes. He also took letters to the Post Office at Horsted Keynes, two miles away, and collected those to be delivered.

With the other servants Charlie attended morning prayers and lustily sang the hymns that Lucy Tait accompanied on the organ. Mrs Benson read from the Bible and led the prayers, and it was all very jolly, especially as the service only lasted fifteen minutes. Charlie loved Mrs Benson because she treated him almost as a grown up, and because she looked like a plumper, kinder version of Queen Victoria.

Soon after Ben's death, Fred's eighteen-year-old manservant was conscripted into the army. Charlie, a good-looking, fresh-faced youth of sixteen was surprised and pleased when Fred asked him if he would take the place of his departing manservant. He accompanied Fred to Brompton Square and from then on went with him on visits all over the country and abroad. They spent some time together at Tremans while

Fred was sorting out his mother's effects, and they were there, with Francis Yeats-Brown, when the Armistice was declared.

On his last evening at Tremans, in the now unfamiliar surroundings, Fred went from room to room, letting the old associations flicker in and out of his mind, remembering his unhappiness when Tremans was first acquired, then his visits, either alone or with friends, over the past twenty years, the sharing of intimacies or the breaks in communication with brothers and sister, the changes in allegiance, the cosy companionship or irritable differences; then the gradual emptying, the unoccupied rooms and the echoing silences as the family grew smaller; until finally there was only the quiet, elderly presence of Lucy and Ben to spread life thinly through the once noisy, busy house.

In the garden Fred found the gardener looking at the new asparagus bed and bemoaning the fact that it was giving promise of its best crop ever. Now there would be no one left to enjoy it.

# CHAPTER SIXTEEN

he death of Henry James in 1916 seemed to Fred, at the time, nothing more important than the regretted passing of a major writer and family friend. James had lived at Rye, in Sussex, in a dignified but modest Georgian house called Lamb House after James Lamb, its first owner, who had built it in about 1723. Fred paid his first visit there in the summer of 1900. He was then thirty-three years old, the author of *Dodo* and a few other novels which had not had nearly the same impact. James had given his famous opinion of *Dodo* when it was sent to him in manuscript form, that he didn't find it as ferociously literary as his taste demanded, and Fred had flinched but carried on with the novel undeterred. On that first visit to Rye, Fred felt honoured but somewhat intimidated. James was one of the most admired authors of the day and he, ever ready to hero-worship, was but a fledgling writer who had not yet hewn out his own style.

In summer Henry James wrote in a room in the garden, close to the house but at right angles to it. It had a bow window looking down the cobbled West Street which, turning to the right, met the disused churchyard and the west front of the church itself. Fred had his days free, and frequently played golf at Camber. Sometimes he walked with James through the town and out to the marshes, and he would listen to the master's musings and speculations. He was only at Rye for a few days, but even in that short time he felt the beginnings of the spell that Rye could cast: Georgian houses of red brick, timber-framed houses, picturesque cottages, cobbled streets, sea beaches, and the leisurely yet busy lives of the inhabitants; above all, the exquisite Lamb House with its walled garden promised contentment and tranquillity. But Fred was young, energetic, striving towards a future as a writer, and needing the world as his schoolroom; Rye was for those who had had enough of adventure. So whatever slight yearnings he may have had towards the Henry James kind of life he put firmly aside.

Since that first visit Fred had been to Rye again to stay with Lady Maud Warrender, a friend who lived at Leasam, a mile outside the town. From her house one could see Rye itself, the marshes and the sea into which they merged. Lady Maud, the sister of Lord Shaftesbury, was often hostess to distinguished people, or people who were on the verge of being distinguished. Edward Elgar was one of them, and Fred wrote four poems for him which the composer intended to set for solo voice, chorus and orchestra. Sadly, for Fred was very pleased with them, they were never performed, and are now lost.

Lamb House, bequeathed to Henry James's nephew, also a Henry James, was let to Mrs Beevor, a widowed American, at a rent of £120 a year. Eighteen months later she, finding the climate of Rye too severe, decided to spend the winters abroad, and asked an artist friend of Fred's called Robert Norton if he would like to use it for a few weeks and make use of the housekeeper she had left in charge. Norton suggested to Fred that they should share the tenancy. Fred was busy with his work at the Foreign Office, and had only his weekends free; but as there was little to do in London, he agreed. He would go down by train on Friday afternoons and return on Monday mornings, taking with him his latest manuscript and a ream of writing paper. Robert Norton painted in the garden room and Fred wrote in the sympathetic atmosphere of the Green Room on the first floor, the room that Henry James had used when it was too cold to work in the garden room. Fred was content. He had an intimate friend, a congenial place in which the friendship could blossom, and an occupation that gave him constant delight.

But the contentment was short-lived. Norton had to go back to America and offered the rest of his short lease to Fred. But Fred was already sharing the Villa Cercola on Capri with John Ellingham Brooks and had every intention of spending his summers there again when the war was over. He could hardly cope with a second holiday home, so regretfully he declined Norton's offer, passing it on to another friend. This time the offer was accepted and someone else took possession of the house that Fred was beginning to think of as his own home.

And that, he thought again, was that, but once again he was wrong. The lease of the Villa Cercola was up for renewal in 1919 and the owner refused to let it on the old terms. Fred and Brooks would have to buy it if they wanted to continue living there. Neither had any intention of doing so: Brooks because he could not afford to buy even half a share, and Fred because he didn't want to be obliged to go to Capri every summer just because he owned property there. He was, at this time, dealing with the disposal of Tremans and the sale of its contents, so it seemed that, for the foreseeable future, his only home would be his house in Brompton Square.

Happily the new occupant of Lamb House now told Fred that he wanted to spend his winters on the Riviera, and would therefore not need the house any further – would Fred consider taking a sublease from October till the end of March the following year, 1920? The answer was immediate, and soon Fred was back in the house for which he had conceived such an affection.

Fred received a visit from Arthur soon after he had installed himself, and again when Arthur was well enough to make decisions and take charge of his own affairs. He liked the change from the Master's Lodge so much that when the lease came up for renewal again he and Fred decided to share it, though the furnished rent had risen to £250 a year. They arranged that Arthur should occupy the house during the university vacations and Fred for the rest of the year. When Arthur was in residence Fred retired to Brompton Square. Arthur felt sad that the old family life had come down to two moderately successful men with no children or wives, sharing a strange house that had no family associations, but eventually he found the house a delightful haven, and he produced three novels, two volumes of reminiscences and an anthology of Greek epigrams during the few years he had left. Fred's output in the next ten years was prodigious.

Soon after the end of the war Fred began to suffer from arthritis, the result of a fall while skating in Switzerland. He thought the first slight stiffness would soon go away, but that was not to be. The disease crept on him slowly, but insidiously. Though it would be some years before reaching crippling proportions, Fred realised that he would get progressively less mobile, and he was determined to do all he could for as long as possible. At the age of fifty-three it was of course natural that he would be less active than when he was younger, but when he was cut off from the games he enjoyed it was a blow. He could still manage his walks, but they became shorter, and he had to give up golf and swimming. His winter visits to Switzerland to skate and ski ended, and he found foreign visits tiring. His writing occupied much of his time, and he played the piano assiduously, setting himself to learn by heart Bach's forty-eight preludes and fugues, though he faltered towards the end, realising that, good amateur player as he was, he had set himself an impossible task. He played chess, and for an outdoor hobby took up bird-watching, which became something of an obsession.

He spent long afternoons in the marshes with his field glasses and was soon familiar with the appearance and habits of the local birds, dunlin, ringed plover and redshank; and he travelled further afield to the north coast of Norfolk, sometimes with Arthur or with other friends, to spend a couple of weeks at the village of Blakeney or the marshes round Cley-next-the-Sea and Salthouse, which were rich in bird life.

He also occasionally stayed at Holkham Hall, the seat of the

Earls of Leicester, a magnificent mansion in a vast park, close to the sea but not within sight of it, and near a cluster of villages all called Burnham. The house was designed by William Kent and completed in 1761, and its interior is more palatial than almost any other house in England. The grounds were laid out by Capability Brown, who also built a large lake to the west of the house. Fred appreciated the grandeur and nobility of Holkham though he was just as comfortable in the modest George Hotel at Cley-next-the-Sea, and Charlie Tomlin much preferred the smaller place where he could not get lost in a maze of corridors.

For several months in 1919 Fred was subjected to a barrage of letters from a dentist's wife in Warwick that left him bemused, irritated and in the end bored. The first one was sent on April 27 and he made the mistake of answering it. 'Each of your books radiates *you*,' the lady wrote, 'and I am acutely conscious of your personality. Where have you learned your fine morality?'

The lady was a clairvoyante named Miriam Harvey, but who sometimes signed herself 'Madeline'. She had seen Fred in a vision after reading *Up and Down* and wanted to enter into an intimate spiritual relationship with him. She was not yet sure what he looked like – 'a dark man, are you, whose hair looks as though it might do with a good brushing? Or you bring a grey-haired man with a stoop, penetrating eyes and a material mouth, with you. Are you either of these, I wonder? Let there be no misapprehension concerning my social status. My husband is a dentist...'

Fred was intrigued enough to ask her if she would tell him what form her clairvoyance took – whether, for instance, it enabled her to see into the future. He said he did not look upon death as a 'rest' state, but as perhaps the beginning of a much higher activity, which he was interested in investigating. He wrote again a few days later, discussing her suggestion of the possibility of meeting ('I regret that as I am going into the country very shortly I cannot now have the pleasure of seeing you'); not yet realising what he was in for by encouraging the lady to hope that their spiritual union might be accompanied by a more earthly bond. Later it seemed that a meeting at the Royal Court Hotel, Sloane Square, where the lady was staying for a few days, was not necessary. His 'shadow' would suffice. She had seen him talking to a fair man – both wearing khaki. Fred had shown the fair man her letter and had said kind things about her.

In her next letter Madeline sent a sealed enclosure. 'If there is a lady in your life with white hair, who is stout, and who sits in a high-backed chair, will you kindly be a trusted messenger and give her the enclosed letter?' Fred returned the letter promptly, with a curt note. 'I have no one to whom I could send it who answers your description.' As it was a year since his stout, white-haired mother had died he must have thought that Madeline's powers had got on the wrong wavelength. However, there is something odd about the situation. In the letter to the lady that Fred had returned unopened (and whose contents she disclosed in a subsequent letter), Madeline had written to Ben and had described her surroundings and her physical appearance very accurately, and had worked out that she was Fred's mother. After one more letter Madeline inexplicably announced that she must go out of Fred's life for ever.

The disappearance lasted only ten days. Madeline bounced back. She had now given Fred the nickname of 'Honour Bright'. She thought she 'saw' him on top of a bus speaking to a man with brown eyes. In his reply Fred refused to accept that it was he, denying that he had ever been on a bus talking to such a person. Then Madeline gave him another persona – 'King Nebuchadnezzar' – and told him she had been searching for him for years. 'You will reply to this letter from across, or near, deep salt water,' she wrote, adding inconsequentially that Fred's favourite colour was pink.

In the next letter King Nebuchadnezzar turns out not to be Fred... Madeline had held one of Fred's letters, written on Tremans writing paper, and by pyschometry had visions of the house and gardens. She prophesied that she would motor there with him in his car, 'scorching' through a town raising the dust until they reached the house and see an elderly man with a sad, clever face and a thin lady in dark clothes waiting to greet them. A few days later she saw Fred standing near a long oak table examining a pile of letters, and she knew he was looking to see if there was one from her.

She returned to her belief that Fred was the man in khaki sitting on the bus, but she had now seen him in another place, standing beside her bed looking straight into her eyes. 'When I meet you in the flesh you must needs be Mr Benson, but for letters and thoughts you shall be Honour Bright.' The next time she saw him he was in the Slough of Despond, walking over grass and deep in meditation. He looked nice in tweeds and stockings, but she was not very keen on his cap. On another occasion he was wearing a dark lounge suit and tie, and once, dining at the Berkeley, she noticed that he was wearing purple socks. One of her fellow mediums, a gipsy called Eva, saw them together in a foreign country on a verandah with palm trees in the background, and that for some reason led to a prophecy about a book he was going to write which would be tremendously discussed and argued about, and which would bring him a lot of money.

In July, during a sitting with Zitta, another medium, she took on Fred's condition with an awful headache so that she had to abandon the sitting. 'Take care, Honour Bright, that way madness lies.

You never will lose your reason. Your will is too strong, but go easy with yourself – learn to cultivate repose.' Fred's mother has now become 'Kindly Light'. 'Be with her as much as you can, for she soon goeth to her rest.' Fred had evidently still not told her that his mother had been at rest for over a year. On July 10 Madeline said, 'I cannot discuss with you the perverse thing your letter implies. I would wish this (letter) to end our correspondence *please*.' Fred had annoyed her in a way which she didn't specify, but far from closing the correspondence she re-opened it the very next day.

She had decided that Kindly Light was dead. She knew there was a sickness about her and she had seen Fred scurrying along like the devil on a motor-bike. Besides, Fred's last letter had been written on black-edged paper – but all this proof went against what Eva had seen: Honour Bright talking to his 'old Lady' again. It was all too much for Madeline; she got very confused.

In many of the letters she insists that she is in deadly danger from forty traitors – 'Ali Baba and the forty thieves' she calls them – and that she is going to be poisoned because she has been chosen to defeat the treacherous forty. They are all mixed up with Winston Churchill, Lloyd George, Sir Edward Carson and the Duke of Westminster (another of her 'shadows'), but not as participants in the plot, it seems, but as part of the army fighting for the Right. She does not say who Ali Baba is – 'though find out what Bonham Carter writes so many notes about.' She mentions that Eva had said, 'That Honour Bright is friskier than wot you thinks for!'. 'I must wait and see, mustn't I?'

In another letter she wrote 'Honour Bright, have you read *Across the Stream* by E. F. Benson? I plonked down seven bob for it yesterday – the clerk at the store wanted me to buy *Up and Down* as well, but I intend to ask the author to give me a copy of that. To Mad Eline. Love from Honour Bright. Wilt?'

After July the letters became spasmodic. In November it appeared that Madeline was ill and dispirited. She gave up her *séances*.

Eva and I are not doing any more psychic work this year and I have promised, also my husband, to write no more unsolicited letters, which promise will not be difficult to keep. I trust I have made myself clear, Honour Bright, but am still rather ill and must remain in bed. Things had to come to an end sooner or later and for my sake 'tis perhaps well that 'twasn't later. May you be happy always – and so I sign myself for the last time Madeline. One by one the shadows have departed – there remains only you to settle up with.

Whether Fred ever did meet Madeline, and if he did, how often, is not clear from her letters, and his to her have not survived. Once she wrote 'You know how well I liked you when I first saw you in the flesh', which may or may not have been literally true. Reading between the lines it is evident, as far as is possible with such incoherent meanderings, that she was falling in love with the imaginary character she had attached to a human being, but in the end she saw how ridiculous the situation was and started to write in a sisterly way rather than in the coy romantic vein she had first adopted.

What Fred thought about this bizarre episode in his life is not recorded. He must have been reluctant to encourage the dizzy lady, yet her letters must have fascinated him at first however difficult it was to decipher her meaning and disentangle shadow from substance, spirit from reality. But in the end he grew bored and cold, finding no more amusement in Honour Bright and his supposed doings, and no further value in any of Madeline's psychic revelations, and very relieved when illness and depression brought her interruption in his life to an end.

# CHAPTER SEVENTEEN

rthur had begun to surface into a sort of life during 1919 and the threat of chronic invalidism gradually receded. During the early part of 1920 Dr Ross Todd persuaded him that it was time to give up the security of the nursing home and put at least a toe in the waters of the real world, so Arthur agreed to visit Fred in Rye for a month, and from there he would go somewhere unfamiliar.

He took a companion with him to help him fill in the hours and combat his wretchedness, but unfortunately the man he chose was quite the wrong type. He was a sickly Roman Catholic writer named Virgo, a former friend of Hugh's, and with a resemblance to the late Frederick Rolfe in his seedy sensualism. But Arthur had promised to help him and this was his way of keeping his word.

Arthur's improvement continued at Rye. To a casual visitor it appeared that there was little wrong with him. He talked well, looked robust and ate heartily. But inside there was still a core of desolation, and an inability to respond to the stimuli of everyday life. He had not resumed writing, and without it he was like a husk of himself.

After Rye he and Virgo went to Hastings, but the three months they spent there were a miserable failure. The two men were utterly incompatible and, without Fred's friendly presence, they could find little to do together apart from playing chess and draughts, and little to say to each other. Occasionally Fred would come over from Rye and the gloom would lift for a few hours, but when he returned Arthur had to make a great effort not to cry, convinced that they would never meet again.

Fred has never been given sufficient credit for the help he gave to Arthur during the long miserable years of his illness, whereas Percy Lubbock and other Cambridge friends have been known as active and patient supporters. It was typical of Fred not to advertise his generosity with time or money. Arthur was, even in the depths of his depression, aware of what Fred was doing and was truly grateful. In April 1920 he wrote to thank him for being so wonderfully good, and wished that he could show his gratitude. He knew that he had caused trouble and anxiety and would never forget Fred's kindness.

After his stay in Hastings Arthur returned to Cambridge for the Lent term, but at Easter he was back in Rye, this time without his companion, and beginning to show signs of his old genial and benevolent despotism. He would suggest a bicycle ride, a walk, or a motor drive, and would sulk if Fred preferred something else. So for Arthur's sake Fred would often fall in with a plan he was not especially keen on. When Arthur arranged for a friend to stay Fred was relieved because it would give him the chance to go to Norfolk again, but rather annoyed at the eagerness with which Arthur welcomed the chance of another companion. After all he had done for Arthur...But he soon realised that the seemingly ungrateful desire for change was another sign of returning health, and he went off to Blakeney for a fortnight with a light heart.

Fred was intensely happy walking along the shingle and among the sand dunes, watching the cockle-hunters digging in the black mud left behind at low tide. With field glasses in hand he stalked the waders and ducks and marvelled at the flocks of migratory birds coming south for the winter from Scandinavia, and the nesting and breeding habits of the terns. Bearded tits, godwits, curlews – Fred grew to know and love them all. At Salthouse he saw an avocet, a solitary bird which had come back to the place where its ancestors had had a breeding colony a hundred years before, and he hoped that it was the beginning of another settlement, but the visitor was shot by 'a cold-hearted wretch', as Fred called him, and no avocet appeared again at Salthouse until many years later.

In August 1922 Fred was at Blakeney again, this time with Arthur, whose doctors, trying to break his psychological dependence on them, had told him that they would not be able to see him for another two months. The experiment was a success in spite of Arthur's efforts to make it otherwise. In his diary he moaned continuously about his abject misery and the precious little he had to show for the money he had spent on doctors over the past five years. Fred found him sour and cantankerous and was glad when it was time to leave, his place as nurse-companion being taken by Percy Lubbock. When Arthur was back in Cambridge his doctors assured him, though he was reluctant to believe them, that he was much better and could extend his social engagements.

He spent Christmas with Fred that year, and noted with concern that Fred was in much discomfort from rheumatism. Not until March 1923 did Arthur admit that his depression was really vanishing. In April he cancelled the power of attorney he had signed six years before, and made a bonfire of all the letters to friends, to be sent only when his reason had collapsed permanently. At the age of sixty-one he looked forward again to a life of productivity, happiness and the companionship of lovely and engaging young men. He was going to make up for the wasted years with an orgy of creation.

At the end of every term he hurried down to Lamb House, taking with him an undergraduate or don, and would spend the time walking, bicycling, playing chess, talking late into the night and, above all, writing: essays, articles, and chapter after chapter of the current novel. His diary had already passed the three million word mark. His weight was increasing rapidly, his legs gave him trouble, neuritis was bothering him, but none of those mattered. Arthur was his old self again.

Since Fred had given up his share of the tenancy of the Villa Cercola he had not been back to Capri. John Ellingham Brooks had rented a much smaller place, the Villa Salvia, and was reasonably content there, although the house had few of the amenities of their former home, and, as there was no spare bedroom, he was unable to put up friends. He wrote to Fred suggesting that he should pay a visit to the island for a few weeks, as the spring was particularly beautiful and so warm that bathing had begun. In England the weather was being beastly, with arctic conditions making life uncomfortable, so Fred sent a telegram to say that he would start southwards immediately.

From Naples he and Charlie Tomlin caught the evening boat to Capri, and Brooks met them on the quay of the Grande Marina. At first Fred and Brooks were not comfortable with each other. They hadn't seen each other for years and had corresponded little. There had, too, been many changes on the island that Fred viewed with horror. Many of the people he had known were dead, Norman Douglas had left, but fortunately Compton Mackenzie was back temporarily and he and Fred went bathing together. Mussolini was ruling Italy and in his passion for order and efficiency had ordered that Capri should be developed. The more new hotels went up and the straighter its roads became, the less there remained of its former charm. There was a plague of motor cars and a greater plague of fashionable English visitors who had taken over Fred's old haunts and made him feel a stranger where he had once felt at home. He did not particularly care for the Hotel Tiberio where he was staying; it was clean and comfortable, but soul-less. He knew nobody and felt oppressed by the insidious menace of Fascism.

Brooks had changed too. Physically he was thinner, older, his features more austere. His joints were stiffening and he could no longer walk or bathe with ease. He had developed something of a persecution complex, quarrelling with friends and then complaining of loneliness. His Hérèdia sonnets had been rejected by a publisher, but instead of being disheartened and resigned to the fact that they were not, even after all the years he had devoted to them, very good, he was convinced that all they needed was more and more polish. He was also translating a selection of Greek epigrams, hypnotising himself into believing that his appreciation of Greek verse, together with an ear for rhythm and melody, were producing gems of pure crystal.

He played an old out-of-tune piano with verve and complete lack of talent. For years he had been trying to memorise Beethoven's sonatas, and still couldn't play a note without the music in front of him. When he was unable to find a word that perfectly translated a Greek original, he would sit at the piano and with stiff joints murder another sonata.

Fred saw that in various small ways Brooks's mainspring, which had kept him busy and enthusiastic in the old days, was running down. Capri, now that he was poorer and almost friendless, was becoming a prison in which he would finally wind down and stop. Fred urged him to return with him to London and stay at his Brompton Square house for the summer, or at Lamb House in the autumn, but Brooks invented reasons for rejecting both proposals. So Fred went home, leaving Brooks on the quayside, a defeated figure, waving jauntily. They never saw each other again.

Back in London, depressed at having lost part of his past which had given him such delight, dejected at the thought of what had happened to an old friend, and aware that his own arthritis was bound to limit his activities more and more in the years to come, Fred began to wonder if he would turn into another Brooks, self-deluded, his talents of limited range, finally failing to achieve his ambitions.

He rejected the word failure from a financial point of view. His books were selling as well as ever, with reprints and popular editions after the first printings were exhausted. He had a large and faithful following of readers, chiefly women, who enjoyed his novels, particularly those dealing with high society. He could go on writing formula stories till the end of time and nobody would complain, and his bank balance would grow ever larger. But was that what he wanted? He wondered what had happened to the young man who had dreamed of becoming a great writer, an entertainer with a deep purpose, a stylist, a passionate advocate of fine feelings. How had he turned into a purveyor of sentimental romances for spinsters without noticing that his dreams had faded and his style turned into clichés? What had happened to the emotions that had really touched his heart, and to the imagination that laziness and facility had stultified?

He looked at his achievements and the exercise was depressing. He had written over fifty books – there they were on his bookshelves – and most of them he could not remember having written; the settings, the plots, the names of the characters even – all meant nothing. Only a

few of the titles struck a chord of memory; only half a dozen still meant
something to him, something he was proud of and willing to defend
because they had artistic integrity. He had felt the characters to be true as
he wrote about them; he had related to their emotions and lived through
their lives. *David Blaize* was the book he felt closest to. *The Luck of the
Vails*, in spite of being over-written in parts, was another favourite. He
also remembered *Sheaves* and *The Climber* with affection, and that was
about all. Fifty books, and only four to rest his reputation on. What kind
of literary career was that? he thought, and in an unaccustomed mood of
self-criticism he was harder on his achievements than he need have been.
But he was in a backwater, and if he were not to flounder there he must
reach the bank quickly and find new flowing water.

Thirty years ago *Dodo* had been published, and that was the
cause of his present discontent. A huge, popular success, it had brought
him fame and money, but it had given him the idea that all he had to do
was sit down and dash off his amusing little stories in order to gain the
admiration of the literary world. Now his career seemed to have reached a
state where he could not move forward on the same lines, but might even
be receding. There were so many novelists who produced one or two
books a year and continued doing so for their writing lifetime, and when
they were dead sank into oblivion. Fred did not want to be another
Robert Barr, Claire de Pratz or E. S. Stevens (whose *The Veil* went into
seven editions), but he knew that his mark was fading and that he would
join the ranks of the great unknown unless he stopped drifting.

His self-examination went deep; it was honest and eventually wholesome. The pleasure he took in writing, the ease and lucidity
of his style, were not enough. He needed to observe more critically and
feel more intensely. In his own words he had not been delving into
himself and others, only turning over the patch of ground he had already
prepared, and setting in it cuttings from his old plants. His characters
bustled about, and talked with sparkle. Some were weak and some noble,
but they lacked blood and guts. He had plastered fake sentiment over his
lack of feeling for his creations; there was absolutely nothing of himself in
them.

The next question was to decide what to do about it. He
could, he supposed, give up writing altogether before readers and critics
were tired of him and crossed him off their lists. But he couldn't face the
prospect of a life without a pen in his hand and a sheaf of paper in front of
him; and as he wrote for profit as well as pleasure it would hardly do to
cut his income so drastically. He must change direction, he decided. He
would not try to stage a comeback with fiction of a higher quality, but
would instead turn to biography and memoirs. Both would need extensive
research, powers of observation and the retentive memory he prided

himself on having. Shadows would have to give way to reality, and the hard work involved would make impossible the lighthearted approach he had previously adopted. He relished the prospect of serious application to his craft, but was apprehensive too. He had been frittering himself away for so long that he might discover there was little genuine talent left.

One of the first books that Fred sat down to write during his early days at Lamb House was an account of the Benson family between 1867 and 1896 – the year of his own birth and the year of his father's death. He called it *Our Family Affairs*, but it was as much an auto-biography as a family saga. Even of the eight photographs, three were of himself. He described the Benson homes at Wellington, Lincoln, Truro, Lambeth and Addington with great detail and affection. The account of his first five years was chiefly a mixture of misty impressions; Beth was the only person who was not just part of the general landscape but a human being with personality. She entered into every memory of those early days.

Slowly, as infancy receded, his parents, brothers and sisters became more solid, more part of a coherent pattern. He was able to describe Wellington College, nursery incidents, his first reading lessons, and his mother as a glorious sunlit figure, but still not as wise and loving as Beth. Nellie and Maggie were still dimmish figures, Martin and Arthur were even more so as they were away at their private school. He remembered visits from his mother's three brothers and from her mother, and the three aunts who were his father's sisters. The only figure still unrealised was his father. It was not until the Bensons moved to Lincoln in 1873 that Edward Benson became real, and the more he was known, the more he was feared. Fred was puzzled about that for he knew that his father loved them all with the tenderest love.

At Lincoln Fred had felt the stirrings of love that was not 'family' love for another person. There was much enjoyment during the Lincoln years; visits to the Bishop of Lincoln at Riseholme, holidays at Torquay and Skegness, and the pursuit of a multitude of hobbies. It was at Lincoln that he and a small boy called Willie Burton had exchanged clothes in the toolhouse, and where he used to stroke his mother's hair as she read Dickens to the children. When the move to Truro came in 1877 Fred was growing into adolescence and became fascinated by the natural world, collecting specimens of all sorts, animal, vegetable and mineral. He experienced the first family tragedy when Martin died, even though it failed to touch him deeply.

Temple Grove followed; three years of learning, growing, playing hard and working little, making friends and beginning to love poetry. Then came Marlborough, a strange new world of widening horizons, more friendships, visits to Switzerland, games, Latin and

Greek. During his second year at Marlborough, when his father had become Archbishop of Canterbury, he was able to describe life at Lambeth Palace and Addington Park and enjoy the sumptuousness of the family's new surroundings. His description of his mother's flowering into manageress, hostess and brilliant conversationalist, yet always with time for her children, is perceptive and loving, lightly amusing over her limitations and deeply understanding of the forces that took her away from her husband in religious matters. Fred described his late teens in ecstatic terms; at the end of which some kind of philosophy had begun to stir beneath the childish enjoyment. The habit of finding pleasure and interest in every experience he underwent now remained part of him for the rest of his life.

Eustace Miles entered his life and they went to Cambridge together. The fun went on, as did the games and, spasmodically, the work. Vacations at Lambeth and Addington, mountain climbing in Switzerland, were all full of wonderful moments. *Dodo* was started in a desultory way. The sunlit path was only clouded over by Nellie's death. After Cambridge and a triumphant tripos came excavations at Chester, followed by Athens and Fred's complete seduction by its beauty. *Dodo* was published to the acclaim of the public and *The Rubicon* to the savagery of the critics. The next three years were divided between Greece and Egypt, and then, in 1896, his father died.

There the book ends, quite suddenly. It is on the whole a bland book, with not much given away, a skilful skimming over the relationship between his parents, the sexuality of his brothers and sisters unrecognised, and his own barely hinted at.

Among the many letters that Fred received after the book's publication was one that gave him special pleasure. It was from Mary de Navarro, the actress Mary Anderson. Fred had fallen in love with her after seeing her play Hermione and Perdita in *The Winter's Tale* when he was an undergraduate. He had kept her photograph in his pocket and thought of little else but her for a long time. Mary de Navarro lived in Broadway in Worcestershire where later Fred visited her and got to know her well. She called the book a really dynamic work – a work of genius. She was entranced by the childhood passages and called the children 'darlings'. Her son at Cambridge was soon to receive a copy with all the Cambridge references underlined in pencil so that, busy as he might be, he would know what parts he must read. 'I feel highly honoured to figure so delightfully in such a book,' she went on, 'and that such an author should ever have liked my work gives me a feeling of real delight. How I love those hero-worshippings. I have had so many of them and can so understand them.' In a postscript she asked Fred for a photograph to put alongside those of all the people she had known and admired, including

Victor Hugo, Henry James, Robert Hichens and Hugh Walpole. And Fred must be sure to write on it....

The long and rambling letter that Fred received from a young Australian music student who lived in Melbourne was typical of many he got from lonely and impressionable young people, who felt that his accounts of friendships with other men helped them to come to terms with their own emotional difficulties. They found comfort in the way that Fred had expressed his own feelings as openly as he could. The young man wrote:

> I have a strong, and maybe unreasonable desire for your friend-ship, even if this does annoy you, you must confess it is an innocent young emotion on my part. You may also add, not without reason, that in face of the facts that you are years and years older than I, of different outlook, living at the Antipodes, it is a foolish and mis-placed one. There is little more for me to add on this theme. Probably you are amused at my asserting that I know what you are like. You will either not understand what I am driving at, and think it all foolishness, or else you will grasp the situation. In defiance of my first letter to you I will say I think there is quite a possibility that had we met in the ordinary way, things would have arranged themselves to my satisfaction....

And so on. This was not the young man's first letter (another had included photographs of himself 'in various attitudes'). Fred had replied to that, chiding him gently about having other topics of con-versation besides himself and giving nothing away, but when he read in the second letter that his correspondent might be coming to England at the end of the year and would like to meet him, Fred decided that the letter should be lost in the post. He could not cope with the heated imaginings of someone less than half his age. A swift cut would be better than a lingering illness, so the Australian pianist faded from the scene.

In late July 1920 *Queen Lucia* was published, and there could not have been a greater contrast to *Our Family Affairs*. Something rather less sweet than sugar had been dropped into the champagne, and the result was noticeably drier. With *Queen Lucia* Fred successfully entered into a new realm of social satire mixed with comedy and tinged with farce. It was a mixture, the ingredients of which he used for five more books in the next nineteen years. With penetrating ruthlessness, he speared his characters' pretentions and held them up for ridicule, though he always tempered his attack with affectionate understanding.

Emmeline Lucas (known as Lucia to her friends) has the

limelight focussed on her in all the six books. Even her formidable rival, whom she does not meet until 1931 in *Mapp and Lucia*, cannot match her in egotism, intellectual pretensions and skilful in-fighting. Lucia is one of the great figures in English comic literature. She is the acknowledged queen of Riseholme (a disguised Broadway in the Cotswolds), a village of false rusticity where crazes, fads and affectations flourish. Lucia lives at The Hurst, a fake Tudor mansion, with a dim husband who writes prose-poems and rarely emerges from the background; she bulldozes her way through the local society, impossible but diverting. All that can be said on Literature, on Music, on Art, is uttered by Lucia – so loudly and persistently that everybody else in the village resigns themselves to echoing her. The only possible rival is her friend Daisy Quantock, who is always making discoveries: Christian Science, Guruism, a Russian princess who can call up almost anybody from the spirit world, and lastly, some beautiful pink tablets to increase her height. Lucia always manages to annexe Daisy's discoveries, but the fireworks are always damp squibs. The guru turns out to be a curry cook who decamps with a heap of valuables, and the Russian princess is a bogus spiritualist wanted by the police. But such setbacks only make Lucia more determined to carry on. She continues to speak her Berlitz-Italian, plays Mozart as Mozart has never been played before, and rules her chief courtier Georgie Pillson with an iron hand in her velvet glove. Georgie is one of Fred's best bachelors. He has many of the characteristics of his predecessors: he is selfish and sentimental, he gossips, dusts his bibelots, and he tries frantically to retain a semblance of youth with dyed hair and a toupé; but his heart is sound, and every so often he rebels against Lucia's domination and asserts his individuality.

Lucia almost comes a cropper when Olga Bracely, world-famous opera singer, arrives in Riseholme and quite unconsciously plays the Bolshevik in Lucia's cultured kingdom. Miss Bracely can do all the things which Lucia only pretends she can do, and the result is that all her intellectual pretensions are shown up before the whole of Riseholme society. Even Georgie turns his worship towards the newcomer. By the time Miss Bracely discovers the harm she's unwittingly doing, out of the goodness of her heart she departs for a long tour of America. Lucia's sway over Riseholme is swaying in a very drunken fashion, but she doesn't know the meaning of defeat. With the departure of her rival she again dons her queenly mantle and is soon treating the absent singer with outrageous patronage. The inhabitants of Riseholme return to their old allegiance, and Lucia's autocratic control.

Fred's knowledge of human frailties are deployed in *Queen Lucia* to full effect. His people go over the top but Fred does not. His style is dry and controlled; the humour comes out of character, situation and dialogue. The monstrous things that happen are funnier because Fred keeps a straight face and holds farce at a distance. In spite of his insistence that the book was a piece of frivolity that had no lasting importance, he was wrong. Lucia will live with Mr Pooter, Jeeves, Mr Polly, Augustus Carp and the Provincial Lady as long as humour lives.

The critics in the main were enthusiastic, welcoming something that would help to make the wet summer more bearable, and grateful that it was not another novel about an erring husband and noble wife. It was called 'a matchless piece of satire', 'a story which touches off human foibles without hurting' and 'witty, satirical and more than a little wise'.

Rachel Ferguson, the Kensington writer, suggested to Fred that she should turn *Queen Lucia* into a play. She thought it the most subtly priceless book of its kind she had ever read, and had read it at least twenty times. She wondered too if Fred would care to collaborate with her. They would have to take tremendous liberties with the book, as it was too lacking in plot for the theatre. She went on to say that the reincarnation of Olga Bracely was an actress called Edith Goodall: that she had the same outlook on life, raciness of speech and kindliness and would be perfect in the part. Fred did not share Miss Ferguson's views on the possibility of success for *Queen Lucia* on the stage and the idea wasn't followed up. That didn't prevent Rachel from being a fervent fan of Fred's for many years.

*Lucia in London* appeared in 1927 and is the only book in the canon where most of the action takes place outside either Riseholme or Tilling. It happens because Lucia's husband's aunt (aged eighty-three and bedridden) has died in a private lunatic asylum, leaving Pepino a house in Brompton Square (No 25 and Fred's house without any change, from the churchyard at the back to the large music room), £3000 a year and a collar of very small seed pearls.

So Lucia deserts Riseholme to establish herself in London society, and with her superb effrontery and devious plottings succeeds in ascending rung after rung, each time kicking away the support that had put her there. Paragraphs in gossip columns announce her dizzy ascent, and Georgie, Daisy Quantock and the rest of her Riseholme friends feel both hurt and incensed at the way she has neglected them. They take to the planchette and ouija board and start a Museum, the *pièce de résistance* a pair of Queen Charlotte's mittens.

Lucia is presented at Court and scrapes an acquaintance with a princess; during her meteoric flight through society she acquires an Ambassador, a Marquis, a Countess and two Viscounts, to say nothing of a world-famous pianist, a flute-playing pugilist and a modern painter. In doing so she becomes so unbearable that when she and Pepino return to Riseholme for a weekend with some of her smart crowd, her old friends are not allowed to meet them, and she, in return, is snubbed by them.

Hermione, the gossip columnist, is really Stephen Merriall, who could be Georgie's double (to Georgie's fury), and the rumour is that Stephen/Hermione and Lucia are lovers – a rumour that she does nothing to dispel. Her cup of happiness runs over when she attends a ball at which there are seven royals and she is able to curtsey seven times.

Nemesis, however, steps in. At Adele Brixton's weekend party after a number of outrageous snobberies that entrance the secret society of Luciaphiles, who hang on her every word, she mistakes her bedroom and enters Stephen's. Both are horrified. For weeks they have been advertising the guilt of their blameless relationship – now they will never be able to resume it; it is all too embarrassing.

When Pepino becomes very ill Lucia leaves London immediately, without any regrets, events having become too sticky, even for her. They sell the house in Brompton Square and Lucia devotes her considerable energies to regaining her position as leader of Riseholme society, which she does by taking over Daisy's crown of Golf Queen, and appropriating her expertise with the ouija board. When the Museum burns down in the night, the prophecy of the spirit of *her* ouija board – he writes 'fire, water, moonlight' quite unmistakably – comes true. Lucia is home again and as triumphant as ever.

# CHAPTER EIGHTEEN

hen Arthur had emerged from what he regarded as a living death his old powers had been recharged. He bounced back into Cambridge life, hungry for a world from which he had been absent for so long; the companionship of young men, the writing of books and stimulating contacts with his colleagues. He had become his old acerbic self, employing all the delicate malice of which he was capable when somebody needed deflating, and enjoying quarrels with his best friends, particularly Percy Lubbock, who had fallen in love with a young artist. The artist painted Arthur, and the result so horrified him that he hid the offending picture in a garret.

Arthur saw less of some of his old friends. George Mallory, Geoffrey Madan, Edward Ryle and Carl Lyttelton had all married and so had become less attractive to him. But, fortunately, there was someone new to dominate his thoughts and his dreams as no one had before: George Rylands, whom he first met in 1923. This was the grandest of all his grand passions. Rylands was handsome, charming and lovable with, according to Arthur, 'thick and curly golden hair and eyes with a dancing smile'. Arthur, weighing eighteen stone, getting lame, conscious of his lack of physical attractions, was completely bewitched by the boy. They spent three golden days in Rye on a couple of occasions, but the intensity of his feelings inevitably began to fade, and as the summer of 1924 advanced the relationship grew cool. Arthur, easily irritated, and troubled by health problems, started to find niggling little faults in his beloved. How could he, turning into old age, and in his physical state, hope to have a lasting relationship with someone so young and desirable? It was foolishness, and Arthur decided to bring the affair to an end with dignity. Rylands got a First and prepared to leave Cambridge; and Arthur said his farewells without a sentimental scene, refusing to show that he had cared for the boy more than he had for anyone else for years. They continued to meet occasionally, but as casual friends, and Arthur's hurt gradually healed.

It was about this time that he consulted Fred on the subject that had, over the years, concerned them both: their predilection for younger men. They talked earnestly about their experiences, but could come to no satisfactory conclusion. Had they been thrown off balance by some sort of moral failing? Were their affairs unnatural, abnormal, were they more paternal than sexual in origin? Did they come from suppression? Had their whole attitude to sex been wrong, and if so, was it due to shortcomings in their upbringing? Was being brought up to regard all sexual relations as being detestable in their very nature the reason for their difference from the norm? How far were their parents to blame? They tried desperately to find answers, but they came out of the same door that they went in. Their suspicions about the deepest truths of their natures had been painfully probed. The wounds remained but they were to be covered up. Arthur was never again to have such an intense affair; and Fred had been content for some time to find his pleasure in old friendships whose romantic ardour had dwindled into calm affection.

In 1924 Arthur, curious to find out how rich he really was, counted his assets, and discovered with a pleasurable shock that his securities were worth over £98,000. He had always wanted to be a wealthy man but had never dreamed of having such a fortune. And by April in 1925 he had received many more gifts from his benefactress, including one of £20,000. His assets had risen to £120,000.

He spent the late summer of 1924 in Rye with various friends, including George Rylands, who was temporarily restored to favour. In September he paid a visit to Horsted Keynes to see Tremans again. He went with Lucy Tait and they saw Beth's grave and called on Marshall, the Benson coachman, who was slowly dying. Arthur had made the journey with some trepidation but was glad afterwards that he had gone. Now he need no longer be afraid of memories. 'They spill their bitterness as a stream drops its silt,' he said.

The new academic year at Cambridge brought a new scholar, Noel Blakiston, to stir Arthur's heart, but not violently and not for long. Shortly before the end of the Lent Term of 1925 he began to be troubled by severe pains in his side which, however, eventually receded. He was at Rye at the time and Blakiston arrived for a visit. They had an intimate talk about platonic love which gave Arthur much satisfaction.

Back in Cambridge the pains returned, together with shivering fits. His doctor diagnosed pleurisy and sent him to bed. He wrote to Fred, telling him there was nothing to worry about, and even joked about the convenience of being ill during May Week because he hated all the festivities that went with it. He refused to stop working, but then he suffered a heart attack, and after a few days of weakness and exhaustion he died just after midnight on June 17. Fred had been summoned by telegram and was at Arthur's side on the Sunday evening. 'Why have you come?' Arthur gasped. Then, 'I'm glad you've come...'

A memorial service was held in Lambeth Palace Chapel two days later.

Much later Fred wrote that he felt no real sense of personal bereavement at Arthur's death because, although they met at Lamb House for a few days each year, and always enjoyed each other's company on those occasions, they had little contact apart from that. He had felt a brotherly regard but no great warmth. Over the years they had grown apart, each with a different way of life, and the age difference had accentuated the lack of close communion that binds friends together.

Fred did himself less than justice when he wrote in that strain. He and Arthur may not have been close, but Fred had been a great source of strength to him during the years of his illness, and had received glowing letters of thanks for his support. All their letters to each other had been warm and friendly, and though Arthur could be grumpy and Fred sometimes less than genial, there were always the family memories that kept them from drifting too far apart.

Apart from his mother and Beth, Arthur had been closest to Hugh, knowing his many faults, but forgiving them because he knew that he shared many of them. He knew that Fred would be a better friend, and reveal none of the selfishness that was at the heart of Hugh's nature, but he couldn't help loving Hugh in a way that he could not love Fred. It was Fred who shared the expenses of Maggie's stay at the Wimbledon nursing home with him, and Hugh who hardened his heart against her, but it was with Hugh that Arthur could relax. He never quite accepted Fred's plunge into the world of high society, feeling that he was trivialising his life and wasting his talents; there was always a slight feeling of irritation towards his worldly brother. Having rejected both religion and the scholarly life, Fred was not being a proper Benson, Arthur thought.

Arthur's will, which he had made in 1922, confirmed his own assessment of his wealth. His gross estate was valued at £112,000, with net personalty only £1,000 less. The executors were Fred, Stephen Gaselee, a Cambridge Fellow and friend, and the Bursar of Magdalene. It was a complicated will. Fred received a straight £13,100, personal effects, family plate and pictures and, after various gifts to the College, friends and servants, two-fifths of the residue of the estate, in trust for life, and a quarter of the three-fifths remaining. So he was very much richer at the end of it all. He was also left all his brother's papers, though Arthur had stated that in diaries and certain biographical studies he had written 'very freely and intimately about living persons and private matters', and he therefore directed that Percy Lubbock should examine these and select portions for possible publication, as long as nothing was made public which might distress anyone concerned. Any proceeds from such a publication were to be shared between Fred and Percy Lubbock. It was

Arthur's opinion that certain parts of his works should be destroyed, and other parts sealed up and not read or examined for fifty years.

It was decided that the Old Lodge, which was too big to be a set of rooms for one Fellow, and was no longer needed by the College, should be pulled down and the site used for more useful buildings. So Fred had to dispose of the contents. All the thousands of books, after some of Arthur's friends had had their pick, were destined for a university institution. In spite of Edmund Gosse's careful searching, there were no valuable rarities among them. The four million word diary was passed over to Percy Lubbock. While examining Arthur's papers Fred found evidence of an Arthur that the outside world had known nothing of: a deep-seated frustration, the feeling of having failed to express his real self; and there was a packet of letters that Fred described as 'very dangerous' and which had to be burned immediately. Fred never divulged in what direction the danger lay and speculation is useless; but it is something to know that at least once in his repressed and blameless life, Arthur had been involved in something so indiscreet that the world was not to be allowed to know the details, even after his death.

Hugh's letters were among the mass of material, but unfortunately not Rolfe's, which Arthur must have destroyed. In fact, many clothes baskets full of unwanted papers of all kinds went to the college furnace, and it took Fred many days to empty Arthur's over-flowing cupboards, shelves, boxes and drawers. It was a saddening experience for him, and a tiring one too, as his lameness made movement difficult and climbing ladders impossible. The weather was chilly, rain filled the gutters, and an air of desolation surrounded the Old Lodge.

Fred was thankful to get back to Rye, to the ministrations of his devoted staff. He was now fifty-eight years old, looking rather soldierly with his clipped grey moustache and short neat hair. His face was drawn but his eyes were as bright and blue as ever. He remained an exuberant host, friendly and gossipy.

About a month after Arthur's death Fred was approached by Edward Ryle, an editor with the publishing firm of George Bell, sounding him out about a memorial volume to Arthur, with contributions by those who had known him well at Eton and Cambridge.

Ryle had been associated with Arthur in both places, at Eton as a valued House Captain and at Cambridge where Arthur was his tutor. At one time he had been one of Arthur's special young men, and Arthur had been thrilled when Ryle had carelessly thrown an arm round him. His only fault, according to Arthur, was that he spent too much time on athletics. When they met again in 1923 Ryle was a staid married man, 'elderly-looking and bald, uninteresting and self-absorbed,' according to Arthur. Ryle had not known of Arthur's observation, obviously, when he conceived the idea of his book. He asked Fred for reminiscences of Arthur's boyhood, early family and school influences, and he wanted to publish quickly while the memory of Arthur was still green. He was amazed at Fred's curt reply to his letter, which said that both he and Sir Edmund Gosse agreed that a year should go by before any tribute was issued. In addition, he did not entirely approve of the project.

But Ryle was not inclined to give up. He had approached a number of people, including Monty James, who agreed to contribute, and work was going ahead. Fred replied by return, insisting that the book should not appear until the following June. Ryle, also by return, informed him that everybody from the Archbishop downwards had said that the book should appear as soon as possible, and all the other contributors had intimated that they would do their best to send their contributions quickly.

Fred challenged Ryle's statement. All the contributors were *not* in accord with him. He was doing his best to see that his own book, *Mother*, was not going to be postponed for the second time. He had put it off once before so that Arthur's *The Trefoil* should not be adversely affected, but this time arrangements for its publication were already far advanced.

The correspondence continued at a brisk rate. Ryle sat down to write a long reply, setting out again all his own reasons, and those of the contributors, why publication of the memorial volume should appear without undue delay, but if Fred was convinced that his book would suffer from the previous or simultaneous appearance of Ryle's, then he would postpone publication. Would early in 1926 be acceptable?

Suddenly there was a *volte face*. Fred withdrew his objections and consented to the October publication. He still refused to contribute or to explain why, but Ryle was grateful for small mercies. Fred's last letter on the subject complained that the tone of Ryle's early letters had been peremptory and rather disagreeable, but he was willing to dismiss the whole matter. Everything, he added rather sourly, was settled to Ryle's repeatedly expressed wishes and he was free to show the letter to any of the contributors.

*Arthur Christopher Benson As Seen By Some Friends* appeared late in 1925, but without contributions from Fred or Sir Edmund Gosse. The correspondence between Fred and Ryle had lasted twenty days, between July 2 and July 22. It was marked on Ryle's part by friendliness and consideration, on Fred's by coldness bordering on incivility, an attitude that often permeated his business letters. This curtness was in marked contrast to the exuberance of his books and his sparkling conversation, as if he could not be bothered to be more than barely civil unless he had an audience.

The book that Fred had been concerned about, *Mother*, was published a few months before the memorial book for Arthur. Arthur had also written a biography of his mother, but had decided not to publish it, although a friend had found the manuscript absorbingly interesting, leaving the field free for Fred. It was the last book Arthur wrote and the friend regretted his decision, especially after reading Fred's book, which he thought less complete than Arthur's.

In *Mother* Fred tells how he found his mother's diaries and made considerable use of them. 'Should any reader think that I have exceeded the limits of due discretion, my excuse must be that I believed it could only benefit him to learn something of the inner history of a life so beautiful as hers.' But the book is really Fred's story, from his father's death in 1896 to his mother's in 1918. Ben is the heroine but Fred fills the foreground. By putting his mother in the background he gives a truer revelation of her character than would have been possible by any more direct or exclusive method. The background was indeed Ben's place in the family. From the age of twelve she had sedulously prepared herself to minister to the future Archbishop's comfort and convenience and to overcome the 'childish ways' which irritated his robust and energetic spirit. Mary Sidgwick married without love, but until her husband died she served him with complete abnegation, and for twenty-two years after his death she lived to sustain and comfort her children. She could not actively share their interests, she did not even sympathise with them. Though she kept an Arthur-shelf, a Fred-shelf and a Hugh-shelf, and would never lend a book from any of them, none of her sons' books, with the exception of *David Blaize*, ever gave her 'one spark of inspiration, one crumb of the bread of life'. Some were too quaint for her, some too worldly, and some were propaganda for beliefs she didn't share.

Troubles came to Ben – family illnesses, Maggie's insanity, Hugh's conversion to Rome and his premature death, Arthur's refusal to apply for the Headmastership of Eton; through all these and other trials the lamp of her serene and noble spirit continued to burn steadfastly in the background. Fred paid an eloquent tribute to her, though with perhaps too much reverence, ignoring the occasions when she could be gushing, over-solicitous and over-righteous.

About the others he is very outspoken. The portrait of Hugh is specially intimate and doesn't err on the side of discretion. Of his own life, and particularly of the days and the environment that inspired *Dodo*, he gives some equally vivid pictures. Apart from some occasional sentimental rhapsodies it is intensely alive.

Ethel Smyth was one of the many appreciative readers who had known Ben personally. She told Fred in a letter that she had just closed – with tears – his book, and wanted to talk to him about his mother. She had been at Tremans two or three weeks before her death and had arranged another visit in order to 'talk things out with her'. Then the news came.... She went on to invite Fred to a recital at which some variations of hers, written for flute, oboe and piano were to be played. The 'divine Goossens is the oboe', but Franselle on the piano was going to be too strong.... Her last comment returned to the book. 'I think you make Hugh more attractive than I ever felt him to be (!) and yet reveal the source of my instinctive unliking... "Whoso loveth not his brother whom he hath seen...etc."'

In 1928 Fred and Arthur's benefactress, Eugenia Langdon of Nottbeck, decided to mark their respect for Arthur by a tangible memorial which took the form of a stained glass window in the south transept of Rye Church. It was done in the style of the windows of Chartres Cathedral; the colours had the richness of jewels, and the brilliant glass mosaics were enclosed in round medallions which contained pictures of the *Omnia Opera*, 'everything on earth, in the sea and the sky, all beasts, birds and fishes that praise the Lord'. Among the birds Fred insisted that there should be an avocet, in memory of the one he saw shot at Salthouse in 1922, a horrible act which he had never forgotten.

Arthur was there in one of the medallions, dressed in his red doctor's gown and kneeling before a low desk. The figures of Archbishop Benson and Archbishop Davidson were also shown; the latter unveiled the window. Randall Davidson had recently retired after twenty-five years in the post. After the unveiling he received the Freedom of the Borough, and was pleased to learn that, by a statute never repealed, he could never be arrested in the streets of Rye.

# CHAPTER NINETEEN

n the mid-twenties Fred's arthritis had taken a tenacious hold of his hip joints, and he was never again able to know freedom from pain or to enjoy easy mobility. At first the trouble had manifested itself by twinges which irritated him by interfering with his enjoyment of golf, tennis and skating; then it progressed steadily to a stage when it was all he could do to hobble about with the aid of two sticks. He tried every remedy that he could think of, or was recommended to try, from the orthodox to the wildly experimental. He was advised to eat plenty of oranges, which he did, but apart from enriching his body with Vitamin C they had no effect on his hips. He had dead bacilli injected into his arm and iodine into his hips; he also took iodine internally. Then followed a course of massage and physical exercises. He went to Bath to drink the waters and Droitwich to float in brine.

While he was there he received a letter from Edmund Gosse referring to the manuscripts and proofs of his books which he had given to Arthur in years gone by. He suggested that Fred should destroy them. 'They offer no interest to posterity, and to descend to a vulgar detail – they have no pecuniary value.' He hoped that Droitwich would set Fred up. 'It does wonders. But beware when you take your walks abroad, that you do not crash through the saline crust. It is said to be extremely dangerous.' He finished with a possible epitaph. 'Pickled Body of Celebrated Novelist exhibited in Butcher's Shop in Droitwich still fresh after many years in the salt.'

Fred was persuaded that having a number of teeth extracted would help; it did not. Nor did a course of X-rays. The doctors of Harley Street took Fred's money and gave him in return hopes that were quickly dashed. He fared little better with the less orthodox practitioners. Religiously he drank herbal teas, wore a band of crystals round his neck and radio-active pads over his hips. It was only when an X-ray photograph showed that osteo-arthritis had reached an advanced and irreversible stage that Fred gave up all the rubbishy treatments and resigned himself to a future of wearisome invalidism.

The amazing resilience that was part of Fred's nature now came to his aid. He refused to despair. The knowledge that a part of his life was over for good did not cause him more than a temporary period of depression. He reasoned that he must remain cheerful because his disability was not serious enough for him to be otherwise. There were still many pleasures to take the place of those he had been forced to give up.

He would not complain to his friends, observing that in general people who groused about their illnesses induced boredom rather than sympathy; and in any case sympathy could only lead to self-pity, and for that there was no excuse.

Skates, golf clubs and tennis balls were relegated to lumber rooms, and field glasses were put away, but there had to be other amusements, ones which demanded little physical effort, like chess, playing the piano and bridge. Writing, of course, was as necessary to him as breathing, and entertaining friends was almost as important. Antique collecting became another enthusiasm; occasionally there was a gem of a find in the antique shops of Rye. He was most excited about finding the fourth century marble head of a statuette of the young Apollo, sitting on a shelf surrounded by pieces of modern junk.

Above all it was the garden at Lamb House that was Fred's chief preoccupation, though he had to subjugate his own wishes to those of Gabriel, the patriarchally bearded old gardener. He set out to create a garden within a garden behind the high walls of Lamb House. Beyond the west end of the property was a secret little enclave in which he had built a wooden summerhouse with two sides open to the garden, and had put down crazy paving and a lawn. He had a stone pedestal built in the middle of the grass and on it placed a marble bust of Augustus. The secret garden was Fred's refuge. He bolted the door that led from the main garden, sunbathed, and wrote his books; on dull days in the summerhouse, outside if the weather was fine, and enjoyed his privacy. Not an inch of the garden was visible from the outside world.

It was in the secret garden that Fred had his one encounter with a ghost. It was a hot day and he and two friends, one the Vicar of Rye, were sitting in a patch of shade near the door in the wall which led to the big garden. Both Fred and the Vicar saw a man pass the open doorway and disappear behind the wall. In the few seconds that it took the visitor to pass by, both Fred and his friend noticed that he was dressed in black and wore a cape which he tossed over one shoulder as he walked by. His face was turned away from them. They jumped up, moved to the doorway but saw nothing. The garden was empty. Some time later the Vicar saw the apparition again but Fred did not, although he was there.

Fred decided to turn the incident into a proper ghost story, and made the unexpected visitor the ghost of a former owner of the garden who had been executed three hundred years earlier for the murder of children. He embellished the tale with an atmosphere of horror, bringing in Taffy to whine with fear, and introducing a strange faint light to illuminate the walls. He read the story through, thought that it had a manufactured air and too much embroidery, and tore it up.

Gradually Fred became a stay-at-home. Rye saw him more than Brompton Square did, and the best houses in London missed him. Weekends at stately homes, too, were rarer. In the past he had stayed with the Earl of Leicester at Holkham Hall, with the Countess of Portsmouth at Whitchurch, with Lady Radnor near Sunningdale, the Sassoons at Lympne, and with the Earl of Athlone and his wife Princess Alice at Brantridge Park in Sussex. Now he avoided large social gatherings and preferred small dinner parties with a few friends. One of the most eligible young bachelors in Edwardian society had become a quiet, withdrawn, middle-aged man; still marvellous company with his humorous stories and acid wit, but with no ambition except to write his books and enjoy life as best he could.

In 1922 Elizabeth Mapp made her first solo appearance in *Miss Mapp*, creating as much stir among the members of the Benson cult as Lucia had done two years earlier. Elizabeth Mapp lived in Tilling, a picturesque little town surrounded by level marshlands and tall reedy dykes. It is on a hill and contains many roughcast and timber cottages, mellow Georgian fronts, cobbled streets and quaint corners. This is an exact description of Rye, and Mallards, the house she lived in, is Fred's Lamb House. It is described as having 'charming little panelled parlours with big windows letting in a flood of air and sunshine, plain, well-shaped rooms all looking so white and comfortable, and a broad staircase with narrow treads.' A flight of eight steps with a canopy of wisteria led to the Garden Room which was built at right angles to the front of the house, from the bow windows of which Miss Mapp could observe the comings and goings of her Tillingite friends.

Miss Mapp was a tall and portly lady in her forties, her face highly coloured, and benign when it was not being creased by rage or curiosity, as it often was. She smiled a lot, showing long white teeth, and her bulgy eyes could shoot out danger signals to anybody trespassing on her territory. She ruled Tilling as Lucia did Riseholme. Her friends were more outspoken, even on occasions rebellious, but caved in with the same unconditional surrender as Lucia's friends did, several counties away.

The chief member of Miss Mapp's court was Diva Plaistow, a dumpy little woman who scudded about like a thrush on a lawn and spoke as though she were a human telegram. She was Miss Mapp's only possible rival. Then there was quaint Irene Coles, a postimpressionist painter, suffragette and socialist. Her hair was cropped like a boy's, she wore knickerbockers and sometimes smoked a pipe. Major Benjy Flint, whom Miss Mapp was determined to marry, and eventually did, was gallant, pompous, a secret drinker, and an old fraud with his tales of service life in India. Slightly less prominent characters included the sable-clad Susan Poppit, forever flaunting her MBE medal, Algernon Wyse whom she later married, Mr Bartlett the Padre who came from Birmingham and spoke in a kind of archaic Scottish, his wife Eva, a sharp though timid little mouse of a woman, and Captain Puffin, the Major's drinking companion, who dies at the end of the book. The book is full of exciting, apoplexy-inducing situations, ranging from the finding of Mapp's secret hoard of food stored up in anticipation of a coal strike, the duel between Flint and Puffin that never took place, the appearance of Mapp and Diva in identical tea gowns dyed the same colour on two occasions, Mapp's discovery of the Major's secret drinking habits, the Wyse-Poppit engagement, to Captain Puffin's death by drowning with his head in his soup, his lungs full of oxtail. At the end of it all Tilling experiences a feeling of flatness that is only lifted by Miss Mapp rescuing Major Flint from loneliness by learning to play golf and going out to the links with him by the 11.20 train.

It is clear that Fred was obsessed by love for his preposterous characters. The claim that he was malicious and bitchy because they were women and he disliked women is patently untrue. Hugh had disliked women, and Arthur had been afraid of them, but Fred liked them, and had many women friends of all ages and types all through his life. Some of them were enchanting, some were intimidating, some sweet and silly, and others shrewd. In his memoirs he wrote about them with sympathy and understanding. But he loved to poke fun at certain types of women, to comment satirically on their snobbery, prick the bubble of their pretensions and laugh at their social antics. That does not make him a misogynist. He performed the same service for men. They came under his searching eye and were as mercilessly dissected as women were. In his comic books men are either wimpish, pompous, ineffectual or effete, and one could say from that that Fred disliked men, which is absurd. In comedy the sex of the characters is irrelevant; what is important is whether they are a source for laughter, and Fred found men and women equally ridiculous.

Fred found that, apart from his arthritis, growing old was quite a pleasant process, now that he was so comfortable in Rye. The thrill of being the life and soul of a party of people round a dinner table had waned, and it was no longer any fun to be at some grand and noisy function where friends, crushed together, had to struggle to communicate. At one time he would have welcomed the chance of waving a magic wand and being carried back to the days of his vigorous and enthusiastic youth, but now he would hesitate. The loss of his physical energy had coincided with the decline of his desire for experiences and love affairs; he was content to know that the old Fred, with his unbounded joy in living and his easily stirred heart, was still there, embedded somewhere in his frail, tired body, as much a part of him as his flesh and bones.

Fred was worried when he found that sometimes he was not enjoying writing as much as he used to, so he began to take more trouble with his work, revising and rewriting more conscientiously, wondering every time whether the book in progress would be the masterpiece he wanted to be remembered by. Fortunately, his enthusiasm returned when it was time for another dalliance with Mapp and Lucia and also when it was time to meet David Blaize and Frank Maddox again.

*David of King's* appeared in 1924 and continued the story of the friendship between the two young men when they were both undergraduates at King's College, Cambridge. If, in *David Blaize*, Fred was portraying himself as David, he had changed roles in its successor. Physically, David may have resembled the young Fred, fair-haired, athletic, with strong brown hands and dancing eyes, but in character they had little in common. David at King's was ingenuous to a degree and so clean-minded that he had reached the age of twenty without the slightest stain on his purity. He had never kissed a girl, let alone done anything more reckless, and he was shocked when his friend Crabtree was found holding hands with the girl in the tobacconist's. Crabtree, or Bags, as he was nicknamed, was sampling everything within sight with a keen appetite, even to the extent of consorting with *cocottes* in Paris. David, of course, called them cocoons and hooted with laughter at the thought of Bags with his painted ladies. 'If I'd got to kiss somebody, I'd kiss one of my friends. You for choice,' he told Frank, 'because I'm much fonder of you than the whole of the rest of them.' Frank replied that David always made him feel as if he had just had a bath with plenty of soap, and the conversation, which could have got serious and truthful if the author had been more courageous, ended in laughter.

Frank was certain that one day David would 'manifest himself in the ways of a man with a maid', and then the private David would be accessible to him no longer. Meanwhile, David had promised himself that he would remain a virgin until his wedding day. 'It isn't manly to cuddle a girl, or soak your mind in beastliness and probably your body as well. It's far more manly not to. When the time comes that I see a girl that I really want, I mean to go to her clean.' Then David confessed, to Bags this time, that he would like to 'do it' too, only he wouldn't.

It is in Frank's character, and in his achievements, that Fred can be more cleary identified: his fondness for younger boys, his knowledge that in the end he would lose his friend to the heterosexual world in which he felt an alien, his departure from Cambridge to work at the British School at Athens; and if Fred was writing of himself as Maddox, it is a valid assumption that David must be based on Vincent Yorke, adoration for whom Fred had confessed in his diary. He had shared rooms with Yorke for two years; they were inseparable during term time and in the long vacations they returned to King's to work together. Yorke's game at Cambridge was real tennis. So was David's.

Then the time came when they knew that boyhood was over and their ways must part. Yorke had grown up quickly and was feeling the need to spread his wings, to choose for himself, to distance himself from the highly-charged world of masculine ardours. 'We've loved each other, thank God,' said Frank/Fred, laying his hand on David's arm, then extending it round the back of his neck. 'I've been first in your life, and you in mine. Soon, now, shouldn't wonder, you'll meet a girl and fall madly in love with her and be frightfully happy.' Which is what Yorke did and eventually passed out of Fred's life. Only once did he refer to him again in his memoirs as the friend whose whistling had caused Mozley to turn back to his rooms, but did not mention his name.

*David of King's* is not all heavy breathing and sentimental renunciation. J. E. Nixon and Oscar Browning, first encountered in *The Babe, B.A.* as Mr Longridge and Mr Stewart, and later described under their right names in *Our Family Affairs*, reappear as Mr Crowfoot and Alfred Gepp, known as A. G. Their antics provide the comic relief and Fred had no difficulty in reproducing the actual words of Nixon and Browning remembered from his far-off undergraduate days, nor in recalling the glee-singing, Tintara wine and Borneo cigars dispensed by Nixon, and the boastful and snobbish monologues of Oscar Browning.

At the end of the book Bags gets engaged to a ripping girl called Ida, David's name appears on the Tripos list with a First, and he and Frank agree that though they must grow apart their old friendship is built into their hearts and will remain there always.

The book was as popular as *David Blaize*, being reprinted three times during its first year and twice more before 1930. It appealed to the same audience as its predecessor; nostalgic and elegiac, it both comforted and saddened its middle-aged readers who would never again know the pain and rapture of growing up.

# CHAPTER TWENTY

f Fred ever felt lonely during the years when he was unable to travel very far from home he had a large number of friends, in and out of Rye, on whom he could call, either for weekends, small dinner parties or for games of chess or bridge. Others he could call on when he went up to London for a short time. One of his closest acquaintances was Canon Fowler who from 1921 to 1942 was the Vicar of Rye, and whom Fred liked for his theatrical behaviour and extravagant gestures. They contrasted with his own line of dry irony with a quiet though telling climax. The canon's chief gift was for mimicry, which Fred found very amusing, even though his imitation of an old and deaf parishioner may have worn rather thin with repetition. They teased each other and occasionally behaved with boyish exuberance. The canon dined at Lamb House every week or so, and at Christmas Fred entertained him, his daughter and Mrs Jacomb-Hood, the widow of the artist who had illustrated two of his earlier books.

Francis Yeats-Brown was a frequent visitor to Lamb House. His marriage to a widow of Russian parentage, in 1938 at the age of nearly fifty-two, was both unexpected and not particularly welcome. Fred preferred his men friends to remain single. When they married it seemed almost as if they were denying the strength of former friendships. He felt the same when Eustace Miles married, and probably even more intensely that Vincent Yorke had deserted him when he too left one world for another.

Yeats-Brown, who had been devastated when *Bengal Lancer* was turned down for the third time, went to Lamb House to receive consolation, and there, sprawling on the grass, doing Yoga exercises to relieve the pressure of work, he revised the book yet again, but this time with Fred at his elbow to advise. It was not the first time he had called on Fred for help. His first book, *Caught by the Turks*, was published in 1919 and was a dismal failure, but it would not have been published at all had he not consulted Fred about every aspect of the story.

Yeats-Brown was assitant editor of *The Spectator* from 1926 to 1928, and introduced Fred to the reviewing team. For many years Fred wrote occasional reviews for the paper. He was present at Claridge's Hotel on October 30 1928 when a Centenary Dinner was given by Major the Hon. J. S. Astor. Among the eighty-six guests were Stanley Baldwin, the Prime Minister; Lord Hailsham, the Lord Chancellor; Lord Hewart, the Lord Chief Justice; and Evelyn Wrench, the editor. Fred's fellow writers included Sir James Barrie, John Buchan, John Galsworthy, A. P. Herbert, Hugh Walpole, H. G. Wells and Francis Yeats-Brown.

Major Archie Daukes was another close friend. He and his wife lived in Egerton Terrace, opposite Brompton Square, and he was instrumental in getting Fred interested in bird-watching. Mrs Daukes, however, was not one of Fred's favourite women because of her habit of interrupting other guests at Fred's dinner parties with irrelevant comments, thus upsetting the ordered flow of conversation.

George Plank, the artist who had illustrated *The Freaks of Mayfair* and designed Fred's bookplate – a pierrot astride a globe with a quill pen in his hand – visited Fred in both London and Rye. He lived in Sussex in a house designed by Lutyens and refused to have electric light installed on the grounds that an oil lamp gave a steadier glow. He introduced Fred to Lady Sackville, mother of Vita. Fred stayed with her at Brighton and the two liked each other immediately.

Radclyffe Hall and Una Troubridge lived in Rye in a succession of houses. In 1930 they took a furnished house in Watchbell Street, after staying for several months at the Mermaid Hotel waiting for renovations to their house (called The Black Boy) to be finished. They became acquainted with Fred and were friends very quickly. He teased Radclyffe Hall by telling her that *The Well of Loneliness* had only achieved notoriety because it had appeared in the summer of 1928 when all London society had left for Scotland or the Continent, and it was only an adverse notice in *The Sunday Express* in a blank week that had brought it to the attention of the public. The two women dined with him and he often visited them at The Black Boy, as did Noel Coward, Lady Gregory, and 'the famous trio', Edy Craig (Ellen Terry's daughter), 'Christopher' St John and Clare ('Tony') Atwood. After an illness Una Troubridge received flowers from Fred. At Christmas 1933 they dined with him. Radclyffe Hall rather shocked the servants when she appeared in men's clothes, except that her shirt was frilled rather than 'boiled'.

Dame Ethel Smyth had kept up her long friendship with Fred, and she was an occasional visitor to Lamb House. Her dress, though mannish, was not as outrageous as that of Radclyffe Hall. A tie, yes, but never trousers.

One of the few cousins that Fred kept up with was the Reverend Stewart McDowall, a science master and chaplain at Winchester. His son was Fred's heir. The chaplain was always welcome, but Fred had reservations about his wife; she was tolerated rather than liked. There were two other McDowall sons; all were on active service abroad when Fred died, and could not attend his funeral.

In March 1935 Queen Mary visited Rye, while she and King George V were staying at Eastbourne. She was an obsessive collector of antiques, some of which she paid for, and at Rye it was arranged that Fred should accompany her round the shops. She had met him before when she had taken her two granddaughters to see the Arthur Benson memorial window in Rye Church. After the shopping had been done Fred asked her if she would like to see Lamb House. He left her with her entourage in order to warn his staff of the royal visit but had only just got back before she was on the doorstep. The door was opened by a startled Charlie dressed, not to receive a queen, but to play golf. Fred took his place to welcome her officially and they had a chat in the Garden Room before she went off to have lunch with friends.

Sometime in 1936 Fred received a heart-broken letter from Hallie Miles, the wife of Eustace Miles. Since his marriage in 1906 he and Fred had met rarely, though Eustace and his wife were always welcome in London and Rye. When Miles left Cambridge he had first travelled round the world in 1892, then had taken a job as Assistant Master at Rugby. In 1900 he spent a year in America as Honorary Secretary of the Tuxedo Tennis and Racquet Club, and while there became Amateur Champion of America at Racquets, Tennis and Squash. So he and Fred, who was busy in Greece and Egypt, saw little of each other, except in 1902 and 1903, and again in 1905, when they were working together on their sports books.

In her letter Hallie Miles explained that Eustace had had to go into voluntary bankruptcy. He had no private debts at all, those he had were in connection with his business and lending money to people who hadn't attempted to repay it. The restaurant was forced to close, and they missed it greatly.

Eustace is ever so brave. So desperate our position has been that E. M. Foods were so pressed by their creditors that Eustace and I have received no fees or salaries for six months. Eustace's private estate was all held by Lloyd's Bank against his overdraft. There was no money coming in at all. I used all my savings to keep things going, then there was nothing for it but to sell all we could spare bit by bit – all Eustace's cups and medals and our old silver and a lot of furniture, books etc. The worst part was being so behind with our flat rent but by degrees I've worked it off up to this Christmas quarter; I've got it all in but £25. But the Bailiff is paying his daily

visit – seven shillings a day till that is paid ... As soon as we've paid
up the rent we are moving to a cheaper flat. I'm going to give up
even a servant in our new flat. I shall have to give Eustace lessons in
Domestic Science, as long as my health allows it I shall be able to
manage ... Do forgive this long letter, Fred. I feel as though I'm
writing to more than a friend, to a brother as you are so interwoven
in our two lives.

Her next letter was ecstatic.

Your wonderful enclosure has brought me to tears of thankfulness
and gratitude. I simply can hardly believe it that this nightmare of
the rent is over for the present. I really cannot thank you enough
but I believe you will be almost as happy and thankful as we both
are to know that you have helped so vitally two of your oldest and
most devoted friends who are almost in despair. The distress, so
rightly called, will be lifted tomorrow and we shall begin a newer
and freer life once more and move as soon as possible. You are
right, the very air seems poisoned. Dear Fred, thank you very
much, Hallie.

At the time of his trouble Eustace Miles must have been
about sixty-eight years old. To go bankrupt and have the bailiffs in was a
devastating blow, and the future looked bleak. But, with his income
from his books and fees from The Pelman Institute, he and Hallie
struggled on for ten more years until his death in 1948.

Now that Fred was living such a quiet life in Rye he
established a daily routine that enabled him to make the best of his
physical limitations and gave him as much time as possible to write. He
would breakfast at nine, after a cold bath run by Charlie, who also put out
the clothes to be worn that day. He would read through the newspapers,
then consult the cook about the day's menus. He had a gourmet's interest
in food and wine. There were two or three courses for both lunch and
dinner, with carefully chosen wine from his extensive cellar. He dressed
for dinner every evening even when he was dining alone.

After he had settled domestic affairs, and perhaps telephoned
his stockbroker or the people he was inviting to dinner on some future
occasion, he went either to the Garden Room or the Green Room upstairs
and began the day's work. He would write for between two and two and a
half hours then break off for a session on his Bechstein piano, playing
Chopin, Brahms or Beethoven. Lunch was served punctually at half past
one then, after a short rest, he would take some exercise. When walking,
golf or bird-watching became impossible he took a slow walk round the

churchyard. Tea was followed by more work, then a hot bath, change of clothes and dinner. After dinner, if there were no guests to entertain, he returned to his desk for another writing session. He then relaxed with a drink or perhaps a game of chess with Charlie.

Fred was determined to make his mark on serious literature; to rank himself with those writers he regarded as his equals. He knew he would never be a Hardy, Kipling or Conrad. He could not achieve his aim by writing more novels because his past efforts would be continually held against him. In their day they had seemed to him good enough, but the moods and trends of the depression years of the 1930's were altogether more serious. Who cared about lords and ladies, however amusingly they talked, in the kind of society that had disappeared after the end of the war? He had no knowledge of working-class life and could not write like Walter Greenwood or A. J. Cronin. He did not have the scientific outlook or the belief in the future that H. G. Wells had, and he had no patience with the cocky brashness of Arnold Bennett. He didn't feel like trying to enter the Galsworthy world of family sagas, nor that of Hugh Walpole. Nobody could be another Barrie – and as for the 'moderns', he didn't understand what Virginia Woolf or James Joyce were trying to do, and shuddered at the thought of even trying.

> No faintest breath of joy ventilates that hell of abysmal boredom in which they sadly caper. These unwearied dissectors strive to exhibit precisely and exactly what we are like inside, showing us something, but if it is the soul we see on the dissecting board it is something so minute, withered and kippered that we wonder if it can indeed be the genuine article. No pulse any longer beats in those flaccid and desiccated tissues, it is as joyless as tripe. If, as H. G. Wells once said, Henry James's novels can be compared to an elephant picking up a pin, then Virginia Woolf and her circle achieve the spectacle of an elephant not picking up a pin.

Such a view of modern literature, though unusually vehement and high-pitched, was in line with Fred's general conservative attitude to the times he lived in, and his habit of regarding the past through a golden haze.

There were so many avenues that Fred could not, or did not want, to explore that he was left with non-fiction with which to ensure his future reputation; in particular, biography. His first serious study was *Sir Francis Drake*, which appeared in the John Lane/Bodley Head series 'The Golden Hind', in 1927. Two years later came *Ferdinand Magellan*, in the same series, and in between Ernest Benn published *The Life of Alcibiades*.

*Sir Francis Drake* was very popular with critics and public. Edmund Gosse was particularly enthusiastic, saying that it was composed with unflagging vivacity and he recognised in it an incessant attentiveness. Although Fred was dealing with familiar matters he never failed to give an impression of novelty. His long practice of the art of fiction gave him the facility of making history amusing. Gosse had genuinely enjoyed the elegant and witty monograph, and had found the information about Queen Elizabeth very illuminating.

When the question of Magellan came up, the Director of Bodley Head was a little cautious. 'The subject,' he wrote, 'is not quite so popular as Drake, though it will undoubtedly make an interesting book.' He offered the same terms, an advance of £200 and a royalty of 12½ per cent rising to 20 per cent after 3,000 copies. Fred accepted. He knew that he was not going to make a fortune from either book, though he was proud of his scholarship and the vigour he had shown in tackling his new role. No longer could he just sit down and let the words pour out. Now he had to surround himself with reference books, file cards and notebooks. The work was exacting and tiring, but at the end of each book he felt triumphant.

*The Life of Alcibiades* shows that Fred's love of Greece had not abated with the years, and Alcibiades was an ideal subject to resurrect that devotion. As boy, youth and man he had a unique charm and distinction which continually earned him forgiveness for his most outrageous escapades. He was vicious, insolent, adorable, detestable, brilliant and fickle. He had the face and body of a god, the wit of Aristophanes; he was the very incarnation of the spirit of Athens.

Fred spent several pages on an exposition of Socratic love and found himself in something of a dilemma. 'It would be quite idle to deny that it was accompanied by a vast deal of unnatural vice,' he wrote, 'but it would be equally idle to deny that it also gave rise to blameless and noble friendships untainted by physical indulgence.' On the whole Fred preferred Plato to Socrates. The former defined the Athenian lover as no carnalist, but one who filled the mind of his beloved with manliness and noble aspirations; whereas Socrates insisted that he was the lover of the body's beauty, though he himself had won the struggle between the higher nature and the lower instincts, and he was purged of fleshly desire. Fred was forced to admit that Alcibiades had not lived up to his mentor's ideals but he skipped over the subject of his hero's numerous male lovers and his 'unnatural instincts'.

The book is extremely readable. Fred's scholarship is unobtrusive, he writes with a great deal of charm, and he describes the death of Alcibiades affectingly. One enthusiastic reader was Randall Davidson, the Archbishop of Canterbury. 'My dear Fred,' he wrote,

'Alcibiades is delightful and I am profoundly thankful to you. It will be a veritable revelation to the young England of today, tho', because they don't any longer learn Greek, care not a bit for classical heroes.'

There had to be a change from serious biography, and *Spook Stories* (1928) and *More Spook Stories* (1934) were a welcome interlude, expressing the highest point of Fred's interest in the supernatural. Monty James had first awakened his interest in the subject, and though he never quite achieved such a mastery of the genre, he became a very skilled practitioner. His first venture into the realms of ghosts was in 1912, when *The Room in the Tower* was published. The title story, a dreamlike tale of vampirism, is the best of the collection. This was followed by *Visible and Invisible* in 1923. *The Step*, printed in a small edition in 1930 by H. V. Marrot, became the first story in *More Spook Stories*.

Fred never quite decided whether or not he really believed in ghosts but his agnosticism was tilted towards a desire to believe that something existed after death that conventional religious ideas could not satisfy. Though he realised that many mediums were frauds he was impressed by many of the things he saw and heard at séances, enough to make him refuse to dismiss out of hand the general view that psychic phenomena were all rot. His own experiences of the paranormal were few and not very convincing, but he pursued his quest with enthusiasm.

Fred was a traditionalist when it came to ghost stories. He kept to a well-tried formula, but within the limits he allowed himself he developed an amazing variety of plots and situations. He was especially convincing in his descriptions of locations, and created an atmosphere that exactly matched the occasion. As a result, the emotions he aroused were genuinely menacing, awe-inspiring or portentous. He set his stories in bleak and wintry places, or by a sullen sea, in remote villages or on wild marshlands, and added to the atmosphere by the weather he chose to accompany the tale. Haunted houses, of course, dominate the scene, but no two are alike. Each has its own smell, its own draughts, its own history and its own ghost. He didn't try to find lucid explanations for his ghosts. By a touch he could produce a hint of explanation that would justify his development where it was fitting that it should be provided, but in the case of the plainly inexplicable he was content not to probe too deeply.

*Spook Stories* and its successors are perhaps more bland to the palate than the earlier two titles, although sensitive scalps will still prick in response to their thrills, and spines still shudder. Three of the ghosts avenge a murder, one foreshadows a murder, one fierce spook monkey kills a surgeon for robbing a mummy of its silver-clamped vertebra, one avenges an eviction by ugly hallucinations, a group of Black Mass celebrants is broken up by the return of its deceased leader, and a Cornish wishing-well first satisfies a jealous woman's spite and then punishes her. *Pirates*, the last story in *More Spook Stories*, is remarkable for its gentleness and charm. In it Fred put all his feelings about the loss of childhood and the impossibility of returning to the past. A life had come full circle, and it had to end with the ghostly return of the protagonist as a child.

If Fred's ghost stories don't quite reach the perfection of Monty James's, they do not fall far short. They are quite different in style and presentation but the horror is often just as graphic and explicit. *The Bus Conductor* was turned into an episode of the classic British film *Dead of Night* and *Mrs Amworth* was filmed for TV. Fred's stories originally appeared in popular magazines. His own favourite among all his short stories was *How Fear Departed from the Long Gallery* which first appeared in the *Windsor Magazine* in December 1911. Altogether he wrote well over seventy ghost stories. Over fifteen years many of them were published in *Hutchinsons' Magazine*, often illustrated by 'Blam' – Edmund Blampied. Between 1923 and 1925 several stories were published singly or in pairs, in small editions, by George Doran, Fred's American publishers. Even the American *Weird Tales* magazine carried his stories.

Two more books of this period which can be bracketed together are *As We Were* (1930) and *As We Are* (1932). The first is another recapitulation of family history, another slant on the Bensons, first met in *Our Family Affairs*, then again in *Mother*, but this time is not limited to family affairs, nor is it a collection of anecdotes about some of the great personalities of Victorian times. It is a detailed, if one-sided, treatment of a period, the second half of the Victorian era to the end of the Golden Age brought about by the savagery of the Great War. The book opens with a chapter about a pincushion. Big as a blancmange for eight people, made of rich crimson velvet and decorated with white glass beads and draped with tassels it stood on a dressing-table in the best spare bedroom in the Master's Lodge at Wellington School. Fred used it as a symbol for Queen Victoria herself (she had visited the school in 1864) and for the age she represented. The picture of the Queen is a version of the full length biography which appeared in 1935. A couple of chapters of family history follow, ending with Edward White Benson accepting the post of Archbishop of Canterbury. Then there is an interlude in which we meet Lady Henry Somerset, whose husband was mixed up in a scandal involving homosexual behaviour, and her sister, who married the heir of the immensely wealthy Duke of Bedford. Lady Henry, ostracised by society, turned to the reclamation of drunken and criminal women. Her sister became a close friend of the Bensons, and went abroad with them to Switzerland. She was one of an eminent group of women who asked the Archbishop to stop the 'moral rot' which was ruining London, the centre of which was the Prince of Wales's set.

Mr Gladstone and Tennyson come under Fred's microscope before he embarks on his own affairs − Cambridge (with more anecdotes about J. E. Nixon, Oscar Browning, Walter Headlam and Charles Waldstein), Athens and archaeology. Then suddenly we are back in society listening to Fred extolling the 'great lady', extinct after the Great War, who, above everything else, was possessed of that 'queer old quality called dignity'.

The three 'ladies of distinction' he writes about are the Duchess of Manchester, Lady Londonderry and Lady de Grey, later Lady Ripon. They were all gracious, imperious, condescending, strikingly beautiful and, by today's standards, appalling in their arrogance and greed, but Fred thought they were marvellous. Two of the many scandals of the nineties were the Tranby Croft affair in 1891, which involved the Prince of Wales, and the trial of Oscar Wilde in 1895. Fred writes of both protagonists with sympathy. He is careful to avoid mentioning the offence with which Wilde was charged, it might have been stealing birds' eggs or defacing a library book. But he brings new information and a perceptive insight into the affair, born out of his personal knowledge of the man.

The Pre-Raphaelites, Whistler, Ruskin, Swinburne, Gosse − all pass before Fred's bright and critical eye; so does *The Yellow Book* and literary figures of the nineties; in particular, Henry James. The book ends with Fred on Capri, not realising the dangers of the assassination at Sarajavo and the imminence of war. When war came 'the old order of secure prosperity smouldered into ash,' he wrote, 'and England will know it no more.'

*As We Are* is the second half of a diptych. In *As We Were* Fred dealt directly with the life of a period, his aim to create a mood and an atmosphere; here he was constrained to put most of what he had to say into the form of fiction, accompanied by a commentary. Much of the book is occupied by an ingeniously devised parable of the passing of a great Edwardian country house called Hakluyt, which was owned by Lord and Lady Buryan. The history of the house and its owners encompasses the decay of the landed class, the growth of Socialism, the questioning of accepted moral standards, and the revolt against the formal etiquette of society. Fred dwells on the chasm that was widening between the war generation and its successors, seeing those who fought as unhappy intermediates. 'They resented the imbecilities of their elders, they detested those who had escaped their own fate and assumed their privileges; they were a generation apart.' He sees society as doomed, agrees that it was time for the aristocracy to go but, paradoxically, regrets all the same the loss of what had been so valuable to the country.

The Hakluyt story engrossed Fred so much that he produced a little masterpiece, but then he had to deal with the actualities of war and the post-war years, and the difficulty was to shift the scene and readjust the lighting. The problem is not entirely or happily overcome. There is a lack of proportion, urbanity and literary grace; instead we get some vigorous and effective journalism and some rather querulous and questionable judgments. There are some sketches of eminent men: Arthur Balfour, Randall Davidson, and two distinguished Germans in England who suffered obloquy during the war. Fred suggests that the philosophic statesman and the political Archbishop had their gifts misdirected, that each should have had the other's job.

Fred then turns to men of letters, and there his prejudices show blatantly. He tries to be fair, but it is easy to see how distasteful he found modern trends in literature. James Joyce is an example of his dilemma: is *Ulysses* a work of supreme genius or a record of unreadable trivialities? There is no doubt in Fred's mind. Similarly with *Mrs Dalloway*, and Joyce and Woolf are contrasted with Henry James, to their detriment. James, Fred claims, had developed the stream of consciousness method, analysed and perfected it forty years before. He fulminates against the flood of novels which were wholly concerned with sex and sexual perversion – 'a pathological deformity of minds rather than a mark of unspeakable moral obliquity' he calls it, though he absolves *The Well of Loneliness*, regarding it as a serious study, able and sincere.

D. H. Lawrence is treated as a tragic genius, an enigma with mutually contradictory solutions: sheer naked sensualism, spiritual self-torture, unbridled carnality, and gnawing emptiness. He hated the beauty that roused desire, the yearnings of his soul, and all men and women who found peace and satisfaction in sexual intercourse. Lawrence feared men and women, whom he both loved and hated, and most of all he feared himself, for they and he were his torturers. It is a penetrating, not unsympathetic picture of Lawrence, but written without the final leap into the heart of the man.

Fred got his own back on Arnold Bennett who had told a mutual friend that Fred could not write. He sent a message back to say that, as he couldn't write, he had sent for one of Bennett's books to read. To his despair he found that he couldn't read either. He grants Bennett one great book, *The Old Wives' Tale*, but he slashes *Imperial Palace* into small pieces with great enjoyment.

The last chapter is a strange mixture of politics, religion, economics and sociology. Many of Fred's conclusions are simplistic. He expresses guarded hopes for the future of England under a National Government, and looks forward to the League of Nations as a pointer towards peace, but, in truth, what Fred really wants is something he can never have: a return to pre-war times when values were solid and revolution only a nervous babbling; when people knew their places in a well-ordered society, and when both family and national unity was a real, not an illusory concept. Fred was out of his depth, and it showed. *As We Are* did not have the same impact as its predecessor.

In 1931, in *Mapp and Lucia* (originally to be called *The Queens of Tilling*), the fearsome couple finally meet. Lucia has been mourning her dead Pepino for an inordinately long time, much to the impatience of her Riseholme friends, who find things dull without her to direct their lives. To help her 'convalescence' she rents Mallards, Miss Mapp's house in Tilling, for three months, and Georgie Pillson rents the nearby Mallards Cottage. Before they take up residence Lucia saves the Riseholme fête from disaster due to Daisy Quantock's inept producing, and rewards herself with the star part of Queen Elizabeth in the pageant.

In Tilling, Lucia and Elizabeth Mapp clash time and time again; there is almost open warfare. Mapp resents Lucia's lordly airs and Lucia is infuriated by Mapp's pushiness and deceitful ways. Lucia is disconcerted by the arrival of Mr Wyse's cousin, the Contessa Faraglione, and the threatened disclosure that she cannot really speak Italian, so she pretends to be ill and Georgie leaves Tilling hurriedly.

When that crisis is over Lucia and Georgie find that they are enjoying life in Tilling so much that they decide to live there permanently. Lucia takes Grebe, a house outside the town skirting the marshes. Mapp sneaks round the kitchen looking for Lucia's recipe for Lobster à la Riseholme when a sudden flood sweeps both ladies out to sea on an upturned kitchen table. They are away for three months, having been picked up by a fishing vessel. During that time Georgie inherits Grebe and Major Flint Mallards. Georgie arranges a memorial service and erects a cenotaph, but fortunately does not take possession of Lucia's house. But Flint buys a car, puts his house up for sale and goes to live at Mallards. When the castaways return at dead of night they see their cenotaph and are shocked. The Major is ejected by an irate Miss Mapp. Lucia and Mapp hold simultaneous public readings of their experiences at sea, but only the Major attends Mapp's function and they end up engaged. Mapp holds a celebration lunch, serves Lobster à la Riseholme and gives the game away; she *had* stolen the recipe. Lucia makes an acid comment and Mapp is again discomforted.

Four years later came *Lucia's Progress* and though Mapp still tries to topple Lucia her efforts are nearly always aborted. Georgie develops shingles and has to grow a beard; as it turns out to be a different colour from his hair he has to dye it and takes pride in his resemblance to *The Laughing Cavalier*. Lucia embarks on a new career, buying and selling shares, with all the aplomb of an experienced financier; the rest of Tilling follow suit and there is intense excitement and rivalry until Lucia loses interest.

A vacant seat on the Town Council is contested by both Lucia and Mapp: they tie at the bottom of the poll. Mapp and the Major have married by now and Mrs Mapp-Flint seemingly innocently gives the impression that she is pregnant and lets out her skirt; but takes it in again when she can no longer fool her friends with her 'wind-egg'. As a result of financial stress she sells Mallards to Lucia who, queen-like, takes up her 'official residence' again. To counter some animosity towards her from her long-suffering subjects she becomes the town's benefactress. She has the organ renovated, plants trees, and confers benefits on the Cricket and Football Clubs, both of which elect her as President. The publicity and the glory bring her the offer of a co-opted seat on the Town Council and she is chosen to be the next mayor. Her last triumph is her marriage to Georgie, though both have decided very firmly that it is to be a marriage of convenience only and that locked bedroom doors will be the order of the night.

*Trouble for Lucia* (1939) begins with Lucia, now Mayor of Tilling, having to decide who shall be her Mayoress. All her female friends try to persuade her to choose them; the married ones send their husbands as emissaries. Mrs Mapp-Flint is finally chosen, on the grounds that Lucia will be able to keep a closer watch on her. After various mayoring ceremonies Lucia opens Diva's new tearooms. She refuses to play bridge for money and is cold-shouldered by her friends. When she relents, the arrival of a policeman at a card party at Diva's causes panic. Lucia and Georgie learn to ride a bicycle, in secret. When they are proficient enough to appear in public Lucia loses control of her machine, is fined for dangerous driving and becomes a heroine. Cycling then becomes the latest craze. Quaint Irene paints a picture caricaturing the Mapp-Flints; it goes to the Royal Academy and is chosen as Picture of the Year, first to the Mapp-Flints' horror and then their joy.

Olga Bracely appears on the scene, and the Tilling ladies all fall for her, appearing in makeup and with waved hair. There is confusion about whether or not Lucia has met Poppy, Duchess of Sheffield. When the Duchess stays overnight at Mallards nobody believes that she was actually there. Lucia reaches the lowest point of her fortunes when Georgie goes off to stay with Olga in France, the Council rejects her offer of her portrait and the duchess snubs her. To relieve her feelings she rounds on her friends and accuses them of disloyalty, and they are suitably shattered. Georgie returns and gossip about him and Olga comes to an end, the duchess comes to stay again, and to make sure there is no mistake this time Lucia invites the whole of Tilling society to dinner. Her troubles evaporate like snow in sunshine and she resumes her reign unchallenged.

The Mapp and Lucia books are rich, subtle and devastating comedies of manners. Fred does not spare his characters, exposing them frequently and gleefully to temporary humiliation, but he always allows them to bounce back again. The absurd and magnificent Lucia is completely fascinating. She has vitality, a high magnetic power, and more hypocrisy and snobbery than her rivals – though they are almost as agreeably awful as she is.

The six novels appeared between 1921 and 1939. It is hard to say that any one is better than any other. The standard of comic writing remains constant, invention never flags, the character-drawing is as scathingly accurate in the last as in the first. They are an important record of a pocket of Edwardian manners that survived into post-war England, exaggerated as it might be. It was an anachronism that Fred helped to demolish, but he did it, not with fury or distaste, but with a humorous, teasing affection, inventing a fairytale world in which there is no war, no depression or poverty, no sex, no class warfare, nor any intimation of the upheavals that were changing the face of society. It was a remarkable achievement, made more so by the fact that Fred didn't fully realise what he was doing, and when it was done he looked on his Lucias and his Tillings as frivolous and amusing exercises that were not intended to do more than provide pleasant entertainment for a few hours.

# CHAPTER TWENTY-ONE

n 1933 Fred, now a well-known and highly-respected member of the community, became a magistrate. Every morning he took his seat on the Bench and dispensed justice with firmness and fairness, and occasionally with impish humour. Most of the cases were of a trivial nature – cycling offences, parking without lights, petty pilferings, neighbours' quarrels and drunken husbands. On one occasion the daughter of a Town Councillor was booked for leaving her car without lights in an unlawful place. She appeared in court before Fred who was in one of his playful moods. He spun out the case as long as he could, in order to entertain the gallery, asking the Town Clerk whether the accused had any previous convictions and whether there were any mitigating circumstances. The angry and embarrassed young woman was eventually fined five shillings.

Fred was incensed to read a letter in *The Times* from a Lord Norris complaining that country magistrates were a farcical body, idiotic by nature and wholly ignorant of the law. Fred wrote a sarcastic letter to the newspaper inviting the noble lord to visit Rye, commit some petty larceny and he would soon see how competently and correctly he would be dealt with. This provoked a heated reply from a County Magistrate from Devon.

> Sir,
> Lord Norris can take care of himself. I have been since 1906 a County Magistrate; there has, I think, since then been a steady deterioration, but in one respect the quality of the Bench has not varied, viz. a complacency, conceit and cocksureness, so well evinced by your letter. I wonder what you know about the rules of evidence – and how many times you have condescended to put pen to paper in taking a note. No sane man would allow *you* to deal with him in any case, whereas in the two instances you suggest, he has the right to a jury. But your letter is typical and in its way rather magnificent.

A choleric outburst; fighting words indeed. Fred replied directly to his correspondent, and in the course of his letter suggested that High Court Judges became atrophied intellectually in old age and were therefore not fit to sit in judgement on their fellow men.

The magistrate replied:

> You know as well as I do that where a man's whole life professionally has been given to the study of a single subject he does not lose, with the passage of years, his knowledge of, or judgement upon, the subject. Those like yourself who play at being a judge or a lawyer as an agreeable if rather pompous diversion for an hour or so every fortnight – between games of ball – are indulging themselves in a performance where the trained mind has no part.

This cutting remark was too near the truth for Fred's liking, and he hastily brought the correspondence to a close. It must have been the only time he had been bested in an exchange of incivilities.

One morning in 1933 Fred received a telephone call from Captain Edwin Dawkes, a local lawyer and the Town Clerk, asking if he could see Fred on an important matter, which turned out to be an invitation from the Town Council for him to be the Mayor of Rye the following year. The members of the Council had been impressed by Fred's performance as a magistrate, by the esteem in which he was held in the town and by his generosity towards good causes. Fred was staggered to receive such an out-of-the-blue proposal, and couldn't help feeling slightly amused. But he expressed himself as highly honoured and promised a speedy decision.

Deep down Fred knew that there was no way he was going to refuse, but he had to counter his instinctive feelings by dredging up all the reasons he could against such a major upheaval in his life. The main one was that he had no knowledge of municipal affairs, nor did he particularly wish to acquire any. He had never been to a Council meeting, nor did he know any of its members. He was ignorant of what they did at their meetings – hospital management, sewerage, the running of the workhouse and the condition of the streets were all closed books; and it all sounded desperately dull. Then there was the fact that he did not live in Rye all the time. Though his visits to London were becoming much less frequent he still had the house in Brompton Square which he needed as a base to entertain his friends. Would his occasional absence from Rye, especially in the summer, he wondered, be a bar to the execution of his Mayoral duties? And would his duties mean that his writing would be adversely affected? And what about having to make speeches on official occasions when everybody knew that he hated speaking in public. Then, still pretending that he was going to refuse, Fred thought up the most convincing excuse of them all. *Lucia's Progress* was due to be published later in the year, and in it, by coincidence, Lucia was going to be elected Mayor of Tilling. Would her preposterous antics, and those of Elizabeth Mapp-Flint, her Mayoress, bring the office into disrepute if people knew who their begetter was and the post he held? He put this last point to Captain Dawkes, who assured him that the Council would be aware of the distinction between real life and fiction.

All Fred's objections melted away when his butcher told his cook that it would be a capital thing for Rye if her employer were to become Mayor. So he capitulated and accepted the Town Clerk's offer, as he had meant to do from the beginning. He chose as his Mayoress Mrs Jacomb-Hood, the widow of his artist friend of many years ago. She lived in Rye and was noted for her devotion to civic duties; and they lived together in 'municipal sin' for the duration of his Mayoralty.

Fred was the 645th Mayor of Rye. He was both awed and amused on the occasion of his investiture in 1934, being unfamiliarly attired in a fur-trimmed crimson robe, with a double chain round his neck and a cocked hat on his head. He walked behind the mace bearers from the Town Hall to the George Hotel and, after refreshments, he and the other Town Councillors went out on to the hotel's balcony and threw bagfuls of pennies down to the street so that children could scramble for them, as children had been doing since medieval times; though in those days the pennies had been heated and the recipients had burned their childish fingers.

Fred took great pleasure in all the pomp and ceremony associated with his office as Mayor, and as Chairman of the many committees he had to attend. He found he had an unexpected gift of diplomacy in dealing with arguments and acrimony and the general contrariness of his fellow citizens who helped him to settle the financial affairs of the town. The celebration of King George V's Jubilee was in the offing, and months of planning ahead were necessary. Fred had to cope with a number of inappropriate proposals, from a new swimming bath which would be a heavy charge on the rates to a scheme for all the inhabitants of Rye to dress in eighteenth-century costume for three days. In the end they decided to hold a festival for children and have a tea party at which commemorative mugs would be distributed, with fireworks to close the proceedings.

Fred was amazed to find himself happily involved in duties which were quite outside his usual orbit. He had not been used to mixing with 'ordinary' people, and any kind of social service had been quite foreign to him; now he readily spent much of his spare time working for the community. He found that the interruptions to his once placid and orderly life were actually stimulating. His interest in writing gained a new impetus, and his infrequent visits to London took on an extra glamour because he could not be there just when he wanted, but when his duties allowed him to escape for a few days. Rye was the busy, humming centre of his life; London was a quiet, almost provincial backwater.

In 1935 Fred was re-elected Mayor of Rye and again he spent his mayoral salary in a few weeks, and for the rest of the year he had to subsidise his outgoings himself, which he did willingly. During June of that year his beloved Welsh collie, Taffy, died. He had been a constant companion for seven years and Fred greatly missed the dog's intelligence, sense of adventure and fierce determination to guard his master's interests.

In the summer of 1935 a new Lord Warden of the Cinque Ports was appointed, and the ceremony of installation was held at Dover Castle, as it had been on similar occasions for 600 years. With the Mayors of the other Cinque Ports and Antient Towns and Limbs of the Cinque Ports, and with assorted Town Clerks, Recorders and mace-bearers, Fred attended the service in St Mary's Chapel where he heard the Archbishop of Canterbury bless Lord Willingdon, the new Lord Warden. Afterwards the Ancient Court of Shepway was held in the grounds of Dover College, and Fred, as Speaker of the Cinque Ports, had to ask the Lord Warden if he would observe the franchises, liberties, customs and usages of the Ports. The Lord Warden promised solemnly that he would, and Fred felt relieved; there was always a chance that the noble lord might have rebelled against tradition and said 'No'.

In the autumn of 1936 Fred was asked if he would continue as Mayor for another year. Now he left Rye on fewer occasions than formerly, and never for more than a week or two, so he could accept the offer with a clear conscience. At least his physical presence would be available, and his attendance at Council meetings would give him an excuse to avoid the winter fogs of London.

The Coronation of King George VI was arranged for 1937. Because he was Speaker of the Cinque Ports Fred could claim his right to attend the King on his Coronation Day in Westminster Abbey. If his claim was granted he automatically became a Baron of the Cinque Ports, an honour which lasted for one day only and did not carry with it the right to a seat in the House of Lords. Moreover, the temporary Baron had to provide his own costume – gold-braided cloak and waistcoat, black breeches and white stockings. Fred, because of his lameness, reluctantly had to forego the honour of standing for hours on end in Westminster Abbey holding a banner, and asked his Deputy Mayor to take his place. Fred boasted later that it must have been the first time that a commoner had conferred a Barony on another commoner of his own choice (even if it was only for a day) without being challenged.

In July 1937 Fred gave the West Window to Rye Church in honour of his parents. He had designed it himself; the idea had come to him when he was sitting in his secret garden a few days before Christmas in 1936. He had had a vision of angels swooping down through the sky to alight on the stable roof at Bethlehem, in the presence of the ox and the ass, the Virgin and Child, and Joseph. The Kings of the East approached across a meadow of flowers from the left, the shepherds from the right. He made a rough sketch while inspiration was still with him. Because his ability to draw was non-existent the angels resembled either moths or aeroplanes, but the intention was clear, and his designer friend Hogan, who had been responsible for the Arthur window nine years earlier, was called in again. The particular shade of blue that Fred insisted on was finally achieved after sixteen attempts to capture the exact colour of the morning glory flower that had blazed over the walls of the Villa Cercola on Capri. Apart from the angels and the Nativity figures the window contained the figures of Charlie Tomlin, disguised as a shepherd, and Taffy, still greatly missed. Fred himself appeared in the bottom righthand corner, dressed in his red mayoral robes.

Dr Lang, Archbishop of Canterbury, came to Rye to unveil the window and the ceremony was attended by the new Lord Warden. There was a civic procession and an Archbishop's procession, and the service had a Christmas theme related to the window, with carols and the Christmas lesson. Fred was not a regular churchgoer, not being a religious man, but he occasionally attended services in Rye Church, and in Brompton Oratory in London. The colours and pageantry appealed to his sense of theatre, he found the music sensuous and the whole atmosphere calming.

An event of 1938 that gave him enormous pleasure was his election into an Honorary Fellowship of Magdalene College, Cambridge, a gesture of gratitude by the College for everything that Arthur had done for the place during his Mastership. The invitation was made by A. S. Ramsey, the Bursar of Magdalene. 'As a distinguished author, you were the most fitting of all living writers to succeed to Hardy and Kipling,' he wrote. Kipling had died in 1936, so the College authorities must have deliberated long and hard to choose his successor. To be in such company as Hardy and Kipling must be, Fred thought, a tribute of the highest order. After he had become an Honorary Fellow he offered to endow the College with enough money to found a scholarship or exhibition, an offer which delighted the body of Fellows when it was announced at a College Meeting.

Fred then asked them if there was anything of his which the College would like to possess and the Bursar said that as Hardy and

Kipling had left them manuscripts of their poems, a manuscript of one of his works would be a splendid acquisition to their archives. Ramsey went on to hope that Fred would soon visit Magdalene and take his M.A. degree; they would make it an 'honourable occasion'. Fred sent them a bound manuscript copy of *As We Are*, which had been published in 1934, and he and Charlie went to Cambridge to receive his degree.

In the same year the Freedom of the Borough was conferred on him, and this again was an honour he relished, as the last Freeman had been Archbishop Randall. The ceremony took place in the Town Hall, where Fred had to present two pennies to the Town Clerk in payment for his Charter of Freedom. Fred fumbled in his pocket for the coins, and there was an amused moment when he thought he had no money on him. A Councillor offered to lend him twopence, but eventually Fred found the fee, handed it over and was given a receipt.

The Mayor then handed over a copy of the resolution and extended to him the 'Right hand of fellowship'. He explained that different customs were observed in the different Cinque Ports. If the presentation had been made at Sandwich the Mayor could have claimed twelve pennies instead of two, but in return Fred would have had the right to sell fish in the street on Sundays. In his address the Mayor went on to praise the countless acts of kindness and generosity that had made so many people happy. Mr Benson, he said, had always presided over Council meetings with incomparable humour and charm; and as for his magisterial activities, the reason why there were so few cases coming before the Rye Bench was probably because of the way Mr Benson administered the law and his persuasive charm towards criminals in convincing them that it was better to be good than clever.

Fred, ever ready to dispense with speech-making, said in his reply that he would express his gratitude in a very simple way, and what he left unsaid he wanted them to credit him with thinking.

To mark the occasion he was presented with a silver model of the *Rose Marie*, the first armed frigate launched by the British Navy in the time of Henry VIII. She had fifteen guns, her captain stood on the deck and there were sailors in the crows' nests. 'Nothing will give me greater pleasure,' Fred said, 'than to have it constantly under my admiring eye on imaginative voyages on the table cloth. After dinner I shall often bewilder the crew by calling "port please".' The ship would remind him of the breezes of friendship that swelled its silver sails.

This last honour was a fitting conclusion to his years of service to Rye. In 1939 he started to write his last book of memoirs which he was going to call *A Few People*. He found it heavy going. His usual fluency seemed to have dried up; the effortless ease of composition eluded him. It worried him. Usually he sent his manuscript, illegible as it was, to a typing agency, and when he received the typed copy he would make any corrections before sending it to the publisher; but now the work advanced slowly, with much revision of the first draft. Not only was he worried about the book, he also started to suffer from the curse which had affected his father, sister Maggie and brother Arthur so alarmingly – the black depressions that attacked without cause or warning, making life almost unbearable until the cloud lifted. Fred was never as severely affected as the others, and it was only when he was old and the constant pain of his complaint made him tired and grumpy that he gave way to moods when nothing was right, his work displeased him, and life wasn't worth living. He grumbled constantly about himself, his aches and pains, but only to Charlie, and Charlie bore it all with patience and good humour. The amazing thing was that none of his friends suspected there was this undercurrent of moodiness and apprehension; to them he was as affectionate and entertaining as ever.

Towards the end of the year Fred knew that there was something wrong with him that was not connected with his arthritis, his lowered spirits or his inability to write at his former rate. He began to lose his appetite and his weight dropped. He felt tired at the times when normally he would have been vigorous, his voice grew hoarse and he was troubled by a persistent cough. His doctor arranged for him to see a specialist at University College Hospital in London. There they suspected cancer. An exploratory operation was performed and the disease was found to have attacked the tissues of his throat. He died on February 29, 1940, a few months before his seventy-third birthday, before any steps could be taken to alleviate his condition. He had smoked twenty to thirty cigarettes a day for many years.

Charlie was at Fred's bedside when he died. Affection as well as the habit of service had kept him there for the ten days that Fred was in hospital. Other friends had called, but there was little they could do and they didn't stay long. Francis Yeats-Brown was one of them. Fred could hardly speak. 'It's such a bore,' he whispered. 'I can't write!'

Fred knew that Charlie was there and was glad of it. The day before he died he turned towards him, smiled and said, 'Oh, Charlie.' Those were the last words he spoke.

'He was my friend as well as my master,' Charlie said afterwards. 'I have lived for nothing but him. Now he is gone and I cannot think what I shall do.'

From the time that Tremans was given up and Fred went to Rye until his death this sterling young man had been at his shoulder, anticipating his needs, guarding him from stress, and providing a strength that the older man drew on gratefully. Charlie was of humble beginnings and though his language and initially his accent were those of his class, he knew exactly how a gentleman should behave, and behaved that way, without ever giving himself airs or pretending to be other than a houseboy who had had the good fortune to become the personal servant of a greatly respected master. He was fiercely loyal and supportive. When Fred was old and tired and in pain he would say, 'I can't do it, Charlie.' 'Oh, yes, you can, sir,' Charlie would reply confidently, and Fred did it. Fred taught Charlie how to play golf and chess, and he was such an apt pupil that the time came when he regularly beat his master at both games.

Fred was buried in Rye Cemetery, just outside the town. The Bishop of Chichester conducted the service. The organist played Bach organ voluntaries, the hymns were 'Jesu, Lover of My Soul' and 'O God, Our Help in Ages Past'. Psalm 18 was sung to Hopkins in C and the Nunc Dimittis to Barnby in E. The chief mourners were various cousins, Charlie Tomlin, Rose Edwards and Ivy Green, cook and housemaid, and George Eton, the gardener.

What Fred had meant to the people of Rye was expressed by the Mayor, Councillor George Marsden, who said:

> He introduced into the Council Chamber the flavour of a unique personality. His delicate sense of humour kept the Council in good temper, and he frequently resolved into clarity and commonsense an atmosphere befogged with prejudice or passion. Though he wore an air of detachment he was far more conversant with the details of civic life and organisation than was commonly supposed. Few persons other than the recipients were aware of his many acts of kindness and charity.
>
> It was a rare pleasure to partake of his hospitality at Lamb House. A meal which, though simple, was a work of art; bland vintages; the severest of old silver; urbane and witty conversation embellished with reminiscences drawn from a widely varied experience; and afterwards, perhaps a stroll in his lovely and beloved gardens. I liked the smaller one best, his sanctum, which combined a classic simplicity with the naiveté of the early Primitives.
>
> In the busy streets of Rye, and in its quiet corners, many potent figures of its historic past still live and hold commune with those who have ears to hear. With these E. F. Benson is now numbered.

Fred would have liked that appreciation, especially the references to his bland wines and severe silver, and he would have chuckled at hearing his secret garden described in such high-flown terms.

# CHAPTER TWENTY-TWO

red's agent sent *A Few People* to Longman, Green about ten days before he died and it was published towards the end of 1940, but under a new title, *Final Edition*. The reviews were unanimously enthusiastic. Fred had at last written the masterpiece it had always been his aim to produce. Detached, yet most attentive, he had passed through life noting insatiably, commenting both seriously and frivolously, and exercising wide-eyed criticism of himself no less than others. What he wrote about himself was always interesting, for he was a highly interesting person, richly endowed by fortune for the pursuit of his vocation. What he wrote about others was either extremely amusing or moving. With its elegant and polished style, *Final Edition* is the last testament of a charming, intelligent, civilised, yet in some ways unfulfilled man who watched life go by from the other side, unable or unwilling to plunge into the moving stream.

There is no trace of age or disabling illness in the book. All through it one is given a sense of intimate contact with Fred's family, and with that part of him he is prepared to reveal. His successes as a novelist were earned too easily in youth, but in later years he took infinite pains to . develop his talent and give it genuine expression; and *Final Edition* completes this aspect of his work as well as ending it altogether. It is rich in humour, anecdote and feeling, produced with courage and an undimmed spirit.

*Final Edition* is principally the story of the Benson family again, from the days at Tremans to the honours bestowed on Fred at Rye and Cambridge. All that has gone before in *Mother* and *As We Were* is gathered together and knitted into a long and harmonious account of the joys and travails of Ben, Maggie, Arthur and Hugh, up to the death of Arthur in 1925. Interspersed with the family history are memories of and anecdotes about some of Fred's many friends and acquaintances: Lord and Lady Battersea at Overstrand in Norfolk, Sir George Lewis (Oscar Wilde's solicitor), Philip Burne-Jones, gifted but dilettante artist with whom Fred laughed a lot, Marie Corelli, fantastically unreal but a primitively genuine character, the strange inhabitants of Capri during the *South Wind* period, Henry James at Lamb House booming at his typist, and many more.

Fred was the last of the Bensons, but he did not grow bitter when he was left alone. He describes his life in Rye and how he came to terms with his disability. 'This has altered my amusements,' he told Francis Yeats-Brown, 'but it hasn't interfered with my happiness at all.' His zest for life is evident in all the stories of his later years.

And yet, detailed and loving as his observations are, one feels that he is standing behind a glass screen, that by putting out a hand one would touch, not living flesh, but a cold surface. Amusement, irony, detachment – he exhibits these in all his writings, but, one wonders, is there too much detachment? Where is shock, outrage, despair? Was he shattered by Maggie's tragic end? Did he feel desolate when Ben died? Was he more affected by Arthur's death than he cared to reveal? Family deaths are described regretfully, lovingly, but coolly, as though the distance in time between the event and the recording of it had been there from the beginning. What of his deepest feelings? His books and his letters reveal tantalisingly little of the Fred who lived behind his observer's mask, and it is not likely that we shall ever melt the ice that is between him and us. He does not intend us to know the secrets of his heart, just as he never revealed his generosity. He remains aloof, an enigma. As a youthful laughing pagan, an eligible bachelor and socialite, and a quiet, almost spinsterish invalid, and as a writer through all these phases, Fred Benson was a very private man.

# APPENDIX

p to the beginning of the First World War Fred wrote effortlessly and relentlessly, publishing two or sometimes three books every year. The pre-war novels were usually a mixture of melodrama and sentiment, touched sometimes with the maudlin. Very few genuine feelings were allowed through the froth and the glitter, the cynicism and the moralising, the smart dialogue and the calculated plotting; but they pleased an ever-growing band of readers.

Fred's first four books have already been commented on. The rest need some critical commentary to show how his development into a writer of stature was patchy and inconsistent, for his net was flung too wide in his efforts to satisfy different segments of his public. But gradually he shed some of his graver faults, and matured in both style and content.

He left Methuen for Heinemann in 1899 and stayed with them for many years, though he had brief flirtations with more specialised publishers for his sports books, or because he had too many finished manuscripts for one publisher to handle in a year. During the war he went over to Hodder and Stoughton and Hutchinson; his later books were shared between Hutchinson and Longmans, Green.

After the failure of *The Rubicon* came the failure of *The Judgment Books*. 'The decline of Mr Benson continues,' said the *Saturday Review*, and *Bookman* was indignant because a grave subject had been spoilt by hysterical sentimentality, and should be passed over in silence.

Frank Trevor, an artist, decides to paint a picture of himself – his whole self, the Jekyll and Hyde of him. He is going to depict the man who loves Margery, his wife, and the man who has led a dissolute life in Paris. As the picture progresses he becomes scared at his obsession with it and is terrified at what is happening; his personality is disappearing and he is getting nothing in return.

His face in the picture is vicious and guilty, and so is the real one. He is raising the ghosts of the past and they are taking over. He knows that as soon as the picture is finished he will die. Confessing everything to Margery he implores her to help him. She leads him to his studio and they look at the picture. 'Can you see the *café chantant* in it?' he asks in a hoarse whisper. 'Can you see Paris, and the cruelty and sweetness and bitterness of it? Can you see Claire in it, the end, the pleasure, the weariness, the – the Morgue, yes, that is where I saw her last...' For answer she puts a dagger in his hand. In a frenzy he stabs the picture and tears it into shreds. The evil spell is broken and Hyde is Jekyll again...

A month or so after Fred's father died in 1896, *Limitations* appeared. Cambridge still occupied a lot of Fred's thoughts and the book opens with some witty talk between two undergraduates, and it seems that we are to enjoy a comedy of university life. But the hero, Tom Carlingford, refuses to read for his Tripos and, in order to become a sculptor, leaves Cambridge for Athens to study the Antique. He marries a saintly Philistine, and battle between incompatible ideals and personalities is soon joined. The wife's ignorance of his art makes her jealous of a more sympathetic woman friend, but that strand of the story is not developed because it would have been unthinkable for Tom to contemplate infidelity. In the end he surrenders his ideals because of the necessity of supporting a wife and child after he has lost his money. When Fred's characters lose their money they usually manage to exist on an income of several thousand pounds a year, but in Tom's case it is different. He has got down to his last fifty pounds, and does not know how he is going to be able to keep on his suite of rooms, nursemaid, and landlady who provides their meals. So he ends up by making little statuettes of goddesses for the London dealers, work which he detests but, having put his art behind him, he becomes reconciled to his lot.

The disquisitions in the book on art and religion are tiresome, and there is too much vacillation between profundity and vivacity. The reviewers found little merit in it and advised Fred to remain content with the success of *Dodo* until a few rejected manuscripts had taught him how to use his undeniable talents.

Only two months after *Limitations* came *The Babe, B.A.*, in January 1897. It had been written earlier than *Limitations* because extracts had appeared in *The Granta*, beginning in January 1896, and that accounts for the book's scrappiness. It was written in high spirits and its aim was simply to amuse. With no attempt at a connected story it is a series of detached episodes set in Cambridge and centred round The Babe,

> a cynical old gentleman of twenty-one years of age who played the banjo charmingly. His particular forte was dinner parties for six, skirt dancing and acting, and the performances of the duties of half-back at Rugby football. His dinner parties were selected with

the utmost carelessness, his usual plan being to ask the first five people he met, provided he did not know them too intimately. With a wig of fair hair, hardly any rouge, and an *ingénue* dress, he was the image of Vesta Collins, and that graceful young lady might have practised before him, as before a mirror. But by far the most remarkable point about the Babe, considering his outward appearance and other tastes, was his brilliance as a Rugby football player...

The Babe was based on J. F. Marshall, a clever fellow from King's who took the Mechanical Science Tripos. He was a fine banjo player and founder of a very successful club which took a large concert party to Oxford and elsewhere. He shared rooms with Eustace Miles and excelled at racquets and real tennis. When Marshall learned that he had got a first he gave a memorable party for a dozen of his friends, at which he produced a special drink poured into a boating mug with a glass bottom. It looked like ginger beer but was actually green Chartreuse.

*The Vintage* (March 1898) was very different from anything that Fred had so far attempted. As a romance of the Greek War of Independence it was not an unqualified success, but it showed promise in an entirely new field. Its chief faults were an over-elaboration of detail and a certain heavy-handed literalness; pruning would have greatly improved its impact. Fred's thorough knowledge and love of Greece and the excellent war scenes, cannot be fully appreciated because the reader has become too tired to care.

*The Vintage* was illustrated by G. P. Jacomb-Hood, an artist who did a lot of work on the serials which *The Graphic* ran. In his book *With Brush and Pencil*, published in 1925, he describes a journey to Greece with Fred for the purpose of collecting material for his illustrations. In southern Greece they were joined by an American photographer called Burton Holmes. They visited the excavations of old Corinth, where Fred discovered in a cornfield the ruts worn by chariot wheels in the rock; then drove to Sparta to pick up a cavalcade of mules, muleteers, cook and guide. They spent days travelling west and north through the mountains, staying in empty cottages or a mountain monastery, and climbing into the clouds to find the remains of the Temple of Bassae, a small edition of the Parthenon, and at Tripotomi Fred's eagle eye for ancient remains discovered inscriptions and carvings in the rock. They spent some days in the old sea-coast town of Nauplia, the scene of some of the incidents in Fred's story, and also visited Tiryns and Mycenae.

Another book that appeared in 1898 was *The Money Market*, a lightweight romance written for Arrowsmith's Christmas Annual, published in Bristol, and is a reversion to the style of *Dodo*. It has perhaps a certain period charm, but its characters are preposterous, particularly those who are excessively good, such as Percy Gerard, the hero, and Blanche, the heroine. When the story opens Percy is engaged to Sylvia, who is incredibly beautiful, but selfish and shallow. Lady Otterbourne, her mother, even more selfish and scheming, is in debt to Jewish money lenders, but Percy bails her out. At the age of twenty-five Percy inherits his grandfather's money, nearly three million pounds, and the magnificent mansion of Abbotsworthy. Then Percy learns that his grandfather has amassed such a large fortune by money-lending. The old gentleman had been the secret owner of the firm that had been dunning Lady Otterbourne. The blow is stupendous, but Percy decides to sell Abbotsworthy and get rid of every penny of the tainted money. He imagines that Sylvia will fully understand and approve of his actions, but when she refuses to marry a pauper (he will only have about £120,000 left) Percy is shattered. He meets Blanche by accident and they discover that their feelings for each other were more than friendly. He has fallen out of love with Sylvia by this time and proposes to Blanche.

In the meantime Sylvia has married the rich American who has bought Abbotsworthy, so that everybody is happy. Goodness has brought its own reward, but badness has done very well too.

*The Capsina*, which appeared in the spring of 1899, was a great improvement on *The Vintage*, to which it is a sequel. The Greeks and Turks are still fighting, and the slaughter of the Turks is quite thrillingly told, with Fred showing a genuine power for vivid and rapid description.

Capsina is a wild Amazonian maiden, chieftainess of the clan of Capsas, and the plot centres on her relations with Mitsos, hero of *The Vintage*. It is not an easy situation. Mitsos is married, and though he and the madly attractive Capsina spend much time together on her little brig, they both behave with the utmost propriety, despite her fire and his impetuosity. In the end Mitsos returns to his loving wife.

In the autumn of 1899 came *Mammon and Co.*, and Fred returned to the style of his first success, having got a little tired, perhaps, of his unappreciated efforts to become known as a historical novelist. In *Dodo* he was merely the amused onlooker; in *Mammon and Co.* he ranges himself unmistakably on the side of the angels.

Lady Conybeare is both heroine and awful warning; she comes to grief in the end and repents, but it is only because she has had a scare. For most of the story she is frivolous and heartless, wears orange chiffon, puts Marie Corelli and parsnips at the head of her list of dislikes, and cheats at baccarat. She is also unfaithful to her financier husband. In an excess of rage the jealous husband knocks her downstairs. This is only

one of the many incidents that lead to her unutterable despair, culminating in a serious illness when the doctors can save either her or her
unborn child. Fortunately Lily Murchison, her angelic young sister-in-
law, prays at her bedside and effects her regeneration.

In Lord Comber, the exquisite young man of thirty who
freshens up his makeup with rouge and antimony pencil in the lavatory of
the Bachelors' Club, looks at himself in the glass and says, 'Not a day
more than twenty-five', we have one of the first portraits of an effete male
character who wanders through many of Fred's books, being bitchy in
the background and snobbishly clinging to the coat tails of society. The
apotheosis of the type is Georgie Pillson in the Lucia books.

Fred always had such a character on tap. Was he trying to
tell us something? Was the character Regie Lister, John Ellingham
Brooks, or another of his gay friends? Or was he drawing a side of himself
that he dared not show to the world or perhaps did not even realise
existed? The only hint we have that there may have been something of
Georgie in Fred is Somerset Maugham's remark that he was 'not an
obtrusively masculine sort of person', but no other commentator has
suggested that Fred ever presented a less than conventionally masculine
front to the world, whatever lurked behind the facade.

Only one book was published in 1900, *The Princess Sophia*.
If it had not been for the two excursions into Greek history Fred could by
now have been called a single book novelist, because here is Dodo again,
but this time dressed up as the Princess of Rhodopé, a small principality
on the Albanian coast. Sophia is bored by her official duties; her obsession
is gambling, and this leads to both matrimonial and political consequences
which Fred treats with more frivolity than seriousness. Her husband and
the Prime Minister plot and counter-plot against her and one another
with farcical complications. Prince Leonard, her son, wins Rhodopé
from her in a game of roulette so that she is forced to abdicate. On taking
the throne Prince Leonard suppresses all forms of gambling, even
knuckle-bones, and sends Sophia off to Monte Carlo with a generous
allowance so that she can continue to indulge her passion for the rest of
her life.

John Maynard Keynes's father wrote to his son (then nearly
seventeen and at Eton) in 1900 that he had read *Princess Sophia* and found
it interesting though not a great work, as 'Benson is extraordinarily
careless on some points'. Apparently Fred talked about golf and bicycling
as if he were describing events happening towards the end of the nineteenth century instead of twenty or thirty years earlier. As applied to the
seventies many of his references were anachronisms.

Arthur once said that inaccuracy was a family failing, but
that Fred was by far the worst. He would shamelessly improve upon any

circumstance or occasion he was relating for the sake of a good story.

Fred openly acknowledged that the germ of his next novel, *The Luck of the Vails* (1901) came from Arthur, who used to tell a version of the story to his boys at Eton, and Fred dedicated the book to him. It was his best effort so far. The style is sombre, direct in its effect, and wholly compelling.

The 'Luck' of the Vail family is a mysterious goblet, encrusted with precious stones, which in the life of the family is alternately lost and found. On the goblet is an inscription: 'When the Luck is found again, Fear both fire and frost and rain'. Young Henry, Lord Vail, finds the Luck by accident, but does not worry about the threat of the legend. At the same time his Uncle Francis, the next heir, comes on the scene. He is an old gentleman of benevolent appearance, rosy-cheeked and with engaging manners. Immediately Henry is assailed by an amazing series of disasters. Uncle Francis, whose habit it is to play the flute at every crisis, is solicitous for his nephew's welfare and rejoices in his hairbreadth escapes. They live in an old house which is full of secret passages through which dark exits and entrances can be made. At the end there is an exciting midnight scene when Uncle Francis turns out to be the villain. He almost succeeds in killing Henry, but fails and dies horribly himself. The Luck is smashed to smithereens so that it can never work its havoc again.

The book is not completely successful as a supernatural story because much of it is a lavish picture of rich, selfish people shot through with the relish which Fred at this early period felt for them; but it is redeemed at the end by the way he fuses wit and terror so perfectly in a finale that is both dramatic and brilliant. Unfortunately, the critics, bored with the rehashes of *Dodo* and unimpressed by the Greek histories, were not inclined to give proper consideration to the originality and vivid imagination that Fred brought to this new approach to plot and character. The *Saturday Review* was typical of many:

> Mr Benson's reputation resembles a wind-bag... every fresh demand on it leaves the thing more limp, flabby and dejected. We believed that in *The Princess Sophia* he had reached the lowest literary depths possible in a man of breeding and education but he has now condescended to write a story which has all the characteristics of a shilling shocker.

Fred was by now so used to such reviews that he was able to dismiss them with a light laugh. At least his readers were faithful and increasing, eager for whatever kind of novel he chose to give them. He was fast entering the ranks of the bestsellers.

*Scarlet and Hyssop* (Spring, 1902) was another return to the manner of *Dodo*, but written with a new ferocity. Fred becomes a social satirist with a whip that flays the manners and fashions of the smart set with sincere indignation. Through the mouth of his heroine, Lady Alston, he calls his characters vulgar and charmless. The book is a tirade against the leaders of society, showing up not only their irresponsibility but also their promiscuity.

The original title was to have been *The Leper*, but Fred eventually decided on *Scarlet and Hyssop* because hyssop is mentioned in Leviticus as a cure for leprosy. 'We are all lepers,' says Lady Ardingly, an old woman in a preposterous wig. 'We are all wrong and bad, and we roll over each other in the gutter like these Arabs scrambling for backshish.'

In 1902 came the first of Fred's collaborations with Eustace Miles. It was called *Daily Training* and was published by Hurst and Blackett in their Imperial Athletic Library series. A greater contrast between Fred's society books and this stern manual could hardly be imagined, condemning as it did over-eating, over-drinking, and 'sensuality', and extolling air, light and work as the three great remedies 'in the pharmacy of God'.

Fred and Miles were ideal collaborators because, though still good friends, their life styles were completely different. Both of them were in robust good health but approached the subject of diet from differing angles. Fred had made meat an important part of his diet while Miles was a vegetarian; Fred smoked heavily, Miles not at all. Fred was a regular games player, Miles was spasmodic, but equally fit. Thus they were able to pool their ideas with good-humoured compromise. 'Many people,' wrote Fred, 'one of the present writers is one, finds that he can work more steadily and with less restlessness when smoking.'

The authors' views on 'purity' reflect the received opinion of the time.

> The greatest harm is done by preachers, schoolmasters and others who warn boys that such habits will lead to immediate decay of the mental and physical powers and early death. What his teacher ought to have taught him was that such practices are the cause of mental and physical decay in thousands, though not immediately. It will appeal to many to know that at the age, let us say, of fifty, a man who has lived purely is, almost without exception, a stronger and more vigorous person than one who, in early manhood, though possibly for a few months or weeks only, behaved like a mere 'brute beast'.

There are nine illustrations of a naked man performing exercises. This is probably Miles himself, though it is impossible to be certain because the figure looks as though his head has been covered by a paper bag; censorship dictated that identification of a naked body should not be possible.

1903 was Fred's most prolific year: six books, three of them solo efforts, and three with Miles. *A Book of Golf* and *The Cricket of Abel, Hirst and Shrewsbury* were further contributions to the Hurst and Blackett's Imperial Athletic Library. The former was only edited by Fred and Miles. It had contributions by J. Braid, J. A. T. Bramston and H. G. Hutchinson, all noted golfers of the time. In the cricket book the two authors discussed the merits and tactics of three of the greatest cricketers of the day. R. Abel (Surrey), G. H. Hirst (Yorkshire) and A. Shrewsbury (Nottinghamshire) were all professionals who had played in sixty tests between them against Australia and South Africa between 1881 and 1909. Hirst was still at the height of his powers.

*The Book of Months*, an April publication, is an agreeable if rather desultory book which is difficult to categorise, being neither a novel, diary, collection of essays, autobiography, nor a gardening book, but an amalgam of all of them; a record of experiences, both material and emotional, with the thoughts to which they have given birth, within the space of one year.

The critics were caught off guard by this change in tempo and direction and did not know what to make of it. Most of them praised it highly, in a rather surprised kind of way; only the *Saturday Review*, never a fan of E. F. Benson, spoke of 'these maunderings on lumbago, and the gibberish he talks in his bath, and above its dreary humour, its wilted sentiment, is the amazing insensibility with which the thing is done.'

Fred had been a passionate admirer of Wagner for many years. He had been to Bayreuth twice, experiencing the Master's genius at source. He had seen *The Ring* in London and had attended countless concerts in which Wagner's music was prominent. His reputation as a Wagnerian was such that when the firm of Dean and Son announced the preparation of a series of romances founded on the themes of grand opera they asked Fred to start the ball rolling with *The Valkyries*.

Fred told Wagner's story clearly and intelligibly and without undue elaboration. He put together the 'romance' with much ingenuity and it reads very smoothly. Naturally, the 'homely prose' − Fred's own description − became somewhat florid. The book lacks the largeness of the epic; it cannot give a real impression of the elemental forces that clash in Wagner's drama.

Fred had a strong dislike of New York and American

'vulgarocracy', as he called the antics of the Four Hundred in the social register. In *The Relentless City*, published in October 1903, one of his characters says, 'I look upon America as some awful cuttle-fish. Its tentacles are reaching over the world. You cannot see it coming because it clouds the wide atmosphere with the thick opacity of its juice, wealth. Then before you know it, it is there, and you are powerless. It has come to England.'

The novel is melodrama at its late-Victorian best. There is a maidenly heroine, the daughter of an American millionaire who is a gentleman without breeding and knowledgeable without being cultured. Her mother, however, is an ambitious climber with the voice of a peacock. The hero is a belted earl who marries the heroine and is content to live on his father-in-law's money. There is an immoral actress with whom the hero has had an early entanglement, and is responsible for the epigram: 'England is the home of linen-washing in public. It is the one industry that remains to us.' The villain is another American millionaire who forges blackmailing letters to the hero, pretending that they come from the actress, thus causing temporary distress to the heroine. The villain dies, inevitably, by violence, being run over by a locomotive in a tunnel. There are a few variations on an old theme, but the book is only made effective by Fred's merciless satire, though the rhetoric of disgust with which New York is presented is not always convincing.

The last book of 1903 was another, and very different collaboration between Fred and Miles called *The Mad Annual*, published by Grant Richards. It is a collection of humorous articles, parodies and spoofs, heavily illustrated by J. R. Monsell. Its humour is surprisingly fresh and sharp. There are no collapses of stout parties, but genuinely funny situations and targets which are hit in the middle. 'The Return of Sherlock Holmes' by Lord Watson is a perfect parody.

1904 saw only one book, *The Challoners*, and Fred at last begins to grapple with the problem of real people. Smart society plays only a small part in the story; Fred has returned to solid ground, with characters of substance.

The central figures are the Reverend Sidney Challoner, an upright and intolerant widowed clergyman (his Italian wife died young), and his twin children Martin and Helen. They are both artistic and brilliant, both determined to explore their individualities. So there is a clash between two forces, the intellectual rigidity that used to burn heretics in the name of love versus the rebellion with which every new generation claims the right to go its own way. The father will not have any book by George Eliot in the house because she was an immoral woman, and he had once walked out of the opera during the first few minutes of the Venusberg scene in *Tannhäuser*. Martin is a musical genius, but his father is opposed to all his son's aspirations and considers his passion for music a sinful waste of time. Helen teaches in the Sunday School and helps in the parish, though, as she says, she is no ministering angel by nature. She stirs her father to bitter anger by getting engaged to a man who does not believe in God. Although the father and children love each other and shrink from deliberately hurting each other the result is tragedy, not of epic proportions, but of misunderstandings and estrangement.

Unfortunately, the end fails to convince because of its melodramatic overstatement. Having made a spectacular success at his début as a pianist Martin is stricken with fever, and all his problems are solved when he dies in his father's arms.

Sidney Challoner bears a startling resemblance to the late Archbishop; his beliefs, method of delivery, his rigidity, longing for affection, and his inability to understand those he loved the most. Everything that Fred had ever known about his father's character, everything he had ever heard him say or seen him do, is reproduced faithfully. It is a brilliant picture of the flawed person who had dominated the young Bensons as Sidney Challoner had dominated his children.

In *An Act in a Backwater*, published at the beginning of 1905, Fred returned, in a literary way, to a quiet cathedral town to recount a story of love and courtship, which he wrote in a gently flippant style, only at the end dropping into sentimentality.

*An Act in a Backwater* did not please the critics as had *The Challoners*. *The Bookman* called it the apotheosis of *Family Herald* fiction and *Academy* hoped that it was an early work of Mr Benson's, slightly touched and re-written in parts – 'certainly a very disappointing piece of work'.

June 1905 saw *The Image in the Sand* which had been lurking about in Fred's mind for several years, and which contains, not only his love-hate relationship with Egypt's past (vivid descriptions of Cairo, Luxor, temples, tombs and deserts), but also his preoccupation with the occult, archaic lore and spiritualistic phenomena. He had steeped himself in the subject of Egyptian magic and writes about it convincingly. The story is all melodrama, but the incredible things happen with convincing force. Horror and excitement, menace and tension are all elements that Fred executes masterfully.

The story opens in Luxor. Sir Henry Jervis is a rich man whose one idea in life is to communicate with the spirit of his dead wife. For sixteen years he has done so in séances, helped by his daughter Ida, who has psychic powers, and by Abdul, part servant, part spiritual master and medium. In the Cairo bazaar Jim Henderson, an occultist and adventurer who has scraped an acquaintance with Sir Henry, has bought an amulet which has magical powers.

In a storm caused by the sirocco wind Henderson and Sir Henry ride to the Temple of Mut, taking with them Mohammed, a medium attached to Henderson. Their intention is to set free the spirit of Set-nekht, once steward to King Set, that dwells in the amulet. By so doing Sir Henry believes that he will be able to communicate more intimately with his wife's spirit. Abdul, who only uses his powers for good, refuses to go with them. In the temple they draw a circle, inscribe the *crux ansata*, swastikas and pentagrams, and put Mohammed to sleep. The spirit immediately materialises as a swathed body with a white, sneering face, wrinkled and evil. Unhappily at that moment Ida enters the temple and, not being inside the magic circle, is possessed by Set-nekht's spirit, and indirectly by Henderson, its master.

The scene then changes to England, where Ida is about to marry handsome Jack Carbery, six feet tall and a wizard at golf, and her future looks set to be happy and conventional. But Henderson returns from his travels, having made a success of his lectures and séances. He uses his hypnotic power to force Ida to come to him when he calls. When she resists, having been given an injection of morphia by Jack's doctor friend, Henderson orders Sek-nekht, spirit of evil potency who still possesses Ida's soul, to bring her to him. In spite of being drugged Ida has to respond to the spirit's bidding. With maniacal force she pushes Jack and the doctor away, and is only overcome when the doctor presses a chloroformed handkerchief over her face. While she is quiet the faithful Abdul finds Henderson and murders him on Westminster Bridge, both of them falling into the water below. The two bodies come ashore the next morning just opposite Greenwich pier. With Henderson dead Ida is released for ever from the awful spirit of Set-nekht.

*The Image in the Sand* is the old story of the struggle between the powers of light and darkness, between black magic and white for the possession of a soul. To Ida's Marguerite, Jim Henderson plays Faust, whose control over the evil spirit he has released is unconditional, and whose power to protect the girl is absolute until the temptation assails him to use the hatred for his own ends.

Melodramatic or not, Fred wrote a powerful story that, outdated in style and dialogue though it may be, grips as fiercely as anything of that genre has ever done.

*Diversions Day by Day* (1905) is an entertaining little book on which Fred and Eustace Miles collaborated, which demonstrates how games like darts, table tennis and badminton can be played by two people in a confined space. The illustrations include nine photographs of Fred or Miles demonstrating their instructions.

*The Angel of Pain*, which appeared in 1906, has at least a

touch of originality about it − one of the characters is trampled to death by the god Pan who appears in the form of a goat. The character so danced on is a hermit living in solitary communication with Nature, talking a ripe philosophy and persuading nightingales to perch on his finger and sing. The other protagonists are Philip Home, a successful City financier with a gentler, less practical side to his nature; Madge Ellington 'a very woman', whose flippant speech hides her deep feelings; and Evelyn Dundas, a brilliant (male) artist and Philip's best friend. Madge and Philip are engaged, though she does not really love him; and when she sits for her portrait to Evelyn she is won over by his fervent appreciation of life and beauty, and she marries him instead. Philip's ardour turns to hatred, he has a mental breakdown and goes to join Tom Merivale, the hermit, to share in his simple life style. Before Tom dies under Pan's hooves he has exorcised Philip's evil passions and helped him to regain his humanity. In the meantime Madge and Evelyn are at a house party in Scotland. Evelyn is accidentally shot in the face, is blinded and disfigured, and since his artistic nature cannot bear ugliness, he drowns himself. Eventually Madge and Philip come together again, and there is the inevitable happy ending. *The Angel of Pain* is a long book. It glances timidly towards the supernatural, but is basically extremely silly.

Later in the same year came *Paul*, with another melo-dramatic scenario; the relations between husband, wife and wife's friend. Theodore Beckwith is a wealthy young man with a withered, contorted body and an equally twisted mind. He wears a 'somewhat glorious' smoking-suit and smokes rose-scented cigarettes; he is also pale, mincing and bejewelled. Norah marries him in order to help her mother out of a financial quagmire. Paul, a fresh, keen and modest hero, becomes Beckwith's secretary. Soon Beckwith discovers that the two young people are in love, and takes an evil delight in playing upon their passions, acting a diabolical part with a friendly face. He insists that Paul stays in his employ to be forced 'to dance on a hot plate'.

On the day after Norah has told her husband that she is pregnant he is killed in a motor car crash. Paul is driving; he had murder on his mind and pulled up at the last moment, but too late. Beckwith is dead. The memory of what he has done turns him into a drunkard, but eventually he gives up drink after wandering into a Communion service at St Paul's Cathedral. He confesses his murderous intent to Norah, who forgives him. They marry and live on Beckwith's money. Paul's final penance comes when he saves the life of Norah's child from being mown down by an express train.

*The House of Defence* was published in 1907. And a strange book it is, its theme the efficacy of the Christian Science treatment of disease. Fred does not hesitate to ridicule the more feeble-minded exponents of the 'Church', nor to disagree with some of its beliefs, but he does not argue soundly or make the conflict an intellectual one. He tells us what we know can happen – that cases of faith-healing occur from time to time – but we have to wait until nearly the end of the book before the climax comes, the miracle that cures the laudanum-soaked Lord Thurso. Bertie Cochrane, the young American practitioner of Christian Science, drinks a glass full of the drug, without the usual sugar and water, and remains unharmed, triumphantly declaring that Divine Love has prevented him from being poisoned. Thurso is so affected by Bertie's action that he throws his own glass into the fireplace, swears that he will never touch another drop, and rushes out into the storm to find a doctor. When the doctor arrives Bertie is as ruddy and healthy as he always was. He ends up with Lady Maud Raynham, his pupil, and Thurso's wife Catherine returns to him when she knows that he is cured. *The House of Defence* proved a very popular book; it was reprinted many times up to 1924.

At the beginning of 1908 came *Sheaves*, though an American edition had appeared at the end of the previous year. The problem posed by the story is a grave one, incapable of solution by human means; it is the problem of death itself. Lady Rye is the character whose remarks illuminate the action. At her country house her still beautiful widowed sister, Edith Allbutt, meets Hugh Grainger, a typical Fred hero, handsome, fun-loving and straight as a die. Less typically he possesses a marvellous singing voice, though he has no wish to use it to become a celebrity. Edith, as 'Andrew Robb', has written a grim, though popular, play, based on her experiences with her husband, who had died a hopeless drunkard. Though there are seventeen years difference in their ages she and Hugh fall in love and marry. In the second half of the book Fred develops the theme of the pathos that lies behind the happiness of their marriage, but instead of finding a solution to the May and December situation, he ducks the challenge and lets Edith, exiled to Davos Platz in Switzerland, die of consumption.

*The Blotting Book* (1908) is a much slighter and less intense affair than *Sheaves*, and is another new departure for Fred. This time he ventures into the realms of the crime story, with good characterisation and authentic dialogue. Mr Taynton, a genial, middle-aged lawyer, plays a sinister and unforeseen part in the plot when Mr Mills, his partner, is found murdered on the downs outside Brighton. A young client, Morris Assheton, comes under suspicion, and the truth is not revealed until the end of a dramatic trial scene. In 1932 the story appeared again in February's *Argosy* under the title *The Way It Happened*.

*The Climber*, also of 1908, is one of Fred's best novels of the pre-war years, and one which later he was proud to have written. He claimed that he had put emotional imagination into it, and remembered it with affection. It is indeed a compelling story. Lucia Grimson, the climber of the title, lives in Brixham with two elderly aunts who are the daughters of a defunct Dean. She is a selfish and shallow-minded woman but she has tremendous *joie de vivre* and manages to charm most people she meets. She achieves a coveted social position as the wife of Lord Brayton by grabbing what she can at other people's expense, but in the end loses her position in society by recklessness, starting an affair between herself and her husband's best friend. Eventually Brayton sues her for divorce and she decides not to defend the case. She loses her lover, husband, and friends, and is forced to return to her aunts in Brixham in disgrace, permanently trapped, with nothing to do but use up the years as best she can.

If one remembers how divorce was regarded in Edwardian times and how bitterly people paid for their transgressions against conventional morality *The Climber* is quite a powerful story with vivid characterisation and a shrewd motivation. The elderly aunts lighten the atmosphere by providing the comic relief; one of them is an early prototype for Elizabeth Mapp.

Fred must have found it a great relief to turn temporarily from sugary heroines and sunny-natured heroes to another factual book which, on this occasion, he wrote without the help of Eustace Miles. *English Figure Skating* (1908) is a guide to the theory and practice of skating in the English style. Fred was an excellent skater, a member of the Skating Club and National Skating Association, and Vice-President of the Public Schools Alpine Sports Club from 1911 to 1928, writing articles for its Year Book. He held a number of medals and was an expert in the English style, which differed from the Continental style much as Association Football does from Rugby.

The book is very long and detailed, and to a non-skater incomprehensible, describing as it does outside back eights, forward changes of edge, the four rockers, reverse Qs and crossing pairs on opposite feet. In the 1928 Year Book of the Alpine Sports Club, Fred's book was recommended as one of the two best books on English Figure Skating.

After the hardness and glitter of *The Climber* it was a relief to many of Fred's constant readers to turn to *A Reaping* (June 1909) which is another work of fiction in a form new to Fred. The thin story that runs through it is barely more than an excuse for introducing the reflections aroused in his mind by the events that happened to him, his garden, the weather, and so forth; and in this book Fred gives himself a wife. It is in fact a kind of diary made up at the end of each of the twelve months. The wife is a conventional figure, but his cousin, nicknamed

'Legs', a young man of twenty, is evidently far more to Fred's liking, a fanatic for life with sandy hair, freckles and a broken front tooth.

Legs is a typical Benson character, and dies in a typical Benson way: his motor bicycle skids and he falls under an omnibus. His last words are, naturally, brave and understanding. 'Buck up, you two, won't you?' he says. From outside comes the dim roar of London and little noises creep about the room. But from the bed there is no sound at all.

*A Reaping* has a glibness about it, leading to slips in grammar and to the use of showy, over-written passages that induces a kind of nervous dislike of even the truest things in it.

*Daisy's Aunt* (May 1910), published by Nelson in their 'New Novels' series, is a sugar-plum story, compounded of best quality ingredients but in the end a lightweight confection that makes the teeth ache with its sweetness. Daisy is a brilliant, spoilt, rather heartless young lady who backs away from sorrow and ugliness because they are bad for the soul. She refuses to marry poor dear patient Willie Carton because, although she is dreadfully fond of him, she could not match his gentle devotion, and she wonders whether to accept instead the older and more dashing Lord Lindfield. Her Aunt Alice advises her to marry the lord in the hope that attraction might blossom into love, but at this moment Aunt Jeanne enters the story. She is a beautiful young widow of thirty, about to be married to Victor Braithwaite, and is upset by Daisy's intentions because she brings disturbing news. It seems that Daisy once had a sister Diana who deserted her husband, then went from lover to lover, to end her days in a little gilded flat to which Lord Lindfield had often found his way. Diana is now dead and only Aunt Jeanne knows the story. She determines to save Daisy from the reprobate lord, and goes out cold-bloodedly to capture him for herself, to her dismay growing very fond of him in the process.

Then follow explanations and recriminations, and a final chorus of praise for everyone. Lindfield 'becomes a man' on the spur of the moment and understands all. Jeanne marries Victor, Daisy and Willie become engaged and they all go down to Aunt Alice's house at Bray for a long Easter weekend.

One of the achievements of *The Osbornes* (1910) is the creation of a couple of characters who are really good yet are neither boring nor over-pious. Edward and Maria Osborne, with their gaucheries and social solecisms, begin by being laughed at but in the end command the reader's sympathy and admiration. Edward Osborne's wealth came from the manufacture of 'metallic hardware' in Sheffield; he was a benevolent employer and became Mayor, declining a knighthood because he was sure that one day he would be offered a peerage. So that his wife can conquer London society he builds a large house in Park Lane. Maria gives lavish parties which attract everyone who is anyone, and many who are nobody, but she welcomes all her guests with equal enthusiasm.

The Osbornes have two sons; Percy, known as 'Per', the mainstay of the family business, and Claude, a young man of staggering beauty and an endearing naivety. Edward rents a large country mansion from the Austells – Lady Austell, her son Lord Austell, and daughter Dora, a family with precarious finances. Dora falls for Claude, they marry, and for a time they are ecstatically happy. The marriage turns slightly sour when she decides that Claude has beauty but very little else, and it is only after she discovers that Lord Austell, her lying and dishonest brother, has been saved from ruin and disgrace by an act of great generosity on Claude's part that she realises his true worth.

All problems are finally resolved when Maria Osborne's serious illness proves not to be fatal and Edward gets his peerage. The best thing about the book is the depiction of true love without sentimentality. The worst is Fred's attempt to reproduce North Country speech.

*Account Rendered* (1911) is a simple study of cause and effect. There is a small cast of only four people, three of them heroic and one devious. Frank Winthrop, a thoroughly nice, attractive boy in the army, is spending his leave with his family on the east coast. Lord Tenby, also a thoroughly good fellow, but a little lethargic, lives nearby with his mother, who has only a small income to exist on. Lady Tenby is a complex character, outwardly the soul of candour, but really insincere and calculating. The fourth protagonist is Violet Allenby, a sweet and pretty girl of twenty who is governess to Frank's small brother and sister.

When Violet suddenly inherits a large fortune it is natural for her to offer the older woman a temporary home and to settle £2,000 a year on her, and it seems to Lady Tenby that Violet would make an excellent wife for her son. To ensure that Violet and Frank do not fall in love she invents an engagement for him, and so Violet shrinks back from their growing intimacy. With Frank not available, as she thinks, she marries Lord Tenby.

Inevitably the truth comes out and Lady Tenby is revealed as a liar. She pleads for Violet's forgiveness but is spurned. Violet and Frank confess their love for each other, but as she is married they must part forever. It is Lord Tenby who finds the answer to the problem. Discovering that his wife loves another, he throws himself over a cliff and is killed, thus paving the way for a happy ending. Yet again Fred resorts to a completely unnecessary death in order to resolve an awkward situation. It is as if he suddenly grew tired of the story, yawned, and thought to himself, 'Oh, I'll kill him off...'

*Juggernaut* (1911) begins as a simple love triangle. Walter Morrison, soon to enter the diplomatic service, is in love with his cousin Margery, but she is in love with Arnold Leveson, the Greek scholar, who is in love with his work, himself, and Margery, in that order. There is also Olive, Walter's sister, who does not love anybody but would not mind marrying Arnold. Arnold's mother is one of Fred's nice women. Walter's mother is one of his nastiest – deceitful, devious, snobbish and utterly selfish. She tries to wreck any hint of romance between her son Walter and Margery (daughter of her brother-in-law and an *actress*) and then between Margery and Arnold. Her plan fails, and the latter couple marry.

Soon little clouds begin to drift over their happy sky. Arnold is so engrossed in writing his books on Egypt and Greece that Margery has to take second place in his life. When she gives birth to their baby (which dies immediately) Arnold is in Greece, but arrives home in a distraught state. Margery thinks it is because of her illness and the loss of their child but really it is because his manuscript has been stolen and his life's work shattered. However, it turns up and he immediately gets wrapped up in his work again, and Margery is relegated to the background. She realises that to save her marriage she must yield all her own needs, desires and will to Arnold's wants. And in the background the faithful Walter waits and loves, knowing all the time there is no hope.

The ending can only be called superficially happy, and one unusual for Fred. If Arnold is the hero he is a most objectionable one, and Margery, a tomboy throughout much of the story, ends up as the doormat to end all doormats.

The last few Edwardian years saw Fred's development into a writer who could, and often did, rise over the average of a tired and over-productive writer of bestsellers and reach a level that put him among some of the best writers of the day. His better books of this period were distinguished by a quiet humour, often touched by a quiet sadness. For the first time he was showing real feelings for his characters, not just standing aside and observing them with a cynical eye. He was on the verge of middle-age, and middle-aged people were beginning to capture his sympathy rather than his scorn. He found himself writing about men and women whose problems were concerned with fading youth and their apprehension of the coming autumnal glow, and doing it with no melodramatic posturing or glib repartee. Nobody commits suicide or falls under a bus; the theme is resignation and acceptance.

The novel that most marks this change is *Mrs Ames* (1912) in which the chief protagonists are all at that age when looking back brings regrets and looking forward brings unease. Mrs Ames leads the social life of Riseborough. She has a rather toad-like face and a dumpy body, but 'very pretty little feet'. Major Ames, her husband, does little but tend the garden and spend a lot of time at his club. Harry, their son, weedy and lank-haired, is at Cambridge, a member of the Omar Khayyám Club, a society of like minds who, behind locked doors, drink wine flavoured with rose petals and read their love poems to each other.

The story begins with a mild scandal; Mrs Ames is to give a dinner party to which husbands have been invited without their wives and wives without their husbands. Clearly such a revolutionary concept cannot be condoned and Mrs Ames must be knocked off her perch. This is achieved, temporarily, by Millie Evans, the doctor's wife, a bored, fading beauty who is longing for something to happen; to her husband she is nothing more than decoration. She, with the clandestine assistance of Major Ames, plans something that will wake up the sleepy town – a Fancy Dress ball – the success of which will give her the ascendancy among their friends. Both the major and the dreadful Harry fall in love with Millie, and she, flattered but not really touched, allows them both to think that their feelings are reciprocated, and the major takes her attitude seriously, being half excited, half scared by the situation that is developing. Mrs Ames, in order to regain her husband's interest, resorts to rouge and hair dye, but he does not notice the transformation.

The Fancy Dress ball is the comic highlight of the book, reaching a delightful climax with the arrival of several Cleopatras accompanied by their Mark Antonys, each couple having kept their costumes a secret until the last moment.

In her effort to be modern and youthful Mrs Ames joins the Suffragettes, and in another comic set piece tries to sabotage the election meeting of the local Tory candidate by chaining herself to a table leg. Her moment of glory ends when they lift up the table leg and slip the chain off...

Major Ames and Millie make arrangements to elope, though neither of them really wants to do so. Millie waits at the station for her lover, but the major has been caught by his wife packing his bag. Her reasoning wins the day and the abortive affairs come to a miserable end. Riseborough is itself again.

*The Weaker Vessel* (1913) contains two women characters who are essentially Bensonian: they may be copied from life, but they do not live. One is the daughter of a viscount and the wife of a country clergyman, and she has all the aggressive qualities that one expects of such women. She lives in an atmosphere of Sunday Schools and choir practices, and she is convinced of her absolute righteousness. She exhibits a monumental lack of humour, and her bright, hard verbosity has a stunning effect both on the reader and on Eleanor, her step-daughter. Eleanor is the heroine who, rebelling against her narrow life in the parsonage, marries Harry Whittaker, an alcoholic playwright who has leapt to fame with his first play. Without any training or experience of life Eleanor becomes a famous actress, portraying subtle and varied parts with consummate triumph, taking London by storm. Also among the characters is Marian Anstruther, the stage siren, who wears rose-madder cloaks, and Louis Grey, a high-minded actor-manager who is in love with Eleanor, but at a respectful distance. Not only is Eleanor a great actress, she is wise, large-hearted and loving, and when she discovers her husband's shameful secret she sets out to save him; and she does not desert him even when the siren influences him to descend even further into the depths of degradation.

Harry injures his spine in a motor accident and will never be able to walk again, and Eleanor gives praise to God for delivering him into her hands – no more naughtiness for Harry, and no more rivals for her. Marian disappears into outer darkness, though not before Eleanor forgives her for being Harry's mistress. The book ends with a hint of spring in the air after a bitter winter. Harry is about to start another play and Eleanor to resume her acting.

*Thorley Weir* (1913) is a simple romance and nothing more. No titled ladies, no society chatter, no supernatural goings-on: it is the story of an artist who finds fame, and of the girl he loves, restored to him after a series of misunderstandings.

*Winter Sports in Switzerland* (1913) could be sub-titled: Everything you want to know about Skating, Curling, Tobogganing, Ice Hockey, Ski-ing and Winter Resorts. The first chapter is a paean of praise for Switzerland – its mountains, snows and pine woods, beginning with a description of the journey from London, and ending with the almost mystical experience of ski-ing on a winter evening at sunset down the mountain in an ecstasy of silence. Then after the lyrical comes the severely practical; detailed instructions on how to be adept at all winter sports, what equipment to use, what clothes to wear, and what to do in the evenings. The comprehensive text is enhanced by forty-seven striking photographs by Mrs Aubrey Le Mond and twelve full page illustrations in colour by C. Fleming Williams. A coffee table book of its period, it is handsomely produced and stylishly written in Fred's most urbane style.

*Arundel* (1914) opens in Peshawar in India but subsequently moves to London.

The story is banal and the prose thick, and there is a lack of the amusing peripheral characters that Fred often uses to lighten a turgid atmosphere. The best scenes are those set in India; they bring out all the scents and colours of the country that Fred had absorbed during his stay there with Francis Yeats-Brown a couple of years before.

*Dodo the Second* (1914) which first appeared as a serial in

*The Ladies' Field* beginning in March 1913, thus twenty years after its famous predecessor, and *Dodo Wonders* (1921) continue the history of the heroine who had astounded the Victorians, her continuing escapades and those of her headstrong daughter, Nadine. They bring the story down from the archaic age of hansom cabs to the era of the taxi, from before the Boer War to the end of the Great War. After the tempests of her earlier years and the wreck of her second marriage Dodo is brought to a happy haven. Her son David is born, the sinister Prince Waldenech is despatched and the faithful, loving Jack gets his reward. Dodo is as full as ever of her unreasonable charm. She smokes, speaks on the telephone and chatters to Jack, all at the same time and with her old abandon.

But she is older and has to face the fact. As her friend Miss Grantham says to her: 'It's an awful thing, Dodo, to be youthful at your age. You remain the same marvellous egotist that you were when you dazzled us all thirty-years ago. You have thought about yourself for fifty-four long years. Aren't you tired of the subject yet?'

Dodo sums herself up with devastating accuracy. 'A thoroughly selfish woman can make herself behave unselfishly just as a greedy person can starve himself, but they remain just as selfish and greedy as before. I've got a dreadful nature, and the only thing to be done is to blow soap-bubbles all over it, so that it appears to be iridescent.' Dodo can feel deeply for a few seconds, then she can feel equally deeply about something entirely different.

*Dodo the Second* and *Dodo Wonders* are more stylishly written than the original *Dodo*, and have a more serious purpose. The inconsequential chatter of brittle characters is still in evidence, but it is not so self-conscious. The young and scatter-brained Fred has given way to a middle-aged moralist.

*The Oakleyites* (1915) is neither a romance nor a comedy; something of both but with a strong streak of tragedy towards the end when Fred loses his way and cannot think how to end the story without a death.

The main story concerns Dorothy Jackson, a single lady on nodding terms with approaching middle age, and Wilfred Easton, well-known writer of romantic novels. He is also unmarried and past his youth. He has recently come to Oakley for peace and quiet and for the sake of his mother's health. Dorothy has scathingly criticised Wilfred's books in her lecture at the Oakley Literary Union, but Wilfred accepts her damning remarks with equanimity; he knows his own worth, and his mother dislikes his books too.

Gradually love seems to blossom between the two quiet people, though it never reaches a point when it can be declared. Whatever it is, it is utterly shattered with the arrival of Dorothy's sister Daisy, who is in the middle of divorce proceedings against her husband. She, Lady Mayton, is one of Fred's most terrifying predators. In the guise of helplessness and despair and frail femininity she makes a successful play for Wilfred, and she has all the other eligible men in the town under her spell too. Her object is simply conquest; she has already decided that she is going to marry the wealthy Lord Willard. Her cunning is such that Dorothy does not see through the 'little girl lost' act until it is too late, and she has lost Wilfred. When she has discovered the trouble that Daisy is causing she confronts her bravely. Daisy departs, and Oakley is left to pick up the pieces of its once peaceful charm. Wilfred's world is in ruins; he has never loved before with such intensity. At this point it would have seemed natural for Dorothy and Wilfred to have gradually grown together again, but Fred does not allow that. Instead, with surprising rapidity, Dorothy falls victim to consumption and dies in Wilfred's presence, smiling at him, 'her secret radiantly revealed'.

The comedy in the story centres round old Mr Audley, an obsessive collector of bric-à-brac, furniture and pictures, and his three daughters, whom he dislikes intensely. One is a passionate Christian Scientist, another a Yoga fanatic, and the third a proselytising vegetarian. They are all after their father's possessions and after his death they each try to outwit the other with various diabolical stratagems; but in the end it turns out that Mr Audley's huge collection consists mainly of copies and fakes.

*The Freaks of Mayfair* (1916) is an elegant and stylish book consisting of twelve character studies of people who live in Mayfair, wittily illustrated by George Plank in Beardsleyish black and white drawings. Most of the characters are preliminary sketches for those who later flit through many of the comedies. The most important is 'Aunt Georgie', an elderly and effeminate gentleman who does embroidery and gives dinner parties for young men with 'waggly walks'. Fred points out that though Georgie is a figure of fun in the society he inhabits he has done less harm in the world than many normal people. He clearly has a soft spot for the type of people that Georgie represents because they appear in many of his books, the supreme example being, of course, George Pillson who marries Lucia.

In 'Quack-quack' Mrs Weston is an idle woman who indulges in one new fad after another, ranging from diets, water cures, Yoga, Christian Science, Spiritualism, and Higher Thought, which sends her walking through wet grass for fifteen minutes each morning. She comes to life again in the person of Daisy Quantock in *Queen Lucia*. In 'The Eternally Uncompromised' silly Winifred Ames marries the wealthy hypochondriac, Sir Gilbert Fallon. Taking her cue from the romantic novels she read as a child, she longs to be compromised –

though only in her head. All her forays into attempted faithlessness fail dismally, due to her essential innocence. 'The Spiritual Pastor' describes the Rev. the Hon. J. P. Sandow, who attends to the religious needs of the Mayfair freaks. He is immensely popular; his fifty minute sermons fill his church every Sunday – he has arranged his services so as not to interfere with tea (Vespers at six), and Compline at eleven (evening dress optional) for those returning from dinner parties. Mr Sandow is a fine dancer, an athlete and a writer of sweet little devotional books, two of which appear every year.

Constance, Lady Whittlemere, 'The Sea-Green Incorruptible', is a woman of such moral probity that doing the 'right thing' is her only reason for living. Her sons (army, church, parliament and diplomacy), are all totally dull. Settled in a large Mayfair house with her companion and a staff of fourteen, her days, weeks and months are rigidly programmed. She takes no interest in the world beyond her own narrow confines and lives a life of self-centred tedium. 'Climbers' deals with two aspects of social climbing, the horizontal and the perpendicular. The former is illustrated by the sad story of Molly Howard-Britten who was prevented from reaching the top of the social ladder because of the disastrous dinner party she gave for a famous Russian pianist who, instead of entertaining on the piano, performed tedious conjuring tricks. The latter is exemplified by wealthy Sarah Whitehand, snubbed by Nittie Costersnatch and the New York 400, who turns to London society in order to reach the social summit. In no time at all she is perched in the topmost branches among the smart set and is able to snub Nittie Costersnatch and get her revenge. 'Sing for Your Supper' is about Leonard Bashton, one of those young men who sing for their suppers by reading the social columns and making themselves agreeable to those mentioned in them. With an income of £600 a year Leonard lives in modest comfort which is greatly enhanced by his social life. He cannot be called a climber, but rather a user of proffered amenities.

In *The Freaks of Mayfair* Fred is on one of his favourite hobbyhorses, severely criticising in a humorous way a world that puts the pretence of breeding and good taste above all the laudable and innocent purposes that should concern mankind.

Coincidence is a legitimate device in fiction, so is dramatic irony; and *Mike* (1916) has both. When the story opens Michael Comber, actually Lord Comber but called Mike, and son of Lord Ashbridge, is telling his cousin Francis that he has just resigned his commission in the Guards in order to follow his first love, music. Mike, with short legs, long arms, enormous hands and ugly face, sees no future for himself in the army, which he loathes. That evening he attends a lieder recital given by Sylvia Falbe and her pianist brother Hermann which whets his appetite for his imminent visit to Bayreuth to hear Parsifal. When he tells his father of his intention to leave the Guards Lord Ashbridge, who is obsessed with social status and spends his time running his large estate in Suffolk, patronising his tenants and yelling about duty, is appalled. Mike's mother, who looks like a camel, is ineffectual and under her husband's thumb; only his Aunt Barbara, married to an American diplomat, is on his side. Mike leaves the family home under a cloud.

Hermann Falbe, the accompanist at the lieder recital, meets Mike on the train to Bayreuth and they become friends. Mike learns that Hermann and Sylvia are half English and half German and live with their English mother in London. After the holiday, back in London, Hermann hears Mike play the piano, and agrees to take him on as a pupil. Mike meets the Falbes' friends at their Sunday evening soirées, and he is inspired to compose his Opus 1: Variations on Good King Wenceslas, which Hermann includes in a concert, to great acclaim. It dawns on Mike that he is falling in love with Sylvia, but she is not yet ready to reciprocate.

Aunt Barbara approves of the Falbes, which pleases Mike, though he is not so taken with his aunt's concern over the political situation in Europe. She feels that England is far too trusting of Germany, and that there are spies about. Mike's mother, Lady Ashbridge, is behaving very oddly and softening of the brain is diagnosed. Mike arranges for her to live in their Curzon Street house, and he moves in with her.

War clouds gather and Hermann sorrowfully returns to Germany where he feels his duty lies. Sylvia, observing Mike's tender care for his rapidly deteriorating mother, discovers that she does love him. On the day of his mother's death war is declared, and Mike decides to rejoin his old regiment immediately, though he marries Sylvia before he crosses to France. The final pages are heavy with anti-German sentiments and there are frequent references to the atrocities committed by the Hun. After an idyllic time in the French countryside Mike goes for his duty turn in the trenches. As dawn breaks the Germans make their attack and as they approach the trenches Mike shoots at a figure about to attack him. He suddenly recognises Hermann and tries to rescue him, getting wounded in the arm himself as he does so. Though fatally wounded, Hermann is able to open his eyes and recognise Mike. 'Lieber Gott, Michael!' he whispers. 'Good morning, old boy!'

Back home the wounded Mike knows that he will have to tell Sylvia about his final encounter with her brother. He tells her exactly what happened, and the strain makes him break down and cry. Sylvia knows why she had to be told and after allowing Mike to shed his tears '...she laid her arm on his neck. "Michael, my heart!" she said.'

When An Autumn Sowing was published in 1917 Fred was

fifty years old and, when the mood took him, a master of his craft. This book shows him at his best, particularly in the skilful way he economises with words in the delineation of his characters. His ear for dialogue is even more acute because he has dropped some of the brittleness which made his earlier women indistinguishable from each other; the wit is as merciless as ever, and he observes his people with as penetrating an eye as he did in *The Climber* and *Mrs Ames*. Mrs Keeling, for instance, is drawn as meticulously as Jane Austen drew Mrs Bennett, in neat phrases which penetrate deep to the heart of the odious lady, and the same is true of her venomous old mother and the ferret-like Mrs Fyson.

Thomas Keeling, pillar of Bracebridge society, whose god is business, but who has a secret retreat, a study lined with books, starts as a pompous and unlikeable bully; but Fred cleverly turns him into a genuinely tragic figure as the correct relationship he has with his young secretary Norah turns into a passionate though secret love. Alice, the Keelings' daughter, an angular spinster of twenty-five, is handled with a sure touch which keeps her from being merely a figure of fun; and the insufferable Mr Silverdale, the new vicar who suffers from amorous anaemia and baby talk, and with whom the silly young ladies of his congregation, including Alice, fall in love, is dissected with Fred's sharpest knife, especially in the scene where Alice almost proposes to him. She then stops being silly and her suffering is genuine.

The scene between Sir Thomas, as he becomes, and Norah, in the bluebell wood where they confess their love for each other, is in a different mood from those of the earlier satirical chapters, being touched with an affecting innocence. Norah leaves the town because the situation is hopeless and Sir Thomas is left with his business, his library, his thick-skinned wife, and his growing love for his daughter. 'He had let himself seek love, and just because it was love and no mere sensual gratification that he had sought, it had, with the full consent of all in him that was worthy of it, been plucked from him. And with its vanishing his secret garden had blossomed with bitter herbs...'

*Mr Teddy* (1917) was written during the war, but contains not a single hint that the country is in turmoil. It is another of Fred's quiet books, with pathos and comedy combining to create a simple charm. On Edward Heaton's fortieth birthday, his shaving mirror tells him that he could easily pass for a man ten years younger. Looking young and feeling young, he is led into a deeply unsatisfying self-delusion. Mr Teddy, as he is known to his Lambton friends, is a painter of real talent but has a chronic inability to finish his paintings, and his studio is full of incomplete portraits. His *magnum opus* is to be a study of Dante and Beatrice, but he cannot find suitable models.

Daisy MacDonald lives in Lambton with her sister Marion,

who is a writer of Christian fiction. Daisy, like Mr Teddy, is, at thirty-
five, approaching the foothills of middle age, and lives in constant hope
that Mr Teddy will ask her to marry him. Mr Teddy's mother is one of
Fred's special horrors: demanding, selfish and deceitful, keeping her son
tied to her apron strings. She dies halfway through the book, but her
nastiness lives on.

The plot stirs into life when Robin, Mr Teddy's young
cousin, comes to stay. He is handsome, amiable, and wins all hearts with
his charming ways. Then Rosemary Heaton, a distant relative of Mr
Teddy, comes to live nearby, and the scene is set for the drama. The
young couple soon become popular and dominate the town's activities,
and Rosemary unwittingly supplants Daisy in most areas of social life; in
the church choir, for instance, where her fresh and true voice is so
obviously better than Daisy's that she takes over as choir leader and
soloist.

Mr Teddy falls in love with Rosemary. He has persuaded
Robin to pose as Dante in his new painting, and now he asks Rosemary to
be Beatrice. It is not long before it is plain that the young couple are head
over heels in love and Mr Teddy's hopes are dashed. Sad and depressed,
he puts himself into the picture as a tortoise just waking up from
hibernation.

Marion develops an incurable disease. Daisy asks her not to
reveal her feelings for Mr Teddy, but Marion manages to do so by
devious means. Then she dies, but the sadness of her death is softened by
the engagement of Daisy and Mr Teddy.

*Up and Down* (1918) is an uneasy book; the motive behind
its writing is unclear. It is partly an account of Fred's movements
between 1914 and 1917 which included the move from Oakley Street to
Brompton Square, partly a war diary mixed with philosophical reflections,
but chiefly a love story, the relationship between the narrator (Fred) and
Francis, the friend of his heart. Unfortunately, it rarely rings true
because, as only he can, Fred frequently goes over the top and wallows in
lush sentimentality; the death of Francis from cancer is distasteful rather
than affecting.

The love story is punctured by long polemics about the war,
personal hatred of the Huns, the righteousness of the British cause, the
bravery of the allies and the brutality of the enemy. There is also much
moralising about religion, mysticism, life after death and spiritualism.

The book opens with Fred and Francis sharing a villa on a
Mediterranean island. Capri and the Villa Cercola are easily recognisable,
but Francis in no way resembles John Ellingham Brooks. He volunteers
for active service when war breaks out, starts out as a private but soon
becomes a Quartermaster-Sergeant. One day, busy among the stores, he

suddenly finds that the tins of petroleum are shining with God, and he becomes a born-again Christian. 'For him no longer in gloomy recesses sat Pan, the incarnate aspect of the cruelty and lust of Nature, but over all the world shone the face of Christ.' Later, Francis accepts a commission and wins the VC (which he leaves in a taxi). When cancer strikes him he dies joyfully, crying in a voice tremulous with exultation, 'Rabboni!'

The most interesting aspect of *Up and Down* is Fred's account of a depression that one day came out of the blue and settled on him. Neither his father, Maggie nor Arthur had ever chosen the words which described the visitation in such expressive terms, even though they had all experienced its horror.

> But when I woke the Thing was there...there was a blackening poison that spread and sprouted like some infernal mushroom of plague. I found that I did not care for anything any more; there was the root of this obsession...it was all one, for over all and in all was the blackness of the pit of clouds...within me was a centre-point of consciousness that only wailed and cried out at the horror of existence...when I went up to bed the nightmare yelled out and smothered me. At one moment I was nothing set in the middle of cosmic darkness; at the next I was cosmic darkness itself, set in a microscopic loneliness, an alpha and omega of the everlasting midnight...

The Thing passed as Fred held on tightly and life began to steal back, and he believed he had done no more than paddle at the edge of such deep waters, and had not approached real melancholia. It seems to have been the only attack of the family malady he had and, if nothing else, it gave him the chance to sympathise with Arthur, who at that time was going through his own hell.

*David Blaize and the Blue Door* (1918) is Fred's only children's story. He tried to write another version of 'Alice in Wonderland', but the wonderland is missing. David is six years old and the blue door is underneath his pillow. When he finds the key and goes through it he embarks on a number of adventures that, unlike 'Alice', have no logic behind their illogicality. In 'Alice' the logic has its own topsy-turvy reality; in Fred's book there is a never-ending stream of fantastic characters and situations that have no relevance to one another even in a climate of irrelevance; some of them in only a few words or a sentence change direction or focus in a quite meaningless way, leaving the reader breathless and bewildered.

Once through the door David finds himself in his games cupboard where the inhabitants of the Noah's Ark have come to life.

Miss Muffet and her spider enter the story, then David becomes an errand boy to a bank, goes to an animals' ball and dances with a giraffe, meets a cow who is a railway porter, and lands up at a hairdresser's where the customers are having their bald heads painted – a mishmash of surrealist incidents that might individually be funny but cobbled together without any connecting thread are definitely not.

One can see how Fred intended his stream of nonsense to have a cumulative comic effect, but he should have thought up a genuinely original setting, leaving Lewis Carroll severely alone.

*Across the Stream* (1919) is another venture into the world of spirits written, not from the point of view of the enquirer friendlily disposed to the idea of communication with the dead, but from the standpoint of the Roman Catholic Church, which believes that such communications, if genuine, come not from the dead but from the devil. Fred's aim is to state rather than solve the subject and to suggest that the dead and the devil alike may be able to come over the stream to the living.

One of the letters that Fred received after the book's publication was from Conan Doyle, who had been sent a copy of the book by John Murray, the publisher. He had read it with conflicting emotions. 'Of course,' he said, 'Spiritualism may have a dangerous aspect but I am sure that in both cases God has given it to be used sanely and with reason and circumspection... your book may warn timid folks off from what seems to me to be a very sacred and blessed domain... Well, anyhow, as a work of art it is a pure joy – so clean cut and fine.'

After the war and up until 1926 Fred wrote eighteen books: of these seven are undistinguished, run-of-the-mill novels unable to compete with such titles as *Queen Lucia, Miss Mapp, David of King's, Our Family Affairs* and *Mother,* all of which appeared during that period. In 1927 *Lucia in London* began a series of excellent titles which included *Spook Stories* and *Paying Guests;* the 1930s saw Fred's major works, the rest of the Mapp and Lucia stories and the serious biographies, culminating in *Final Edition,* his consummate piece of workmanship.

The little clutch of secondraters, belonging to the first half of the 1920s, are *Robin Linnet* (1919), *Colin* (1923), *Alan* (1924), *Colin II* (1925), *Rex* (1925), *Mezzanine* (1926) and *Pharisees and Publicans* (1926). They may be a tribute to Fred's industry, but not to his talent. He seems to have been marking time, waiting in a literary limbo, content to drift along. The seven books are either exceedingly silly or exceedingly sentimental or just dull.

*The Countess of Lowndes Square* (1920) is a book of short stories which Fred wrote to relax after *Our Family Affairs.* The fourteen stories, which had already appeared in various magazines, are slight stuff, dashed off without much application or imagination, and deal with blackmailers, cats, spooks and cranks. The Countess of Lowndes Square herself, though the wife of an earl, is a criminal and a blackmailer. In spite of the generally frivolous tone of the stories there is an elegance of style that catches quite neatly the delicacy of the best French writers. Fred asserted in his introduction that the ten best short stories in the world would probably all be French, and the million worst would be American: precision and economy as against opulence and amateurishness. He had attempted to emulate the former and for once had put aside the verbosity that made some of his romances so difficult to read.

*Lovers and Friends* (1921) is set during the war, although the war is only peripheral to the story. The love that Bernard, Lord Matcham, feels for his wife Celia is not reciprocated, but he hopes that in time her attitude will change. His obsession with her began when he noticed her uncanny resemblance to a marble head he had acquired, a thing of beauty in the Greek archaic style, and by persuasion and bribery he had got Celia's eccentric father to consent to the marriage. Things are placid enough until Celia meets Victor Vincent, a peripatetic politician who gives lectures at dinner parties on the countries he has visited. Victor's boorishness first repels then attracts Celia, and she falls in love with him. Then Celia, now a mother, has to face the problem of telling her husband her true feelings. This she bravely does, but not until the news comes that Victor has been lost at sea in a torpedoed ship bound for Athens. Bernard has long guessed the truth and has come to terms with it. Celia asks him to forgive her, but he says love takes forgiveness for granted.

'Love goes through forgiveness like a train through a wayside station, at full speed, not noticing. Forgiveness is a speck of rain in a day of sun. It dries off before you notice it.'

The book does not stray outside its social *milieu*. Although there is an air raid scene it is treated rather amusingly; and there are casual references to the Russian Revolution. Two soldiers among the minor characters remind us of the business of war: jolly Tommy is blinded, and handsome Jimmie loses his legs, but neither boy seems particularly worried, and Tommy marries Violet, Celia's sister-in-law.

*Peter* (1922) is a slight and over-written love story which, however, does not contain very much love. Peter Mainwaring is poor, which means that he works at the Foreign Office, lives with his parents, takes tea at the Ritz and visits the opera with the insatiable Mrs Trentham and her entourage of sycophantic and pretty young men. On one occasion, during a performance of *Parsifal*, Peter meets Silvia Wardour, the daughter of wealthy parents, and he marries her for her money, not for love.

The marriage enables him to enjoy Mrs Wardour's money, and when she makes over to him her country mansion and her fashionable

London house, he accepts quite shamelessly the gifts as his right. Silvia continues to love him whilst knowing in her secret heart that he is not in love with her. Peter discovers accidentally that she is pregnant. He finds that he is hurt and upset that she has not told him the news immediately and is forced to examine their relationship anew. The climax comes when their country house catches fire and Silvia is trapped on the roof. After a perilous crawl along a parapet Peter rescues her. At this critical moment she decides to tell him the news, but Peter disconcerts her by telling her that he already knows; and having risked his life to save her he realises that love has come at last.

The coming together of character and situation in *Paying Guests* (1929) creates a comic masterpiece, worthy to stand alongside the Mapp and Lucia books; indeed, in the reality and understanding behind the humour, maybe surpassing them. It is certainly one of the best books in the whole range of Fred's works, tightly constructed, with characterisation diverse and sharply etched, the humour arising out of character as much as situation, and the dialogue richly comic yet true to the speaker.

The paying guests are resident at the Wentworth Guest House in Bolton Spa, a superior establishment magnificently detached, with tennis courts, a croquet lawn and soon to have a third bathroom. The sisters who run it, Mrs Oxney and Mrs Bertram, also take part in its social life. The principal guests are the irascible Colonel Chase, an ex-Indian Army fitness freak whose life is dominated by his attempts to break both his own walking and cycling records, and genteel Miss Grace Howard who sees herself as a kind of Renaissance woman with her improvisations on the piano and the atmospheric water colours with which she keeps the Arts alive. Mrs Bliss, the epitome of smugness, maintains that there is no such thing as illness, and that life is controlled solely by 'Mind', all illness being 'Error', and takes the spa waters purely to satisfy her husband. There is the frightful Mr Kemp, the worst of Fred's hypochondriacs, who keeps his daughter Florence in total subjugation to his whims, Mrs Holders, who delights in putting down the Colonel, and Tim Bullingdon, severely arthritic but equally cynical and ready to join Mrs Holders in her machinations. There is much of Fred in his character.

There are a dozen or so minor characters who help to build up the comic climaxes, one of which concerns the mysterious loss and recovery of the Colonel's pedometer; another, the hilarious concert given in aid of the Children's Hospital when the Colonel's finest hour turns out to be his darkest, and Miss Howard's improvisations do not go as planned. Miss Howard also figures prominently in the account of the unexpected success of her one woman show of water colours, and in the mystery of her Queen Anne family seat in Tunbridge Wells which turns out to be a boring semi-detached in Station Road.

There is tenderness in the account of Florence Kemp's breakaway from her tyrannical father and her entry into a deeply satisfying and overtly expressed lesbian relationship with Grace Howard who, to his amazement, has rejected the Colonel's offer of marriage; but, lightness is all, and the story bubbles away merrily until the final pages, which provide one of the most mischievous of all Fred's denouements.

*The Male Impersonator* is one of The Woburn Books, published by Elkin Mathews and Marrot in 1929, in an edition of five hundred copies for sale, each signed by the author. Fred was in good company: other titles included those by G. K. Chesterton, T. F. Powys, D. H. Lawrence, Henry Williamson and Robert Graves. Fred's is a slight effort of twenty-five pages. It concerns Miss Mapp and Diva Plaistow of Tilling, and their endeavours to find out who is the Lady Deal who has taken 'Suntrap' in Curfew Street. The plot, if it can be dignified by such a name, is thickened by Miss Mapp's discovery that Lady Deal was formerly a male impersonator in the music hall, and so is beyond the pale as far as the Tilling ladies are concerned. But it turns out that the lady ensconced in 'Suntrap' is *not* Lady Deal, but her old governess, and the male impersonator is *not* the Lady Deal who has bought the house, but a former holder of the title. Diva finds out all this before Miss Mapp does and – here Fred brings in a touch of originality – for once holds the cards in her pudgy little hands. Though Fred's style is as suave as ever his skills were not over-taxed by this mild little story.

At first *The Inheritor* (1930) seems to be a light and romantic account of Cambridge days for the gilded youth of the period during May Week, when King's boat has finished at the head of the river. A young don, Maurice Croft, makes sure that the undergraduates do not get out of hand by preventing them lighting a bonfire, which would have meant the leading spirits being gated. Maurice, Steven Gervase, an undergraduate whom he specially favours, and the six feet four Merriman, nicknamed the Child, make an attractive threesome. The imminent departure of the Child signifies the break-up of the group and they are all aware that life will never be the same again. After the celebrations Steven and the Child go rowing in the early hours of the morning, and here the writing has many homo-erotic overtones which indicate the nature of the relationships between the leading characters.

> The Child... had stripped to shirt and trousers. At the other end, facing him and above him, sat Steven, the red stripe of his pyjamas black in the dim light, while the jacket with its missing button lay open at the neck, and, slipping down his arm, left one shoulder

bare. The muscle of it, alternately taut and slack, rippled under the skin as he pressed on his paddle and withdrew it.

The boys bathe naked, struggling playfully in the water, and then, at Steven's instigation, they make a sacrifice to the gods of the river and the night by burning twigs, withered herbage and tobacco from their last cigarette.

After the Child has left Cambridge Maurice and Steven feel an indefinable affinity, and gradually Maurice learns about his friend's background, of the horrifying curse that has dogged his family for many generations, the curse that turns the first-born son into something that is barely human – goatlike, hirsute, and unable to speak or understand. Steven himself appears to have escaped: he is golden-haired, blue-eyed and beautiful. He tells Maurice how, as a child, he had a glimpse of an uncle – only four feet high, with chest covered in dark hair, a beard, and two horns coming from his forehead. The creature was quickly caught and led away. Steven felt drawn towards the misshapen old man, but he was not allowed to see him again and could not attend his funeral which followed soon after the meeting. Maurice does not know that though Steven may have overcome the curse as far as his appearance goes, the evil thing lurks deep in his psyche.

Maurice spends the summer at Trenair in Cornwall where Steven lives with his mother, a Cornish woman whose ancestors had power over animals, and he remembers how once on a Cambridge river bank Steven showed how he could charm a squirrel out of a tree and make it snuggle up to his face.

Trenair is a strange place. There is no church, deadly henbane grows in profusion, and there is a great circle of monoliths and a line of grave-like mounds. Then there is Steven's simple-minded half-brother Tim, a bastard of extraordinary beauty, who prances about semi-naked playing bird-song on his home-made pipe. Maurice notices the resemblance between Steven and Tim, but does not guess the cause. He becomes aware of the pantheism which has gripped the whole community, and he is shocked to discover Steven's total indifference to all human feelings. Steven and Tim, he decides, are animistic creatures absorbed by the dark and hidden mysteries of nature.

When Steven realises that Maurice has no desire to follow him into his esoteric world he drops him, as he has dropped the Child, and it is not until Steven has married and inherited his uncle's fortune that they meet again. Believing that his erstwhile friend has re-entered the real world Maurice joins him and his pregnant wife Betty at Trenair. Slowly Betty Gervase also senses something of the horror that lies behind the face of the pleasant countryside. She begins to loathe Tim, who adores Steven and follows him everywhere, and she feels instinctively that the monoliths and graves are the source of a great evil.

Even though it is well signalled the climax produces a violent shock. Betty gives birth to a bleating monster, and Steven is completely unconcerned when it dies.

There is only one way for the story to end. Steven and Tim become part of the nature they have always worshipped by poisoning themselves with henbane. *The Inheritor* is a magnificently successful venture into the occult, even surpassing *The Luck of the Vails*.

If ever there was evidence that it was right for Fred to concentrate on biography rather than on fiction it is *Charlotte Brontë* (1932), a model of what a biography should be. One would have thought, even in 1932, that there was little left to say about the Brontës, but Fred made this book fascinating, not only by finding out new facts about the family, but by his insight into the characters of such intensely individual people. Based on the evidence of Charlotte's own letters, for the first time we have a true and poignant picture of the tragic family.

One of the striking qualities of the book is its credibility. Without bravado, Fred puts most previous biographers in their places. They made their contribution, even Mrs Gaskell with all her evasions and omissions, but they did not tell the whole truth: or the truth as they saw it was twisted by their own fanciful theories; and Fred writes with such assurance and marshalls his evidence so aptly that one feels that this must surely be an authentic picture of what the Brontës were.

Although Charlotte must have been a very uncomfortable person to live with, because of her intolerant opinions, Fred makes her an attractive figure for her loyalty to the family, her complete integrity as a writer, and for her avoidance of the lionising that she could have had after *Jane Eyre*. He also brings out well the pathos of the last year of her life, the happiness she was beginning to enjoy before an untimely death cut the story short.

Only in his assessment of Anne's talent as no more than mediocre does Fred fall short of his clear-sighted and balanced view of the achievements of the Brontës.

In *Secret Lives* (1932) the snobbery of middle class England is again deflated with affectionate but deadly satire. We move from Tilling and Riseholme to Durham Square in London (Brompton Square, of course), but the ladies of the square are just as provincial as those of Tilling, and if Miss Mapp had been missing from Tilling her place could have been taken by Mrs Mantrip without any sense of loss. Mrs Mantrip is the doyenne of the square and of the railed garden in its centre. Her clergyman father had bought up all the houses as an investment and in doing so had rescued the square from the shames of prostitution – thus serving God and Mammon. Mrs Mantrip is writing a life of her estimable father, but somehow has never managed to get past the chapter headings.

Her best friends, with whom she has many a battle, are Elizabeth Conklin, devoted to her ten Pekinese dogs which pull her around like a balloon with ropes attached, and Jimmie Mason, the square's auntie, a crashing snob who persists in over-stretching his youth and whose tongue has discovered the secret of perpetual motion. Lady Eva Lowndes, clairvoyant, who sees the most amazing auras, and her husband, Captain Lowndes, who no doubt would have been interesting if he were allowed to say anything, are among the other inhabitants of the square.

Then Miss Susan Leg comes to live at No 25, and the square buzzes into life. She is obviously rich, but equally obviously not out of the top drawer (caviare on scones at tea time...) so it is doubtful if she can be admitted to the innermost circle. Besides, she is addicted to the loudest gramophone and wireless music she can turn on, and is driving the square mad. There is a mystery about dumpy little Susan Leg. Who is she? Mrs Mantrip would love to find out.

Who, too, is Ulrica, the gossip columnist? And Rudolph da Vinci, the best-selling romantic novelist, author of 'Apples of Sodom', scorned by Arthur Armstrong, the stern literary critic, but secretly adored by Mrs Mantrip — why does she think he is Susan's butler's nephew? Why did Rudolph not turn up at the Regency Palace Hotel in Brighton? Susan Leg was there, and Arthur Armstrong, and Ulrica...

A series of farcical scenes of misunderstandings, recriminations and dawning recognitions bring the mystery to an end, and Mrs Mantrip and Susan Leg become bosom friends. At Susan's Christmas party Mrs Mantrip says, proposing a toast to her hostess:

> We have all of us, I expect, a secret life unknown to the world, but when, by accident or design, these secret lives of ours come to light, how seldom, alas! does it happen, as in the case of our beloved hostess, that instead of there being discreditable exposures, we stand revealed, as she has done, in a blaze of added glory, of fame, not infamy.

Fred's secret was quickly revealed: Susan Leg could not have been anybody but Marie Corelli, and Arnold Bennett was the literary critic who said of *The Brothers Karamazov:* 'Most people regard it as a classic. My answer is monosyllabic. Rats.'

Fred's subtitle of his *King Edward VII* (1933) is 'An Appreciation', and that is what the book is. 'Hagiography' would perhaps be too strong a word, but the King is certainly presented in the most favourable light that Fred could manage. Edward's background was, of course, the reason for his later rebellion against acceptable conduct, and the 'moral rot' that the Marlborough House set was accused of had its roots in the repressive upbringing that Queen Victoria and her husband considered necessary for the heir to the throne: but the defects in his character must have been there from early in his development, and these have not been sufficiently explored.

The watchword of Prince Albert was 'Never relax', and, aided by the queen, the Consort did not for a moment relax from trying to make his eldest son a carbon copy of himself: unbendingly upright, austere in his habits, devoted to literature, science and, above all, duty. Fred explains, with perhaps too much sympathy for the young man, how the Consort's efforts failed completely, and how his son became a roistering, gambling womaniser, popular with all but the most rigid members of the Court, and thought of as a 'gay dog' by the common people.

The relationship between the earnest Prince Consort and the genial heir apparent is very vividly described, and so is his mother's lack of appreciation of whatever gifts he had. If he had been allowed more responsibility and trained more sensibly for his future role he might, in time, have given up some of his more bizarre habits. Fred is at his best telling the story of Edward's kingship – his relations with other monarchs and with statesmen, and his growing realisation that life was not all women, drink, shooting pheasants and taking the waters. In the end he gave great service to the country. His skill in dealing with his cousin the Kaiser of Germany and as a diplomat among the other nations of Europe made up for many of his earlier excesses.

Fred captures the whole pageant of an age that began with Victoria's accession and ended with Edward's death. As an historian he may not show enough impartiality but as a scene and portrait painter he is superb.

In *Travail of Gold* (1933) Fred's stock figures re-appear more colourful, preposterous and snobbish than ever. The dialogue is smarter, the opulence of everything more magnificent and vulgar, even the heroine is more tender, modest and priggish than others have been; and Christopher Merivale, the aspiring playright, is every one of Fred's heroes who has started out as an idealist and become spoiled by success.

Nancy Cornish is a struggling actress and Christopher Merivale is in love with her. He writes for her a highly romantic play called 'Travail of Gold' which nobody will put on. Nancy's career takes off, but Chris stays earthbound. He gets in with the smart set led by Wee Violet Angus, an immense and immensely rich woman, obviously based on Lady Charles Beresford whom Fred had known in the early years of the century, with her wigs, false eyebrows and Watteau Shepherdess frocks of turquoise blue. Princess Olga, the greedy Russian, Bobbie Lucas, bank Chairman, who is like a malicious Georgie Pillson, and Chris's stepmother, whom he hates for taking him away from Eton and who is the kind of social climber that Fred has drawn so frequently, are other members of the cast, and they swirl around, chattering like drunken parrots.

Chris eventually does find fame and fortune with plays that crackle with cynical brilliance, and he and Nancy drift apart. To take Nancy's place comes Irene, another actress who resembles her in every way but character, for she is as hard and insincere as he is. Chris brings their passionate adventure to an end when he realises what a tough adversary she can be. 'I never knew anyone so essentially mean as you are,' she tells him, 'or one who so devoutly worships money for itself. But we're both damned, I expect, for I'm just as hard as you.'

Later Chris takes out the nearly forgotten manuscript of 'Travail of Gold', written for Nancy, and sees how the play, full of love and sacrifice, can be re-fashioned into a black comedy. He has finally burnt his boats; love of money has killed all other kinds of love.

*The Outbreak of War, 1914* (1933) was written as part of Peter Davies's 'Great Occasions' series, and Fred found himself in the company of John Buchan, Martin Lindsay and Helen Simpson. It is a rather strange mixture of politics, history and autobiography; encompassing the short time between June 28, 1914 when the Archduke Franz Ferdinand, heir to the Austrian throne, was murdered at Sarajevo, the capital of Bosnia, to August 4, when Britain declared war on Germany. The events leading up to that dramatic climax are written from an entirely personal standpoint – one might almost think that the war had happened to spoil Fred's plans. When the assassination occurred Fred was on Capri, arranging for more furniture to be sent from Oakley Street to the Villa Cercola; he was also hoping to go to the Wagner Festival at Bayreuth.

The situation did not seem to be critical, but he returned to England and visited his mother at Tremans. Arthur and Hugh were there too. He relates other bits and pieces of family history, some new, others already recounted in other books; homely things that emphasised the difference between life in England and the upheavals all over Europe. Interspersed with the personal recollections is a detailed account of every move taken by potential allies and potential enemies, every threat, headline, diplomatic move, argument, rumour and ultimatum that Fred culled from a number of books dealing with the origins of the First World War, and from contemporary newspapers and periodicals.

Fred makes the events of those fateful weeks as clear as

anyone could. The form he chose was original, but the execution has uneasy touches. The common people have been left out. It was their war, and without their reactions to it the story is incomplete.

*Raven's Brood* (1934) is the most bizarre book that Fred ever wrote and was probably done on the rebound after some of his heavy biographies or because he wanted to prove to himself that he could do without the aristocracy, smart talk, town houses and innocent young heroines. It bristles with sexuality from the moment we meet John Pentreath, farmer and religious bigot, at his Cornish farm near Penzance. In the first thirty pages there are references to fertility rituals, phallic symbols, lustful boilings in the blood, trollops, shrews, whores and harlots, a cockney strumpet, witchcraft, lascivious leers, 'natural manhood stirring', a menopausal false pregnancy, and all seasoned with a touch of blasphemy. Never has there been such bucolic lust. John Pentreath, whose first wife died in childbirth, has been forced to marry Mollie Robson whose mother had dealings with the dark powers. Mollie, although almost past the age to bear children, yearns to produce a son for him, but he, though eternally randy, lusts after Nancy, his widowed daughter-in-law, who lives with them. Nancy's handsome son Dennis lusts after Nell Robson, Mollie's niece and the family servant.

John Pentreath's religious mania manifests itself in ranting prayers and excessive drunkenness. He believes that his yearning for Nancy is reciprocated and is driven mad whenever he sees a nosegay in the hollow between her firm, generous breasts. Nancy, however, sneaks out of the house at night in order to visit an artist for whom she poses in the nude. John develops a hatred of Dennis, jealous of his youth, although he is not averse to a bit of vicarious fulfilment. 'My God, Dennis,' he says to his grandson, 'you've got the Pentreath muscles over your loins same as me. Twins, lad, get you twins when you take a wife for yourself, and show yourself a man...'

But Dennis is not yet ready for that and spends his time swimming and wrestling with Willie Polhaven. 'There were half a dozen Willies in the village, but Polhaven got to be known as Dennis's Willie, and the folk looked with kindly eyes on the male attachment.' Willie insults Dennis's mother and the two youths fight, but during it Dennis, who is winning, says to himself, 'God, how I love that chap.' Afterwards, as they lie on the sand after bathing, they are almost shy of each other, 'as if their fight had made lovers of them'.

Dennis, however, grows out of this phase and eventually marries Nell, but Willie never turns to women ('I reckon it's a kink in me, and not like to come out!'), and takes comfort from the parson's sermon on David and Jonathan and their love, 'wonderful, passin' the love of women.' In the gallery of Fred's equivocal young men none is more openly homosexual than Willie Polhaven.

Mollie is determined to get pregnant by her husband. First she tries the supernatural, sacrificing a cat on the old stone altar in the woods and smearing its blood on her breasts. She is observed by Dennis who hurries home, shaken and puzzled. Later that evening Nancy puts a plate of scraps on the floor. 'Pussie's not been in all evening,' she says, 'and him usually so keen for his supper.'

'Out mousing, maybe,' says Mollie.

Mollie's next plan involves Nancy. Knowing how he lusts after her, and that Nancy sneaks out regularly to see her artist lover, she tricks her husband into Nancy's bed by imitating her voice. In the darkness John thinks he is with Nancy, but when he is about to return to his own room Nancy returns unexpectedly, and he discovers that he has been bedding his own wife. In his rage he punches Mollie viciously in the stomach, but she forgives him because obviously their sexual bout has been good. At the midsummer revels she forces him to join in the fertility dance. Dennis and Nell dance too, but a little unnecessarily because she is already pregnant.

At last Mollie announces that she is pregnant too, but as the pregnancy advances she becomes thinner as Nell blooms and swells. When the doctor sees her it turns out that it is not a baby inside her but a large tumour. Just before she dies, her mind in confusion, Dennis shows her his and Nell's new born son, and lets her believe that the baby is hers. Then she dies happy.

In John's twisted mind Dennis is responsible for all his troubles and he determines to kill him. He sets fire to the house, thinking that Dennis and his family are asleep inside. But the couple are once again at the leaping and dancing ceremony, and the house is empty. They see the fire from a distance, but when the fire engine arrives only the stone walls remain, and John Pentreath's body lies among the ruins.

It is easy to make fun of *Raven's Brood* and wonder why Fred departed so drastically from his usual style to write a cross between *Precious Bane*, *Women in Love* and *Cold Comfort Farm*, but at least it does have atmosphere and is compelling in its overheated way. Fred's faithful readers were not amused, though.

*Queen Victoria* (1935) is one of the most successful of Fred's attempts to get away from easy fiction. In choosing Queen Victoria as a subject he was on firm ground. Both his parents had known her, his father as spiritual counsellor, his brother had edited her letters, he himself had been part of the society that fringed the court. He had a natural sympathy for the late Victorian era in which he grew up, and as a young man frequently met some of the minor royals at dinner parties and country house weekends. So he had a unique insight into his subject and it is obvious that he enjoyed writing about her. In Fred's eyes there is something of the Tilling ladies in her; a combination of Lucia and Miss Mapp in the way she bulldozed a path through her hosts of relations and the politicians, both home-grown and foreign, with whom she crossed swords. Some of her schemes were sensible, some were ludicrous. She interested herself in everything, even the Jack the Ripper murders. She was dogmatic and humourless, but had great common-sense and a will of iron. Behind the dignity and the aloofness she was a very human creature. Monarchy had not been popular when Victoria came to the throne, but after a reign of sixty-three years no monarch had ever been so affection-ately regarded, her position so firmly established.

She gave the devotion of a love-starved heart to Albert, her Prince Consort, whom she had thought so beautiful when she first saw him. For twenty-one years she relied on his goodness and wisdom, bore him eight children, and bowed willingly to his ideas on child-rearing, on duty, and on foreign policy. To all intents and purposes he was the Crown.

When he died in 1861 her domestic happiness was shattered. She retired into an impenetrable seclusion. Not for three years did she show herself in London and then it was during a drive from Buckingham Palace to Paddington Station. She was full of morbid self-pity and of hypochondriacal fears for her health. By 1866 the resentment of the people against her invisibility was getting serious. That the public should wish to see her she fully understood, 'but,' she wrote,

> why this wish should be of so unreasonable and unfeeling a nature as to long to witness the spectacle of a poor widow, nervous and shrinking, dragged in deep mourning alone in state as a Show . . . is a thing she cannot understand, and she never could wish her bitterest foe to be exposed to!

But in February 1867 she opened Parliament without any nervous crisis. . .

It was not until her reappearance, when she again took her full share in public duties, that her unpopularity began to decrease and the glory of her reign really began; and the expansion of the Empire and the welfare of her people absorbed her energies right until her last years. When she was eighty she went on an exhausting tour of Ireland, and she was working until a fortnight before her death.

Fred writes of the Queen affectionately but not as a syco-phant; his style is easy and humorous where lightness is needed, and clean and direct when politics and international affairs need explanation. The book is a model biography, and if he had any doubts about his standing as a literary figure *Queen Victoria* was one of the books of his later years that put such fears to rest.

In *The Kaiser and English Relations* (1936) Fred develops a new and convincing theory to account for the Kaiser's character and actions. It is that William II suffered all his life from an inferiority complex which may have sprung from the trauma of being born with a withered arm; and as he grew older, his relations with his grandmother Victoria and his uncle Edward tended to emphasise and then confirm this. In the face of their self-control and the liberalism and good sense for which they stood, William, with his crippling disability and his background, which was the opposite of liberal, felt crude and inadequate. To Victoria, he was the son of her favourite daughter, and she was patient with his shortcomings, but to Edward he was an arrogant foreigner who happened to be a family connection and who caused a great deal of trouble. Fred develops an extraordinary picture of these powerful people whose family quarrels had almost as much to do with bringing on the war as the economic factors and trade rivalries of the period.

Fred tells the story of the Kaiser from his childhood to his retirement at Doorn after the war and it is a fair picture, with a witty, often devastating analysis of the man and his actions. As an energetic old gentleman Fred believes he was happier than ever he was on his Potsdam throne, and he asks us to imagine what the Kaiser's life would have been like if he had been allowed to live it entirely in the role of countryman; and he suggests an amusing picture of an intelligent but pigheaded gentleman farmer who has his nose in everybody's affairs and his finger in every public pie.

*Old London* was published in America by D. Appleton-Century, in 1937, but never in England. It was part of a series of which Edith Wharton's *Old New York* was another part. *Old New Orleans*, *Old Chicago*, *Old Philadelphia* and *Old San Francisco* were later additions. Each title consisted of four long short stories, of just over a hundred pages each, and issued in a slipcase. Each of the four told a separate story, each of a different period, and introducing characters familiar to that period and sensitive to its spirit. Of the Georgian period in *Old London* we get 'Portrait of an English Nobleman'. He is Lord Stoke, a pompous peer with an estate in the country, a large family and a mistress in London whom he marries when Lady Stoke gets run over by a brewer's dray in Piccadilly. 'Friends of the Rich' has a mid-Victorian setting. A socially aspiring family, with money and little else, is taken up by a grasping aristocrat who exploits the Acton family mercilessly until she is bested by an Acton daughter. 'Janet' is Victorian. When widowed she plans to add to her slender means by dress-making. Her sisters-in-law and her children are shocked at the idea, so, instead, she makes economies in every aspect of daily life, but when she dies her family learns just how self-sacrificing she has been. The Edwardian novelette is called 'The Unwanted'. Dorothy Vincent is a meddling spinster who irritates everyone who has dealings with her, in particular, sick Auntie Alice, the vicar, and Sylvia and Toby, a happily married couple whom Dorothy is convinced have fallen out. The end is both cynical and sad. Dorothy is repulsed all along the line but cannot understand why her efforts to help meet with such opposition.

In *Daughters of Queen Victoria* (1939) Fred tells the story of Queen Victoria's five daughters – two of whom were still alive when the book was published, and he was able to use unpublished letters and memoirs to provide new light on a remarkable family. The Queen's eldest child was Victoria, Princess Royal, who married the Crown Prince of Prussia. As the Empress Frederick she only ruled for ninety days after many troubled years in her adopted country. She was an ardent, impetuous statesman, implacable in her hatred of Bismarck, and her life was soured by the animosity of her father-in-law, the old Emperor William, and later by that of her son, the ex-Kaiser. Her sister, Princess Alice of Hesse, had a very different character, full of love and consideration. Epidemic and death ravaged her family but her courage never failed her.

Then there were Princess Beatrice, Princess Louise and Princess Helena. They all suffered bereavement and tragedy but all found firm and unfailing comfort in their mother, and in turn gave her obedience and devotion. Queen Victoria's own story is retold gracefully, the unlikeable aspects of her autocratic ideas softened by Fred's sympathy for her.

Fred goes into the intricacies of the royal marriages and their effects on European affairs in great detail, and makes clear how personalities dominated politics and how the fates of countries and people were influenced by the whims, hatreds and weaknesses of their royal rulers.

Fred tried his hand spasmodically at writing plays, either with original plots or adaptations of his books, but with no driving enthusiasm; more as a diversion than a desperate desire to achieve eminence in the theatre. A few were produced for one performance only. *Aunt Jeannie* was licenced to be staged in December 1901 at the Theatre Royal in Birmingham. *Dodo* was performed at the Scala Theatre in London on November 26, 1905; *The Friend in the Garden* at the Savoy on March 7, 1906; *Dinner for Eight*, a one act play, at the Ambassador's Theatre on March 23, 1915 – this is the play that Maggie found quite amusing – and, after a thirteen years silence, *The Luck of the Vails* was staged at the Devonshire Park Theatre in Eastbourne on February 13, 1928. The typescript copies of these plays are in the Department of Manuscripts in the British Library. *Aunt Jeannie* was published in 1902 and *Dinner for Eight* in 1915. Copies are very elusive.

The productions were, in a theatrical sense, a form of 'vanity publishing'. They were social occasions, the audience consisting of friends of the author, friends of the cast, members of society with an afternoon to spare, and a sprinkling of managers and agents on the lookout for new talent. But none of the latter were sufficiently interested to arrange a commercial run for the play in proper conditions; and whatever ambitions Fred had for a career as a dramatist quietly folded and died.

# INDEX

*A Book of Golf*, 171
*Account Rendered*, 179
*Across the Stream*, 190
Addington Park, 27, 38, 40, 55, 58, 123
Adeline, Duchess of Bedford, 46, 148
*A Double Overture*, 47
*A Few People*, 159, 162
*Alan*, 190
Albert, Prince Consort, 11
Albert Victor, Duke of Clarence, 33, 34
*An Act in a Backwater*, 173
*An Autumn Sowing*, 186
*Angel of Pain, The*, 174
*Apostles, the*, 34
*A Reaping*, 177
*Arthur Christopher Benson as Seen by Some Friends*, 132
*Arundel*, 182
*As We Are*, 148, 159
*As We Were*, 148, 162
Athens, 44, 45, 49, 55, 123
*Aunt Jeannie*, 203

*Babe, B. A., The*, 48, 140, 165
Barney, Natalie Clifford, 64
Bayreuth, 67, 75
Beerbohm, Max, 32
Beesly, A. H., 26, 28, 29, 38, 42
*Bengal Lancer*, 93, 141
Bennett, Arnold, 145, 150
Benson, Arthur Christopher, 11, 12,
    14–17, 20, 24, 27, 33, 34, 34, 36, 39–41,
    46, 52, 54–58, 61, 65, 66, 69, 79, 82–84,
    87–91, 94, 104–106, 112, 117–119, 122,
    128–131, 133, 134, 162, 163, 169
Benson, Christopher, 11
Benson, Edward Frederic, passim
Benson, Edward White, 9, 11–13, 15–18,
    20, 23, 26–28, 30, 31, 33, 37–39, 41, 44,
    46, 47, 55–57, 61, 122, 123,
    134, 148,
Benson, Margaret (Maggie), 11, 13, 17, 18,

24, 27, 40, 41, 44, 45, 47, 49, 53, 54,
    58–61, 65, 66, 70, 78, 84–90, 107, 122,
    162, 163
Benson, Martin, 11, 13, 17, 20, 41, 122
Benson, Mary (Minnie, Ben), 10–13,
    16–18, 22, 27, 39–41, 45, 46, 54–62,
    65–67, 70, 74, 78, 80, 82, 84, 85, 86,
    88–90, 101, 106–108, 133, 162, 163
Benson, Mary Eleanor (Nellie), 11, 13, 17,
    24, 27, 30, 38, 40, 41, 122, 123
Benson, Robert Hugh, 11, 13, 14, 17, 24,
    39–43, 55, 58, 59, 61, 65, 66, 79–82, 87,
    88, 90, 91, 130, 133, 162
Beresford, Lady Charles, 74, 75
Beresford, Lord Charles, 74, 75
Bevan, Gladys, 66, 78, 84
Blakeney, 112, 118
Blakiston, Noel, 129
Blampied, Edmund, 148
*Blotting Book, The*, 176
*Book of Months, The*, 171
Bradford, Rev. E. E., 51
British School of Archaeology, 45
Broadway, Worcs., 123
Brompton Square, 98, 99, 108, 112, 137
Brooks, John Ellingham, 52, 63, 64, 93, 94,
    111, 119, 120, 168
Brooks (Goddard), Romaine, 64
Browning, Oscar, 31, 33, 36, 140, 149
Burne-Jones, Philip, 52, 162

Cairo, 59
Cambridge, 14, 28, 33, 38, 40, 43, 79, 101,
    104, 105, 118, 123
*Cambridge Fortnightly*, The, 35
Canterbury, Archbishop of, *see* Benson,
    Edward White
Capri, 52, 55, 60, 63, 94, 119
*Capsina, The*, 58, 167
*Caught by the Turks*, 141
*Challoners, The*, 172
Chancery, The, Lincoln, 15

Charlotte Brontë, 195
Chester, 42, 43, 123
Chitchat, The, 34
Cley-next-the-sea, 112, 113
Climber, The, 121, 176
Colin, 190
Colin II, 190
Colles, William, 58
Cooper, Elizabeth (Beth), 12, 13, 40, 55, 60, 61, 80, 87, 122
Corelli, Marie, 71, 162, 167
Countess of Lowndes Square, The, 190
Crescent and Iron Cross, 96
Cricket of Abel, Hirst and Shrewsbury, The, 171
Cust, Henry, 34

Daily Training, 170
Daisy's Aunt, 178
Daukes, Major Archie, 142
David Blaize, 15, 20, 29, 51, 99, 101, 102, 121, 133, 140,
David Blaize and the Blue Door, 189
David of King's, 139, 140
Daughters of Queen Victoria, 203
Davidson, Randall, 59, 134, 146, 150
Davidson, Michael, 51
Dawkes, Captain Edwin, 155
Decemviri Debating Society, 35
Desire and Pursuit of the Whole, The, 83
Deutschland Uber Allah, 96
Dinner for Eight, 89, 203
Disraeli, Benjamin, 18
Diversions Day by Day, 174
Dodo, 27, 39, 41, 43, 45–47, 72, 110, 121, 123, 133, 203
Dodo the Second, 182
Dodo Wonders, 183
Donaldson, Stuart Alexander, 79
Douglas, Lord Alfred, 32, 50
Douglas, Norman, 63
Doyle, Conan, 90
Druitt, Montague John, 34

Edgar, Mr, 23
Edwards, Rose, 161
Egypt, 49, 53, 55, 58, 123
Egyptian Exploration Fund, 53
English Figure Skating, 177
Eton, 24, 33, 54, 79, 105
Eton, George, 161
Eton Mission, 55

Ferdinand Magellan, 145
Ferguson, Rachel, 126
Fersen, Count, 63
Final Edition, 162
Ford, Lionel, 34
Fowler, Canon, 141
Freaks of Mayfair, The, 142, 184
Freedom of the Borough, 159
Friend in the Garden, The, 203
Fry, Roger, 35, 36

Gabriel, 136
Galloway, Countess of, 67
Gaselee, Stephen, 130
Gladstone, Mr, 43, 56
Gladstone, Mrs, 56
Glennie, Alfred Edward, 26, 29
Gosse, Sir Edmund, 131, 132, 135, 146
Gourlay, Nettie, 14, 53, 54, 66, 78
Graeco-Turkish War, 62
Granta, The, 165
Greece, 53, 123
Green, Captain Leonard, 51
Green, Ivy, 161
Grindenwald, 75

Hadrian the Seventh, 82
Hall, Radclyffe, 142
Hare Street, 81, 91
Harvey, Miriam (Madeline), 113–116
Hatshepsut, Queen, 54
Hawarden, 43, 55, 56
Headlam, Walter, 34, 149
'Helmsworth Preparatory School', 100
Helouan, 59
Hérèdia, 63
Hichens, Robert, 32, 50
Hogarth, D. G., 54
Holkham Hall, 112, 137
Holmes, Burton, 166
Horsted Keynes, 65, 88, 89, 108, 129
House of Defence, The, 175
House of the Resurrection, 61, 79, 87

Image in the Sand, The, 53, 173, 174
Inheritor, The, 193
Initiation, 83

Jack the Ripper, 34
Jacomb-Hood, G. P., 166
Jacomb-Hood, Mrs, 141, 156
James, Henry, 43, 44, 110, 149, 150, 163

James, M. R. (Monty), 20, 21, 33, 35, 39, 104, 132, 147
Joyce, James, 145, 150
*Judgment Books, The*, 164
*Juggernaut*, 180

*Kaiser and English Relations, The*, 202
Karnak, 53, 54, 58, 61
Killick, Hallie (Miles), 29, 143
*King Edward VII*, 196
King's College, Cambridge, 24, 28, 31, 32, 42, 139
Knowles, Sir James T., 55

Lady Margaret Hall, Oxford, 16, 40
Lady Sclater's Fund for Wounded Soldiers and Sailors, 97
Lamb House, Rye, 29, 110, 111, 112, 119, 136, 137
Lambeth Palace, 26, 38, 39, 58, 65, 123
Langdon of Nottbeck, Eugenia, 134
Lang, Dr, Archbishop of Canterbury, 158
Lawrence, D. H., 150
Layman, Beatrice, 84, 85, 89
*Life of Alcibiades, The*, 145, 146
*Light Invisible, The*, 80
*Limitations*, 165
Lincoln, 11, 15, 16, 17, 18, 20, 122
Lis Escop, 18, 19, 20, 47
Lister, Regie, 49, 50, 52, 76, 168
Lord Warden of the Cinque Ports, 157
*Lovers and Friends*, 191
Lubbock, Percy, 69, 104, 117, 118, 128, 130, 131
*Lucia in London*, 126
*Lucia's Progress*, 151, 156
*Luck of the Vails, The*, 121, 169, 303
Luxor, 50, 54, 58, 59
Lyttelton, Carl, 128

Mackenzie, Compton, 64, 119
*Mad Annual, The*, 172
Madan, Geoffrey, 89, 128
Magdalene College, Cambridge, 79, 158
*Male Inpersonator, The*, 193
Malet, Lucas, 43, 45
Mallory, George, 128
*Mammon and Co.*, 167
*Mapp and Lucia*, 125, 151
'Marchester', 100
Marlborough, 24–27, 29, 38, 42, 100, 122
*Marlburian, The*, 28, 37

Marshall, J. F., 166
Martin, Francis, 10
Mary, Queen, 143
Masterman, Charles, 96
Master's Lodge, Wellington, 11, 12, 148
Matterhorn, 38
Maugham, Somerset, 63, 64, 168
McDowall, Rev. Stuart, 142
*Mezzanine*, 190
Middleton, Professor, 31, 42
*Mike*, 185
Miles, Eustace Hamilton, 28, 29, 31, 38, 39, 52, 100, 123, 141, 143, 144, 166, 170, 171, 172, 174
*Miss Mapp*, 137
*Money Market, The*, 166
Monsell, J. R., 172
*More Spook Stories*, 147
*Mother*, 75, 132, 133, 148, 162
Mozley, H. M., 31, 32, 140
*Mr Teddy*, 187
*Mrs Ames*, 180
Munthe, Axel, 63
Mylne, Caroline Charlotte (Tan), 16, 17

Navarro, Mary de (Mary Anderson), 123
Nichols, Beverley, 98
Nixon, J. E., 32, 140, 149
Norton, Robert, 111

Oakley Street, 84, 89, 98
*Oakleyites, The*, 183
Old Lodge, 79, 104, 131
*Old London*, 202
*Osbornes, The*, 93, 178
Oswald, Sydney (Sydney Lomer), 51
*Our Family Affairs*, 122, 124, 140, 148
*Outbreak of War, 1914, The*, 198

Pain, Barry, 36
*Paul*, 175
*Paying Guests*, 192
*Peter*, 191
*Pharisees and Publicans*, 190
Pirates, 19, 25
Pitt Club, 34
Piz Palu, 42
Plank, George, 142
*Poland and Mittel-Europa*, 97
Portofino, 92
*Princess Sophia, The*, 168
Priory, The, 86, 88

*Queen Lucia*, 124, 126
*Queen Victoria*, 200

Radnor, Lady, 69, 92, 137
Ramsey, A. S., 158, 159
*Raven's Brood*, 199
Red Cross, 62
*Rex*, 190
'Riseholme' (Broadway), 125, 126, 137
Riseholme, Lincs., 16, 122
Risley, John Shuckburgh, 26, 29
*Robin Linnet*, 190
Rolfe, Frederick (Baron Corvo), 82, 83
*Room in the Tower, The*, 147
Ross, Robert, 32
*Rubicon, The*, 47, 48, 123, 164
Rye, 110, 118, 137, 142, 144, 157
Rye Church, 134, 158
Rylands, George, 128, 129
Ryle, Edward, 128, 131, 132

Salthouse, 112, 118
Sarajevo, 94, 149, 198
*Saturday Magazine*, 25, 27
*Scarlet and Hyssop*, 170
*Secret Lives*, 195
Sen-Mut, 54
Sharrock, Canon, 90, 91
*Sheaves*, 121, 176
Sidgwick, Arthur, 10, 12, 36
Sidgwick, Henry, 10, 12
Sidgwick, William, 12
*Sir Francis Drake*, 145, 146
*Six Common Things*, 47
*Sketches from Marlborough*, 37, 38
Smyth, Ethel, 13, 40, 41, 103, 133, 142
Somerset, Lady Henry, 148
Somerset, Lord Henry, 50
Speaker of the Cinque Ports, 157
*Spectator, The*, 141
*Spook Stories*, 147
*Step, The*, 147
Stephen, James Kenneth, 34, 35
Stevenson, Charles, 31

TAF (Twice a Fortnight), 35
Taffy (Fred's dog), 137, 157, 158
Taffy (Maggie's dog), 60, 66
Tait, Archbishop, 107
Tait, Lucy, 13, 44, 54, 58–61, 65, 66, 78,
    85, 86, 106–108, 129
Temple Grove, 20–25, 33, 100, 122

Temple of Mut, 53
Tennant, Margot, 46, 47
Thessaly, 62
*Thorley Weir*, 182
'Tilling' (Rye), 137
Todd, Dr Ross, 85, 90, 105, 117
Tomlin, Charles, 108, 119, 143, 144, 158,
    160, 161
*Travail of Gold*, 197
*Trefoil, The*, 132
Tremans, 65–70, 78, 80, 85, 94, 106, 108,
    109, 129
Trinity College, Cambridge, 9
Troubridge, Una, 142
Truro, 18, 26, 38, 122
Turner, Reggie, 32, 50

*Up and Down*, 113, 188

*Valkyries, The*, 171
*Venture of a Rational Faith, The*, 54, 84
Victoria, Queen, 11, 34, 62, 76, 148
Villa Cercola, 63, 64, 93, 95, 111, 119
Villa Salvia, 119
*Vintage, The*, 45, 53, 58, 59, 166, 167
Virgo, 117
*Visible and Invisible*, 147

Wagner, Cosima, 67
Wagner, Richard, 67, 75, 171
Waldstein, Dr Charles, 31, 42, 149
Warrender, Lady Maud, 110
Waterfield, Ottiwell Charles, 20, 21, 22
*Weaker Vessel, The*, 181
Wellington College, 9, 11, 15, 16, 18, 76,
    122
*Well of Loneliness, The*, 142, 156
*White Eagle of Poland, The*, 97
Wilde, Oscar, 32, 50, 63, 149
Wilson, Henry, 34
Winchester, 60, 65, 78
*Winter Sports in Switzerland*, 182
Woolf, Virginia, 145, 150
Wordsworth, Bishop, 11, 15, 16
Wordsworth, Elizabeth, 16

Yeats-Brown, Francis, 52, 92, 93, 141, 160,
    163
Yorke, Vincent Wodehouse, 31, 32, 38, 49,
    52, 140, 141

Zienal Rothorn, 38